groundswell

CHARLENE LI

JOSH BERNOFF

groundswell

winning in a world transformed by social technologies

harvard business review press • boston, massachusetts

Copyright 2008 Forrester Research, Inc.

Printed in the United States of America

12 11 10   13

No part of this publication may be reproduced, stored in or introduced into a retrieval system, or transmitted, in any form, or by any means (electronic, mechanical, photocopying,
recording, or otherwise), without the prior permission of the publisher. Requests for permission should be directed to permissions@hbsp.harvard.edu, or mailed to Permissions,
Harvard Business School Publishing, 60 Harvard Way, Boston, Massachusetts 02163.

Forrester and Technographics are registered trademarks of Forrester Research, Inc. All
other trademarks are the property of their respective companies.

Library of Congress Cataloging-in-Publication Data
Li, Charlene.
  Groundswell : winning in a world transformed by social technologies / Charlene Li and
Josh Bernoff.
     p. cm.
  ISBN-13: 978-1-4221-2500-7
  1. Online social networks—Economic aspects. 2. Information society—Economic
aspects. I. Bernoff, Josh. II. Title.
  HC79.I55.L48 2008
  303.48'33—dc22

                                                                    2007048659

The paper used in this publication meets the requirements of the American National
Standard for Permanence of Paper for Publications and Documents in Libraries and
Archives Z39.48-1992.

To Bill Blue

contents

part three. the groundswell transforms

introduction

Rick Clancy seemed worried.

Rick is a fifty-ish, powerful-looking man with graying hair and, until today, a confident manner that always reflected his control of the situation. In his role as head of communications for Sony Electronics, we'd seen him deal with tough business reporters, nasty competitors, product recalls, and more than one cranky company CEO, all with grace and confidence.

We were meeting him for breakfast before an all-day meeting. He was grappling with a force he didn't understand, one that was growing all the time. Bloggers. Discussion groups. YouTube. Consumers whom he'd never met were rating his company's products in public forums that he had no experience with and no way to influence.

All were assaulting his company's cherished brand, and traditional PR tools were as useless as a broadsword against a rain of poison darts. Rick had decided it was time to take matters into his own hands, to become a blogger himself. For this veteran of almost two decades of managing his company's image, the goal looked daunting. It looked like the unknown.

From where we sit, Rick Clancy is a symbol. He and thousands of corporate executives just like him are now dealing with a trend we call the groundswell, a spontaneous movement of people using online tools to connect, take charge of their own experience, and get what they need—information, support, ideas, products, and bargaining power—from each other. The groundswell is broad, ever shifting, and ever growing. It encompasses blogs and wikis; podcasts and YouTube; and consumers who rate products, buy and sell from each other, write their own news, and find their own deals. It's global. It's unstoppable. It affects every industry—those that sell to consumers and those that sell to businesses—in media, retail, financial services, technology, and health care. And it's utterly foreign to the powerful companies and institutions—and their leaderships—that run things now.

Simply put, the groundswell is a social trend in which people use technologies to get the things they need from each other instead of from companies. If you're in a company, this is a challenge.

The groundswell phenomenon is not a flash in the pan. The technologies that make it work are evolving at an ever-increasing pace, but the phenomenon itself is based on people acting on their eternal desire to connect. It has created a permanent, long-lasting shift in the way the world works. This book exists to help companies deal with the trend, *regardless of how the individual technology pieces change*. We call this groundswell thinking.

why we wrote this book

At Forrester Research, we provide strategy advice to clients all over the world. Since we wrote the Forrester Report "Social Computing" about the groundswell trend in 2006, the pace of change has been accelerating, and the number of clients asking us questions about it has been increasing. The noise around the topic has been growing, too. With all the books and articles about blogging, communities, and wikis, it's hard for company strategists to know where to start. We wanted to give our clients, and the world, a clear perspective on the *whole* trend, not just pieces of it, with a clear set of strategic recommendations. We also wanted to bring to bear the assets we've accumulated from analyzing the effects of technology on business for more than a decade: consumer data, real client stories, and a focus on measurable business success. Finally, we wanted to package it up in a highly readable format, with real stories of the *people* who make the groundswell such an amazing place, to provide a little insight into the psychology behind what's happening.

what's in this book

We've structured the book into three sections. Basically, the first section tells what the groundswell is and lays out the basic tools you need to understand it. The second explains what to do about it. And the third helps you use it to succeed within your company. These three parts include twelve chapters:

Chapter 1: Why the Groundswell—and Why Now? is a call to action. In it we show how the groundswell can threaten institutions like companies and brands as customers draw strength from each other.

Chapter 2: Jujitsu and the Technologies of the Groundswell lays out our basic premise that you can turn the groundswell to your advantage, like a jujitsu master who turns the force of his opponent to his own advantage. In this chapter we describe the component technologies of the groundswell and show both how they threaten companies and how you can benefit from them. Finally, we analyze how to evaluate new technologies as they come along.

Chapter 3: The Social Technographics Profile introduces a key data tool. The Social Technographics Profile lets you examine any group of people—Australians, first-time mothers, or your customer base—and see in exactly what ways that group is participating in the groundswell. This type of analysis should be a primary element of any groundswell strategy.

Chapter 4: Strategies for Tapping the Groundswell starts the second part of the book, focusing on strategy. We define the four-step POST process for creating strategies—people, objectives, strategy, and technology—and reveal why starting with the technologies is a mistake. And because objectives are paramount to success, we define the five primary objectives for groundswell strategy: listening, talking, energizing, supporting, and embracing. Each of these is described in the chapters that follow, with an emphasis on the ROI of each technique.

Chapter 5: Listening to the Groundswell explains how to use the groundswell for research purposes with tools like private communities and brand monitoring. We demonstrate with case studies from the National Comprehensive Cancer Network and the car company Mini.

Chapter 6: Talking with the Groundswell shows how to use the groundswell for marketing and PR, with techniques like user-generated video, blogs, and communities. The case studies feature Blendtec, the company behind willitblend.com; Ernst & Young in Facebook; HP's blogs; and Procter & Gamble's community for young girls, beinggirl.com.

Chapter 7: Energizing the Groundswell illustrates a key strategy—charging up your best customers and enabling them to recruit their peers. The techniques highlighted in this chapter are ratings, reviews, and communities, with case studies featuring the online retailer eBags, the email services company Constant Contact, and the toy company Lego.

Chapter 8: Helping the Groundswell Support Itself is about saving money and gaining insight by helping your customers support each other. We demonstrate this through CarePages, a network for hospital patients; Dell's community forums; and a wiki from the big consulting company BearingPoint.

Chapter 9: Embracing the Groundswell explains how to accomplish the most powerful goal of all—including your customers as collaborators in your company. In this chapter we see surprising customer collaboration stories from Del Monte Pet Products, the Canadian grocery retailer Loblaw, the sales application company salesforce .com, and the French bank Crédit Mutuel.

Chapter 10: How Connecting with the Groundswell Transforms Your Company starts the third part of the book, focusing on transformation. It pulls all the previous techniques together and answers this question: how can I get my company positioned to embrace groundswell thinking? We examine how Dell and Unilever gained advantage by implementing many of these techniques and embracing the influence of the groundswell in multiple settings.

Chapter 11: The Groundswell Inside Your Company examines how the same trends that empower customers in the groundswell also empower employees in your company. We look at how wikis, blogs, and social networks within companies can enhance the productivity of a global organization, with a peek into how this works at Best Buy, Organic, Bell Canada, Avenue A/Razorfish, and Intel.

Chapter 12: The Future of the Groundswell forecasts the next steps in the groundswell trend. We'll tell you how demographic and technology forces will create a disaggregated, collaborative, fluid world within the next ten years; how it will affect companies; and what you should do to prepare.

What you're about to read comes from hundreds of client interactions and thousands of hours of collaboration and analysis, all turned toward a single goal: preparing professionals and executives to thrive in the rapidly changing world of social technologies. Like Sony's Rick Clancy, you may find it a strange world to navigate, but there's no going back. We'd like to invite you to enter the world of the groundswell.

part one.

understanding
the groundswell

1. why the groundswell— and why now?

When he woke up on May 1, 2007, Kevin Rose had no idea he was about to have the most interesting day of his life, courtesy of an uprising of his own customers.

If you have a caricature in your head of a new-age Internet entrepreneur, Kevin probably fits it. He started his company, Digg, at age twenty-seven. At the time of our interview, he sported a day's growth of stubble and a worn gray-green T-shirt. When he speaks, you hear the familiar slacker cadences of Keanu Reeves. But if you listen, you realize this guy is sharp. Really sharp. *BusinessWeek* put his picture on its cover.[1] He understands the massive surge in people-driven phenomena on the Internet as well as anyone else we've ever met. That's what makes what happened on May 1 all the more surprising.

Digg.com is a site where members vote and comment on news stories. Anyone can join. You click on a news story anywhere on the Internet to "digg" the story, and Digg features on its home page the most popular stories. Digg's readers digg not just news stories but also blog posts and other Web sites—anything that's new. There are complicated algorithms that account for recency and help prevent fraud, but that's the basic idea. Given the enormous fountain of news bursting forth from the Internet every day, Digg is one way to sort through what's important, as rated by votes from readers like yourself.

Six months before the events of May 1, Kevin had told us, "It's a strange feeling to wake up in the morning and think, 'What the hell is going to be on the front page?'" That proved to be prescient.

It started when a blogger named Rudd-O put this on his blog on April 30:[2]

Spread this number

09 F9 11 02 . . . Wanna know what's so important about it?

The movie industry is threatening Spooky Action at a Distance for publishing that number, specifically with copyright infringement.

I had no idea a number could be copyrighted.

Anyhow, what is it? . . . It's the HD-DVD Processing Key for most movies released so far.

Translation: the encryption for the new high-definition DVD format had been broken.[3] With appropriate technical skill, a person could now make copies of these supposedly uncopyable supersharp DVDs, and Rudd-O was crowing about it.

For Digg's technology-savvy audience, this was like catnip; within one day, fifteen thousand Digg members had voted for the story. As a result, a link to the secret encryption key was prominent at the top of Digg's home page for everyone to see.

As you might imagine, this didn't sit too well with the movie industry. AACS LA—an organization backed by companies including Disney, Warner Bros., Sony, Microsoft, and Panasonic—had created the encryption that Rudd-O claimed had been broken, and the organization decided to respond. As Michael B. Ayers, an attorney at Toshiba who is chairman of AACS LA, explained to us, "We have a legitimate right to enforce. The only reason to distribute [this key] is for circumvention"—that is, to get around the copy protection. So naturally, Michael had AACS LA's lawyers send a cease-and-desist email to Digg. Now remember, Digg itself hadn't broken any copyrights or hacked any code—the site was just responding to members' requests regarding the most popular news stories, as always. But rather than risk a crippling lawsuit, Digg removed the link (and posted an explanation on the Digg blog).[4]

But lawyers and entrepreneurs aren't the most powerful force on the Internet. People are. And people, empowered by technology, won't always go along. Media isn't neatly boxed into little rectangles called newspapers, magazines, and TV sets anymore. People connect with other people and draw power from other people, especially in crowds. Even Internet wizards—like Kevin Rose, whose strength comes from those crowds—are at their mercy. So what happened next was, in hindsight, inevitable.

Once the number was taken off Digg, other bloggers tracked down the number and reposted it on their own blogs. By the time Kevin woke up on May 1, there were 88 blogs that mentioned the number. By the end of the same day, there were 3,172.[5] Over three hundred thousand people listened to a soulful acoustic guitar rendition of the twenty-hexadecimal-digit encryption code in a YouTube video posted by "keithburgun."[6] Digg member Grant Robertson likened the event to a quip from *NewsRadio*, the 1990s TV show: "You can't take something off the Internet. That's like trying to take pee out of a swimming pool."[7] The controversy became news, and reporters started posting news stories about it on the Internet.

Many of these blog posts and news stories were in their turn also noted on digg.com and immediately began their march up the rankings. Digg's management dutifully removed the ones that mentioned the forbidden code, but as in any game of Whack-a-Mole, the vermin pop up faster than you can smack them.

The next day Digg gave up. Founded on the idea that its members would be in charge of what was news, Digg found that its members wouldn't go along with its decisions. Caught between a lawsuit and its own audience, Digg bowed to the greater force: the audience. Kevin wrote this on the company's blog that same evening:[8]

Digg This: 09-f9-11-02-9d . . .

by Kevin Rose at 9pm, May 1st, 2007 in Digg Website

Today was an insane day. And as the founder of Digg, I just wanted to post my thoughts . . .

In building and shaping the site I've always tried to stay as hands on as possible. [But] we've always given site moderation (digging/burying) power to the community. Occasionally we step in to remove stories that violate our terms of use . . . So today was a difficult day for us. We had to decide whether to remove stories containing a single code based on a cease and desist declaration. We had to make a call, and in our desire to avoid a scenario where Digg would be interrupted or shut down, we decided to comply and remove the stories with the code.

But now, after seeing hundreds of stories and reading thousands of comments, you've made it clear. You'd rather see Digg go down fighting than bow down to a bigger company. We hear you, and effective immediately we won't delete stories or comments containing the code and will deal with whatever the consequences might be.

If we lose, then what the hell, at least we died trying.

Digg on,

Kevin

By the next day, there were 605 news stories[9] about how Digg took down the link and then reversed its decision. By asking that the story be taken down, the representatives of the movie industry had created a whirlwind of publicity, ensuring that it could *never* be taken down. People, by moving together on the Internet for a moment in time, had created an irresistible, ineradicable groundswell.

what happened to digg and aacs la is emblematic

Let's take a step back for a second and examine what happened on May 1, 2007.

First, people on the Internet showed they were in charge. Any individual can be stopped, co-opted, bought off, or sued. But the Internet allows people to draw strength from each other. Digg's members and the bloggers who posted the forbidden key weren't part of some secret society; most of them didn't even know each other. But blogs, sites like digg.com, and the Internet in general allowed them to connect to each other, to feel unafraid, and to be powerful.

Second, the online world swamped the offline world. People on the Internet overpowered the entire movie industry and all its legal apparatus. Real-life physical-world products, in this case HD DVDs and HD DVD players, were affected. The Internet is not some sandbox that can be walled off anymore—it is fully integrated into all elements of business and society.

Third, the people involved weren't stupid or clueless. AACS LA includes incredible engineering talent; Michael B. Ayers is a very thoughtful attorney. The movie industry understands technology. Kevin Rose "gets it" about the Net. None of this made any difference.

This is no isolated incident. Here are others from around the globe, some now famous. (Many of these, and others, were documented in Ben McConnell and Jackie Huba's book *Citizen Marketers*[10]):

- Pilot Gabrielle Adelman and photographer Kenneth Adelman decided to photograph the entire California coastline (see their work at www.californiacoastline.org). Singer Barbra Streisand insisted that photos of her house be removed, which was about as effective as trying to get rid of a hornet nest by hitting it with a baseball bat. Of course, the resulting publicity caused people to copy the photo and post it to sites all over the Net, easily found using Google Image Search on "Barbra Streisand house." Mike Masnick, a blogger for Techdirt, coined the term *Streisand effect* for events where attempts to remove content from the Internet cause it to spread broadly instead.[11] So not only is Barbra Streisand's house still visible online—now her name has become synonymous with futile attempts to remove content from the Net.

- More than a million viewers have watched a YouTube video posted by law student Brian Finkelstein,[12] who filmed a Comcast technician who fell asleep on his couch in 2006, waiting on hold for help from the Comcast home office to fix an Internet problem. This video is now the top result when typing "Comcast" into the search box on YouTube.

- New Line Cinema took on a movie project titled *Snakes on a Plane* that it planned to complete and release in 2006. Word got out, fan sites spread, and before long, *Snakes on a Plane* belonged to the Internet. In the absence of any actual marketing materials, fans created hundreds of unofficial T-shirt designs at cafepress.com.

An unauthorized blog, Snakes on a Blog,[13] became a focal point for fan activity; 8,360 other blogs and Web sites link to it. Fans insisted that the movie include this line for Samuel L. Jackson, star of the movie: "I have had it with these mother-fucking snakes on this mother-fucking plane." New Line had lost control of the movie and its marketing; knowing it had to court these hard-core fans to succeed, it changed the movie, added the line, and lost the film's PG-13 rating in the process.

- Jennifer Laycock, a breastfeeding advocate and operator of the blog thelactivist.com, wanted to raise money for a breast-feeding charity. She created a T-shirt with the slogan "Breast Milk: The Other White Milk" and had sold a total of eight dollars' worth when a letter arrived from (you guessed it) the National Pork Board, requesting that she stop because her "slogan . . . tarnishes the good reputation of the National Pork Board's" trademark, "The Other White Meat." But Jennifer Laycock is no ordinary mom—she's also an expert in Internet marketing. She documented the event on her blog;[14] soon more than two hundred other blogs were linking to it.[15] The pork board saw a PR disaster in the making and rapidly negotiated a settlement *and* took up a collection among its employees to help Jennifer's charity.

- In April 2007, a blogger working at a Dunkin' Donuts supplier in South Korea posted an entry titled "Truth About Dunkin Donuts," including accusations of food preparation in unsanitary conditions and a picture of a rusty boiler that allegedly contaminated Dunkin's doughnuts. In a Korean version of the Streisand effect, Dunkin' Donuts was able to persuade the site hosting the blog to remove the item, but it couldn't stop the spread of the conversation in reactions from other bloggers.[16] The entire episode was covered by the *Korea Times*,[17] surely not the end point that Dunkin' was hoping for.

What happened to these companies will happen to you. Your company's customers are talking about your brand right now on MySpace, probably in ways you haven't approved. Your support representatives' conversations with customers will show up on YouTube, and so will your TV commercials, intercut with sarcastic commentary. If your CEO has any hair left, he or she is going to tear it out and then ask for your help in taming this torrent of people expressing themselves. But this movement can't be tamed. It comes from a thousand sources and washes over traditional business like a flood. And like a flood, it can't be stopped in any one place. Often it can't be stopped at all.

This is the movement we call the groundswell. And while you can't stop it, you can understand it. You can not only live with it; you can thrive in it. That's the point of this book.

what is the groundswell?

Let's define our terms.

In 2006, Forrester Research released a report called "Social Computing."[18] We had identified a trend happening online. People were using tools to link up with each other in various ways, and those trends were threatening to companies.

Already in this chapter we've talked about blogs and member-driven news sites, like digg.com. The groundswell trend also includes social networks, like MySpace and Facebook, and user-generated content sites, like YouTube and Helium. Tools like del.icio.us, which lets people see and share Internet bookmarks with each other, are part of the trend, as are sites like Wikipedia, where people build a content resource together. (We'll describe all these technologies and more in chapter 2.) But we try to take a broader view of this phenomenon, one that encompasses not just today's technologies but the fundamental change in behavior now happening online. The groundswell is:

A social trend in which people use technologies to get the things they need from each other, rather than from traditional institutions like corporations.

Looking at it this way, you can see that the roots of the groundswell reach way back before MySpace. On eBay you buy from other people instead of a store. Craigslist lets you find a job or a babysitter without searching through newspaper want ads. Linux is an operating system created by engineers working together, rather than depending on a big company like Microsoft. Rotten Tomatoes lets you make moviegoing decisions based on reviews from other regular people. BitTorrent helps people get music from each other without going to a music store, just as Napster did in 2000.

Compared to the way things were in 2000, though, the trend of people connecting with and depending on each other online is clearly accelerating. That's why now is the time to understand the groundswell, where it comes from, and where it's going.

why the groundswell is happening now

The groundswell trend is not a flash in the pan. This is an important, irreversible, completely different way for people to relate to companies and to each other.

Why is it happening now? The groundswell comes from the collision of three forces: people, technology, and economics.

First, people. People have always depended on each other and drawn strength from each other. And people have always rebelled against institutional power, in social movements like labor unions and political revolutions. But the rough balance between the scale economies of institutions and the rebellion of their constituents has shifted because of the advent and spread of social technologies.

Technology, the second force driving the groundswell, has changed everything as far as people's social interactions are concerned. For one thing, nearly everyone's online—in 2006, that meant 73 percent of Americans[19] and 64 percent of Europeans,[20] for example. People's connections are fast and ubiquitous—more than half the Americans online have broadband connectivity, along with every office worker, and connections on mobile phones and TV set-top devices are common. Why does this matter? Because software that connects people can now *assume* that masses of people are there to connect.

These ubiquitous connections have led to a fundamentally different kind of software. It's far more *interactive* because the software can depend on having a powerful machine with a fast connection at the other end. And it's *people-aware*—with people connecting all the time, applications like Facebook or MSN Messenger can connect people directly with each other.

This new class of software is so different that Internet observer Tim O'Reilly has dubbed it "Web 2.0." But as powerful as it is, the technology is just an enabler. It's the technology in the hands of almost-always-connected *people* that makes it so powerful.[21]

Along with people's desire to connect and new technologies, the third force driving the groundswell is simple online economics: on the Internet, traffic equals money.

By 2007, twelve years into the Web era, online advertising had reached $14.6 billion in the United States alone[22] and approached €7.5 billion in Europe.[23] Advertisers know that traffic indicates that consumers spend their time and attention online and act to translate that attention into advertising power. It's not even necessary to sell the ads—you can sign your site up for Google AdSense and let Google sell the ads for you and share the cash. While advertising is not the only way to make money online, it's growing so rapidly that any venture that creates significant traffic can count on revenues.

These three trends—people's desire to connect, new interactive technologies, and online economics—have created a new era. This is the fast-growing phenomenon we call the groundswell. Not only is it here; it's evolving rapidly—creating an incredible challenge for corporate strategists.

why you should care about the groundswell

In 1941, the great science-fiction writer Theodore Sturgeon wrote an amazing short story called "Microcosmic God."[24] In it a scientist named James Kidder secretly creates a new form of life—a rapidly evolving race of three-inch-tall intelligent creatures called Neoterics. Because Neoterics have faster metabolisms and brains than humans, they experience a generation in about eight days, and James watches them develop a civilization equivalent to humankind in less than a year. As he subjects them to stresses and puts obstacles in their path, the Neoterics invent ways around these obstacles, which he turns into commercially successful inventions in the real world. He even puts groups of Neoterics in competition with each other to motivate their inventive instincts.

The Neoterics outpace any human research lab since they try, fail, and adapt so much more quickly than ordinary slow-paced humans. As in all mad-scientist stories, the creation gets way beyond the control of the creator.

This is an apt metaphor for the current state of the Internet. Web 2.0 technologies and the masses of people who connect to them allow for rapid prototyping, failure, and adaptation. For example, technology marketing whiz Guy Kawasaki put a new venture called Truemors—a site for sharing rumors—together in seven weeks, for a total investment of \$12,107.09.[25] Online entrepreneurs are highly competitive, and speed can create a dominant edge because whoever gets to an idea first gets first crack at the visitors (and the traffic). The result is an evolution of new ways for people to interact, moving forward at a blistering rate.

In attempting to deal with this rapid innovation, traditional businesses are as overmatched as ordinary humans compared to Neoterics. Offline, people don't change behaviors quickly, so companies can develop loyal customers. Online, people can switch behaviors as soon as they see something better. It's the force of these millions of people, combined with the rapid evolution of new technologies by trial and error, that makes the groundswell so protean in form and so tough for traditional businesses to deal with.

What does this mean to you? It means the groundswell is coming to your world very soon (if it's not already there).

If you work for a media company, look out. Advertisers are shifting more and more of their money online. The groundswell is creating its own news sites (like Google News or Digg). The very idea of news is changing, as bloggers jostle with journalists for scoops. People take entertainment properties like TV shows and movies, rip them off the airwaves and DVDs, hack them, and repost new versions on YouTube or Dailymotion.

If you have a brand, you're under threat. Your customers have always had an idea about what your brand signifies, an idea that may vary from the image you are projecting. Now they're talking to each other about that idea. They are redefining for themselves the brand you spent millions of dollars, or hundreds of millions of dollars, creating.

If you are a retailer, your lock on distribution is over. People are not just buying online; they are buying from each other. They are comparing your prices with prices all over the Internet and telling each other where to get the best deal on sites like redflagdeals.com. As Chris Anderson, author of *The Long Tail,*[26] has pointed out, shelf space creates far less power when there's nearly infinite selection online.

If you are a financial services company, you no longer dominate flows of capital. Trading happens online, and consumers get financial advice from message boards on Yahoo! Finance and the Motley Fool. Companies like Prosper allow consumers to get loans from each other, instead of from banks. PayPal makes credit cards unnecessary for many transactions.

Business-to-business companies are, if anything, *more* vulnerable to these trends. Their customers have every reason to band together and rate the companies' services, to join groups like ITtoolbox to share insights with each other, or to help each other out on LinkedIn Answers.

Even inside companies, your employees are connecting on social networks, building ideas with online collaboration tools, and discussing the pros and cons of your policies and priorities.

The groundswell has changed the balance of power. Anybody can put up a site that connects people with people. If it's designed well, people will use it. They'll tell their friends to use it. They'll conduct commerce, or read the news, or start a popular movement, or make loans to each other, or whatever the site is designed to facilitate. And the store, or media outlet, or government, or bank that used to fill that role will find itself far less relevant. If you own that institution, the groundswell will eat up your profit margins, cut down your market share, and marginalize your sources of strength.

if you can't beat 'em . . .

Amazingly, some businesses aren't eroding away, trying to fight the groundswell. They're thriving in it.

It isn't comfortable at first. The groundswell is filled with threats, as people like Digg's Kevin Rose and Toshiba attorney Michael B. Ayers found out. Things happen rapidly. But the first step to understanding the groundswell is to dip a toe in it. And once you've done that, you can begin to see where your company can, potentially, gain some advantage.

One man who realized this was Bob Lutz. Bob is in his seventies. He's toiled for the auto industry since his early thirties. (Before that, he was a fighter pilot.) He's worked for Ford; he's worked for Chrysler, where he was on the board of directors; and he joined GM in 2001, as vice chairman for product development.

Toward the end of 2004, three years into Bob's tenure at GM, things were going poorly. The stock was in free fall. Customers weren't warming to the new product lines, and neither were the auto critics who traditionally make pronouncements on what's hot in the auto business. Bob—one of GM's best communicators, a dynamic, articulate leader who is passionate about products—wasn't getting his message across.

Bob needed a way to speak directly to the people who were still open to GM's message. So as the auto show approached in January 2005, he decided he wasn't too old—and GM wasn't too stodgy—to try something new. Bob started a blog called FastLane (you can read it at fastlane .gmblogs.com). Time from decision to launch: three weeks. Pretty amazing for an old-line Detroit automaker.

The first entries were a bit stiff—not at all like most of the bloggers out there. But Bob's first post got 121 comments from readers. People wanted to hear what GM was saying. There were critics, but there were also enthusiasts. Here's what one FastLane reader, for example, said about the new Pontiac GTO:[27]

> The GTO is a great car. I've driven it and loved it. I know the price shocks some people. But if you drive the car, you can see that the money has been spent under the sheetmetal. Of course the sheetmetal could use a fresher designer. Something that really says GTO. Not quite a performance value, but a great car, if you can get your hands on it.

Within a few weeks, Bob was off and running, penning posts with titles like "Quick Missive from The Show Floor" and "Best in Class? Taste for Yourself." This guy was born to blog. He just needed the technology to catch up with his innate desire to communicate. Here's how he put it, just four months after starting the blog:[28]

What began as an experiment has become an important means of communication for GM. It has given me, personally, an opportunity to get much closer with you, the public. Often, I find your comments insightful and compelling. At times your criticism is harsh. But the fact that you have remained interested and continue to have faith in our efforts to develop great products is a worthy motivator.

FastLane hasn't revolutionized GM. It hasn't changed the competitive dynamics with Japanese automakers or turned the auto industry's troublesome dealer channel into pussycats. But it has revolutionized the way GM *communicates*. GM no longer needs to be concerned that auto industry trade magazines and expensive TV commercials are the only way to communicate with customers, dealers, employees, and investors—it has a direct channel. Searches on Google for items like "Chevrolet Volt" lead readers directly to the appropriate blog post in the first page of results. GM can now react quickly to news items, criticisms, and even recalls without seeming petty. It can float test balloons about new car ideas and see what the reaction is. And even better, every posting gets hundreds of comments, which generate new ideas for the company.

That's groundswell thinking in action.

If Bob Lutz can join the groundswell, so can you. Whether it's starting your own blog, adding ratings and reviews to your site, marketing through social networks, or enabling your customers to support each other, you *can* gain advantage from the groundswell. You can master groundswell thinking.

To turn the technologies of the groundswell to your advantage, you need to understand them. Chapter 2 explains the neat trick of making the groundswell your ally, including all the technology pieces and how they fit together.

2. jujitsu and the technologies of the groundswell

After you've read chapter 1—or even if you've just been reading the newspaper lately—you might think the groundswell is mostly a problem. After all, businesses and other institutions are built on control, and the groundswell weakens and undermines control. Groundswell phenomena—like unhappy customers posting videos on YouTube, or MySpace members with their own interpretation of your logo—don't fit well with corporate PR and marketing plans.

But the groundswell is like any other human activity. If you understand it, you can work with it or even thrive in it. This is groundswell thinking.

Groundswell thinking is like any other complex skill—it takes knowledge, experience, and eventually, enlightenment to get there. Think of it as a martial art. In fact, think of it as jujitsu,[1] a Japanese martial art that enables you to harness the power of your opponent for your own advantage. If your attacker comes at you with a big, clumsy lunge, he ends up on the ground—and the faster the lunge, the harder the thud.

This book, then, is a jujitsu manual for managers. Like martial arts *sensei*, we will teach you the techniques of the groundswell. First, you will learn about the forces at work in the new online world. Then we will give you the tools to engage with those forces. Finally, we will arm you with the techniques you can use to turn those forces to your advantage.

the big principle versus the component technologies

This chapter is about the technologies involved in the groundswell. It's important to understand these technologies, but the technologies are the detail, and it's tempting to get sucked into the detail. So many words have been written about blogs and blogging, social networks, and user-generated content that you might think that understanding those technologies will equip you for the new world.

Wrong.

First, the technologies change rapidly. And second, the technologies are not the point. The forces at work are. Like the jujitsu master, you must understand *how bodies move*, not just learn a single block or throw. You must develop a feel for the groundswell.

With that in mind, here's the principle for mastering the groundswell: *concentrate on the relationships, not the technologies.*

In the groundswell, relationships are everything. The way people connect with each other—the community that is created—determines how the power shifts.

groundswell technologies and how to use them

In this chapter we will group groundswell technologies according to how people use them and what they mean for you and your company. For each we will explain briefly (1) how they work, (2) how many people use them, (3) how they form part of the groundswell, (4) how they threaten institutional power, and (5) what you can do about them. The descriptions of the technologies are basic because we want to concentrate on the relationships, not the technologies themselves. Remember as you read this chapter that the techniques here are tactics—we explain how to combine them into cohesive strategies in chapter 4.

At the end of this chapter, having described all the key activities people are participating in now, we'll include a bonus: a plan you can use to evaluate new groundswell technologies as they appear.

people creating: blogs, user-generated content, and podcasts

Self-expression used to be either private (you made paintings, wrote poems, or composed songs for yourself) or difficult (you struggled to sell, publish, or perform those creations). Not anymore. First, the tools to create and edit text, audio, and video on a PC are cheap and easy for nearly anyone to use. And second, the groundswell provides ample ways to show off your work so that other people can easily find and consume it.

HOW THEY WORK. A blog is a personal (or group) journal of entries ("posts") containing written thoughts, links, and often pictures. People can publish their videos (one form of user-generated content[2]) on sites like YouTube and their articles on Gather or Helium. If you think of yourself more as a radio or TV commentator, you can create podcasts and regularly distribute those audio and video files through sites like Apple's iTunes. People can listen to these audio segments individually or subscribe to have the files downloaded to their computer or iPod. Some bloggers have also created video blogs, like Martin Lindstrom on the *Advertising Age* site.[3] Nearly all these forms of expression encourage commentary; for example, both blogs and YouTube videos enable visitors to include their own comments on what's been written and posted.

PARTICIPATION. Blog reading is one of the most popular activities in the groundswell, with one in four online Americans reading blogs (see table 2-1).[4] In Japan it's even more popular; more than half of online adults read blogs at least monthly. South Koreans are more likely than residents of any other country to blog; more than one in six online South Koreans is a blogger. Video viewing is also popular, but there are far more video viewers than video creators. Podcasters and even podcast listeners are rare, reaching only 11 percent of the online population in America and less in other countries.

HOW THEY ENABLE RELATIONSHIPS. The authors of blogs read and comment on others' blogs. They also cite each other, adding links to other blogs from their own posts. This interlinking creates relationships between the blogs and their authors and forms the *blogosphere*.

TABLE 2-1

Percentage of online consumers using blogs and user-generated content

	United States	United Kingdom	France	Germany	Japan	South Korea
Read blogs	25%	10%	21%	10%	52%	31%
Comment on blogs	14%	4%	10%	4%	20%	21%
Write a blog	11%	3%	7%	2%	12%	18%
Watch user-generated video	29%	17%	15%	16%	20%	5%
Upload user-generated video	8%	4%	2%	2%	3%	4%
Listen to podcasts	11%	7%	6%	7%	4%	0%

Figures include consumers who participate at least monthly.

Source: 2007 Technographics surveys.

The echo effect in the blogosphere means that for any given topic, there's a sort of running commentary. The cross-linked blog posts cause these posts to rise in the Google rankings because of the importance Google places on links in its search algorithms.

Similarly, amateur video posts can reference each other and include comments. YouTube makes it easy to see multiple videos created by the same author—you can even subscribe to that author's channel to keep up with what he or she is adding.

HOW THEY THREATEN INSTITUTIONAL POWER. Blogs, user-generated video, and podcasts aren't regulated, so anything is possible. Unlike journalists, bloggers may sometimes mix fact and opinion, report rumors, and fail to disclose conflicts of interest. Few YouTube video uploaders check first with the subjects of their videos for permission and copyright violations are rife. Companies frequently need to police employees who post unauthorized content about their employers and their jobs.

HOW YOU CAN USE THEM. First, listen. Read blogs that talk about your company and see what people are saying. Blog search engines like

Google Blog Search and Technorati can help you determine which blogs have the most influence. Search YouTube, Dailymotion, MetaCafe, and other video sites for what the groundswell is saying about you, or use a cross-site video search engine like Yahoo! Video.

If you want to get serious about monitoring, work with services, like TNS Cymfony and Nielsen BuzzMetrics, that monitor blogs, videos, and online discussion groups for mentions of your company and your competitors and gauge general sentiment.

Next steps: start commenting on those blogs or videos, or prepare to create your own. Sun Microsystems and Microsoft encourage employees to blog within guidelines intended to prevent problems like unauthorized financial or material disclosures. Blogs are a valuable tool, not just for communicating to the world, but for getting feedback, as we described at the end of chapter 1 in the discussion about GM. We (the authors) share a blog—you can read it at groundswell.forrester.com. We used our blog to test out ideas for this book, to get suggestions and examples from the outside, and once the book was done, to promote it.

Podcasting has yet to really catch on. Even so, companies like IBM and Purina are experimenting with podcasts for their customers.

For some brands, uploaded content can create a bigger impact than a commercial and do it far more cheaply. For example, Ray-Ban got nearly 3 million people to watch its video "Guy catches glasses with face," in which Wayfarer sunglasses are thrown and caught on a man's face in increasingly unlikely settings.[5]

These tactics make the most sense as part of a corporate strategy of listening to the groundswell, as we'll describe in chapter 5, and talking with the groundswell, as we'll describe in chapter 6.

people connecting: social networks and virtual worlds

If you want to see the seething, connected variety of the groundswell, join a social networking site (SNS) like MySpace or Facebook, which have tens of millions of members already. There's a social network for every audience: LinkedIn targets working professionals, Piczo is popular with young girls, Brazilians join Google's orkut, while hi5 and Bebo dominate in Europe.

HOW THEY WORK. Members of these sites maintain profiles, connect with each other, and interact. In addition to updating profiles, one major activity on social networking sites is "friending," a mechanism by which people acknowledge relationships with and keep up with their friends or acquaintances. Led by Facebook, social networking sites are also becoming a platform for mini-applications. This expands the scope of what friends can do with each other, from managing event invitations to playing Scrabble.

For those who want to go beyond a simple profile, the groundswell provides virtual worlds. Second Life is a popular 3-D simulated environment with more than 10 million members.[6] Cyworld hosts a similar environment in Asia and is expanding into North America. Other worlds, like WeeWorld, are two-dimensional. Either way, participants can express themselves by how they look and what they wear; a fifty-year-old fat and balding technical writer can be a muscular stud in a black turtleneck or a buxom Barbie if he wants.

PARTICIPATION. One in four online American adults visit social networking sites at least monthly (see table 2-2). These sites are extremely popular in South Korea, where one in three participate, because of the country's high broadband penetration and community-focused population. Participation is far lower in Germany and France.

HOW THEY ENABLE RELATIONSHIPS. Social networking sites and virtual worlds are by definition *about* the facilitation of relationships with technologies. On MySpace people often post comments on each

TABLE 2-2

Percentage of online consumers visiting social networking sites

	United States	United Kingdom	France	Germany	Japan	South Korea
Visit social networking sites	25%	21%	3%	10%	20%	35%

Figures include consumers who visit at least monthly.

Source: 2007 Technographics surveys.

others' profiles and share their favorite pictures and music for others to see. Facebook has a news feed on the home page of each profile with updates from friends—alerts like "John added a photo to his profile." SNSs connect people who've moved apart even as they enable people who live close together (like college students) to keep up with one another. They also help create new relationships and are filled with subcommunities like "Yale University Students" and "Clergy Chicks," which is a group for female ministers on Facebook. In Paris there's even a social network called Peuplade (www.peuplade.fr) whose sole purpose is to connect people with others in their own neighborhood—amazingly, people use this social network to make friends and hang out with folks who live right around the corner.

HOW THEY THREATEN INSTITUTIONAL POWER. SNSs suck up a lot of time; 22 percent of teenagers check in *daily*, for example.[7] This time spent threatens, among others, media companies, which is one reason why News Corp. bought MySpace. Fads can spread rapidly through SNSs, displacing, undermining, or (sometimes) boosting brand awareness.

HOW YOU CAN USE THEM. To get comfortable with the dynamics of social networks, join one.

As for companies, many have put up profiles on SNSs that get "friends" just like any other participant—for example, Victoria's Secret has over two hundred thousand friends on MySpace (www.myspace .com/vspink), and over fifty thousand South Koreans made friends with Pizza Hut on Cyworld. This is most effective if the brand profile has badges, backgrounds, and buddy icons that SNS members can post on their own profiles and share with friends.

Many companies are experimenting in virtual worlds—for example, you can test-drive a Pontiac in Second Life, and Skittles is advertising in WeeWorld. These activities have generated publicity, but so far any value beyond that is unproven.

Some companies with enthusiastic communities have created their own networks—for example, salesforce.com created its own social network so that customers can connect with people in similar industries or departments. Webkinz (a site from the plush toy company Ganz) lets kids furnish their animals' online homes and interact with each other in these spaces.

We discuss strategies that use social networks and communities for listening in chapter 5, for marketing in chapter 6, and for energizing your best customers in chapter 7. Communities are also ideal for enabling customers to support each other; we describe that strategy in chapter 8.

people collaborating: wikis and open source

Most of the activity in the groundswell is uncoordinated—people individually pursue their own interests and connections, and the groundswell emerges from the interactions. This mimics the real economy. But when members of the groundswell decide to work together explicitly, the results are powerful because of the advanced collaboration tools now available, starting with wikis.

HOW THEY WORK. Wikis (from the Hawaiian word for *quick*) are sites that support multiple contributors with a shared responsibility for creating and maintaining content, typically focused around text and pictures. The largest and best known, of course, is Wikipedia, the nonprofit people-generated encyclopedia with over 2 million articles. There are plenty of other, more specialized wikis, including Conservapedia, a conservative version of Wikipedia, and wikiHow, a collection of how-to articles ("How to win at Monopoly," "How to do a Shove It on a skateboard"). Anyone can edit a wiki, which you'd think would result in chaos. However, in all but the most controversial cases (for example, articles on political figures like George Bush), the collective contributions represent a consensus view, based on a shared set of conventions (in Wikipedia, for example, the main convention is "neutral point of view"). The community of contributors notices changes and acts to preserve or reverse them based on the ideals of the community.

The same sort of cooperation drives other forms of online collaboration, including open-source software products like Linux (a version of the Unix operating system), Apache (a Web server), and Firefox (a Web browser). In open source, technically adept developers combine their efforts to build, test, and improve software products, and the code is available for all to see. Before you scoff at this form of development, recognize that Linux now underpins many Web servers and consumer electronics devices, including TiVo; Apache is the dominant Web server software on the Internet;[8] and Firefox has gone from zero to over 25 percent market share in less than two years.[9]

PARTICIPATION. While over 22 percent of online American adults say they use Wikipedia at least monthly, only 6 percent contribute to a wiki once a month. We haven't yet collected data on wiki editing outside the United States.

HOW THEY ENABLE RELATIONSHIPS. Wikis include "talk pages" parallel to each page where contributors discuss (and sometimes fight over) what ought to be included. Contributors can also view each others' profiles; those that contribute the most often get more respect from others in the community. In open source, the developer community vets and decides on which bits of computer code will become part of the standard release. In a very real way, these communities are collaborating to define the content of creative efforts that many millions of people will use.

HOW THEY THREATEN INSTITUTIONAL POWER. Wikipedia is universally known and frequently used: it's the eighth-most-popular site on the Web, according to Alexa.[10] This makes Wikipedia a classic example of groundswell power—the masses determine what's on it, including the image presented for companies. For example, as of this writing, the page for Nike Inc. includes sections on human rights concerns and advertising controversies, topics that Nike's PR department would rather weren't included in a "definitive" description of the company.

HOW YOU CAN USE THEM. Since Wikipedia pages typically appear within the top few results on Web searches, what they say matters. Companies should carefully monitor pages that describe them or their products.[11] Making changes is tougher because Wikipedia discourages people or companies from contributing content about themselves. But some companies, including one financial services firm we interviewed, have managed to make factual corrections, and other companies have even added articles about their new products. These contributions survive only when the contributing company behaves transparently. The best approach is to make your case in the "talk pages" on Wikipedia.

You can also deploy wikis on behalf of your company, forming your own customers into a mini-groundswell. For example, eBay has a wiki where its members provide tips on topics like "buying and selling antiques" (www.ebaywiki.com). Reuters deployed a wiki so its readers could build a financial glossary (glossary.reuters.com).

Companies have also found wikis to be useful *internally* as a collaboration tool for teams working on a document or specification, for example. This book was researched and written on a wiki; the coauthors, editor, and others all contributed content and links to a shared repository that any of us could reference or edit.

We feature additional examples of how people support each other in more detail in chapter 8 and talk about internal tools for collaboration in chapter 11.

people reacting to each other: forums, ratings, and reviews

Forums—with posts and responses threaded together—are older than just about any other social technology; they even predate the Internet. And ratings and reviews have become so commonplace online that many may not realize those tools represent part of the groundswell trend. But forums, ratings, and reviews are so easy to set up and to use that they're now part of a wide variety of sites, from media to retail to product support.

HOW THEY WORK. A wide variety of discussion forums are available all over the Web. Typically, once people become members, they can log in and post any question or comment or they can respond to questions and comments posted by others. The comments and responses form "threads" that visitors can perceive as conversations. Yahoo! and AOL host forums on various topics; there are also freestanding forums, like tivocommunity.com for TiVo enthusiasts, and forums run by companies, like Intuit's quickbooksgroup.com forum for small-business owners using its QuickBooks product.

Reviews are becoming even more common than forums. Amazon was among the first sites to leverage reviews; now reviews are spreading to retail sites of all kinds, from electronics to garden tools. Media sites like CNET and travel sites like TripAdvisor have made reviews a central element, while other sites, including Rotten Tomatoes (for movies) and Epinions (for nearly everything), contain nothing but reviews and ratings. Members of eBay even rate each other. At ExpoTV, owners of products upload their own video reviews of items from cosmetics to remote car-starters.[12]

In a classic example of the groundswell applying its techniques to its own content, you can even rate the reviews themselves. For example, an Argentinean reviewer who gave a five-star rave to *Harry Potter and the Half-Blood Prince* on Amazon got 884 people to vote that her review was helpful[13]—fans loved how she wove her passion for *Harry Potter* into the review.

PARTICIPATION. Around one in five online Americans and Japanese participate in discussion forums (see table 2-3). Reading ratings and reviews has become common—one in four online Americans and Germans, one in five British, and 38 percent of Japanese read them. While far smaller percentages actually write ratings and reviews, those people generate enough content to help everybody else.

TABLE 2-3

Percentage of online consumers using forums, ratings, and reviews

	United States	United Kingdom	France	Germany	Japan	South Korea
Participate in discussion forums	18%	12%	11%	15%	22%	7%
Read ratings and reviews	25%	20%	12%	28%	38%	16%
Post ratings and reviews	11%	5%	3%	8%	11%	11%

Figures include consumers who participate at least monthly.

Source: 2007 Technographics surveys.

HOW THEY ENABLE RELATIONSHIPS. Discussion forums are basically a slow-motion conversation, enabling people to respond to each other online; frequent posters in many forums get to know each others' tendencies well, although they likely have never met.

Forums and reviews succeed partly because they let people show off. For example, Harriett Klauser, Amazon's top reviewer, reads two books a day and has reviewed over fourteen thousand. She's well known to publishers, who send her fifty books a week.

HOW THEY THREATEN INSTITUTIONAL POWER. Before consumer reviews, companies only had to worry about influencing experts—the reviewer at *Car and Driver*, for example, or the restaurant critic at the *Los Angeles Times*. Now one buyer with a problem will point out that your digital camera's screen isn't bright enough, your hotel smells funny, or your animated video is boring even for four-year-olds.

HOW YOU CAN USE THEM. For retailers, ratings and reviews are great—they boost buy rates. We quantify this in chapter 7 as an example of using your customers to energize others. We talk about the supportive power of forums in chapter 8.

For companies whose products and services get rated, ratings and reviews are instructive. Brand monitoring, as we describe in chapter 5, finds random mentions of brands. Ratings and reviews are more focused. If an appliance manufacturer finds a reviewer on buzzillions.com saying that his oven's door melts on the self-cleaning cycle, then the manufacturer has a quality problem, not a review problem.

people organizing content: tags

Classifying things is central to the way people organize. One typical organization is a *taxonomy*, where every individual thing has a spot. For example, in the taxonomy of species, *Homo sapiens* goes into the mammal slot, while *Tyrannosaurus rex* goes with the reptiles. But taxonomies depend on an expert's opinion. A classification system for the groundswell has to be more flexible than this, as David Weinberger explains in his book *Everything Is Miscellaneous*.[14] That's where tags come in.

HOW THEY WORK. Consider a Web site where NASCAR fans discuss race standings. You might classify it "NASCAR" and "discussion group," while we would classify it "forum" and "fan phenomena." This loose, overlapping classification of tags is sometimes called a *folksonomy*, a term coined by Thomas Vander Wal.[15] A folksonomy depends on the opinions of the folks out there, not on the experts.

Tags have become the standard way that sites add people-driven organization. Digg, which we discussed in chapter 1, is a tagging site—you tag ("digg") which news stories you prefer and decide into which category they should go. Del.icio.us, a simple downloadable application that's now part of Yahoo!, goes one step further. Del.icio.us allows you to bookmark any Web site and mark it with any classification tag you want. The bookmarks, instead of being stored on your computer, are stored on Yahoo!'s servers, and others visiting the site can see your tags (if you let them) or search for sites with common tags. A similar service, StumbleUpon, was acquired by eBay in 2007.

Once you look, tags really are everywhere in the groundswell. Flickr lets you tag your photos. Blogging tools like WordPress let you tag your blog posts. YouTube lets you tag your videos. And in many of these cases, visitors can add their own tags as well.

PARTICIPATION. Tagging isn't for everyone—14 percent of South Koreans do it, but participation is lower in other parts of the world (see table 2-4). Even so, keep an eye on this activity—after all, those who classify and organize the online world will determine how we see that world.

TABLE 2-4

Percentage of online consumers using tags

	United States	United Kingdom	France	Germany	Japan	South Korea
Use tags	7%	2%	9%	10%	6%	14%

Figures include consumers who use tags at least monthly.

Source: 2007 Technographics surveys.

HOW THEY ENABLE RELATIONSHIPS. Relationships based on tags are subtle. You can use them simply to classify your stuff and to help with searches and then ignore the social aspect completely.

But tags define individuals. Suppose you notice that someone has tagged Red Sox pitcher Curt Schilling's blog on del.icio.us as "celebrity blogger." If this catches your eye, you might want to know what else she has tagged as a celebrity blogger. Now even if you've never met the person doing the tagging, you can follow her choices on the Web.

Del.icio.us has a feature that makes this highly visible. It's easy to publish your newly tagged sites daily as a blog post made up of a series of links and descriptions. This blog post says, in effect, "This is what I saw today; here's what I thought of it. Maybe you'll find it interesting." Your tagging becomes a form of shared self-expression and a chronicle of what you've paid attention to.

HOW THEY THREATEN INSTITUTIONAL POWER. Tagging seems innocuous, but of course, you have no control over how people classify you or your products. If you make farm equipment, you might classify the product page for your cattle prod as "livestock," but somebody else might classify it as "animal cruelty." And it's not just classification you don't control—it's value judgments. One of the most popular del.icio.us tags on walmartingacrossamerica.com, a blog, is "fake"—referring to the fact that the blog was unmasked as a construction funded by Wal-Mart's PR agency, Edelman.[16] Wal-Mart can't do anything about that. The way companies classify the world is often the source of their power (is Subway "healthy food" or "fast food"?). Tags undermine that power.

HOW YOU CAN USE THEM. The first thing you should do is to go to del.icio.us and enter your company's site in the search box. For example, if you do this for target.com, you find that (as of this writing) 297 people have tagged it. After searching for your company's site, click on the result that comes up, and you'll see how people are classifying your company. Obviously, you can do the same thing with your product pages, your competitors' sites, and recent news articles about your company. By looking at not only how your company is tagged but also *who* is tagging it, you can learn a lot about how people perceive you. You can use this information, for example, to buy search words on search engines and to change the language you use when talking to customers.

There's no rule against tagging your own content. Start a del.icio.us account, and tag your company's sites and other related sites according to your view of the world (for example, if you define your company's category as "CRM software," tag your site and your competitors' sites with that term). You can do the same with photos you upload to Photobucket or Flickr and with your own blog posts. This will help people who search on these terms find the photos, blog posts, and Web sites you think they should.

Another way to use tagging is simple: organize the Web. In creating this book, we used del.icio.us to create a set of tags for each chapter, neatly organizing Web sites and articles we'd found. You can follow our work yourself by visiting del.icio.us/thegroundswell. If you want to organize your own collection of Web sites, for yourself or for sharing, tagging is the perfect tool.

accelerating consumption: rss and widgets

You might get the idea from all these groundswell elements that groundswell consumers would be overwhelmed with a flood of content. Start with the e-mail we all get every day, and layer on top of that updates from Facebook pages, blog posts, YouTube videos, and tagged items of all kinds. Then add the groundswell elements you bump into when browsing, like ratings, reviews, and Wikipedia entries. The deeper you get into these technologies, the more help you need finding the right bits of content quickly. That's what RSS and widgets are for—by giving people the ability to consume and process more social content, they accelerate the action of the groundswell.

HOW THEY WORK. RSS stands for Really Simple Syndication. Since the acronym isn't very explanatory, try this: RSS is a tool that brings you updates. Instead of going *out* to blogs, news sites, auction sites, SNSs, and other sites that you want to monitor, RSS brings the updated content to *you*.

Think of RSS as a system with two elements: a transmitter and a receiver. The transmitter generates a *feed*—an updated list of everything new coming from a site. For example, an RSS feed might be the posts from a blog, the articles on a newspaper site, new photos posted by a member of Flickr, stock quotes, updates from basketball games, tagged items on del.icio.us—anything that changes regularly. Any site can host a feed of content that changes over time.

To see the RSS feed, you need a receiver, which is known as an RSS reader. While there are a bunch of RSS reader programs and RSS-driven Web pages—including FeedBurner, Netvibes, and Pageflakes—you can also view RSS feeds on personalized home pages from Google and Yahoo! or on the latest versions of browsers like Firefox or Internet Explorer.[17] Either way, the RSS reader organizes the feeds into areas of your screen and, in some cases, tabs. You, the consumer of all this information, get to see everything that's new in one place and to click on and view anything that looks interesting. Your RSS reader will look different from somebody else's, depending on what content you've added. Web sites that support RSS feeds typically feature a distinctive orange square transmitter-style icon that you can click on to subscribe to the site's feed.

Widgets, like RSS readers, are mini-applications that connect to the Internet. But unlike RSS, widgets typically have a specific function. For example, a weather widget on your desktop could keep you up to date on the local forecast, or a gas price widget could deliver updated reports from local gas stations. Using Web 2.0 technologies, widgets can be highly interactive. Some are designed to run on your Windows or Macintosh desktop; others appear on Web pages or even your mobile phone. Many are designed to sit on pages in blogs or social networks so other visitors can see them. Widgets for Google home pages and Windows Vista are called, idiosyncratically, "gadgets."

PARTICIPATION. Fewer than one in twelve Americans say they use an RSS feed (see table 2-5). But the impact of RSS will be felt far more widely than that. There are 23 percent of online consumers in the United States using personalized home pages—and they're using RSS

TABLE 2-5

Percentage of online consumers using RSS

	United States	United Kingdom	France	Germany	Japan	South Korea
Use RSS	8%	3%	5%	4%	0%	1%

Figures include consumers who use RSS at least monthly.

Source: 2007 Technographics surveys.

feeds, whether they know it or not. As Internet Explorer 7 and Firefox become more widely used, consumers will become used to those browsers' "smart bookmarks," which include RSS-updated headlines right in the bookmark. And we believe the ubiquitous orange squares on Web sites will begin to raise RSS consciousness over the next five years.

Widget use is harder to measure—about 10 percent of online U.S. consumers report that they regularly use a desktop widget like Yahoo! Widgets or Apple's Dashboard. But Web-based widgets are every-where—they appear frequently in MySpace and on blogs. In June 2007, comScore reported that worldwide, 21 percent of online con-sumers have interacted with a Web-based widget.[18]

HOW THEY ENABLE RELATIONSHIPS. RSS is the grease that lubri-cates the groundswell. While subscribing to an RSS feed isn't by itself a social activity, it enables social activity to happen efficiently. A person using RSS can realistically subscribe to more blogs, monitor more social networking pages, and generally stay connected more than other people.

Widgets are social because they spread. If you put a widget on your Web page or SNS profile page, others will see it. Typically, these widgets include a "get this widget" button so others can install it on their pages.

For example, SplashCast makes a widget that can display constantly updated picture and video feeds. Imagine that a political candidate de-cides to put updates of his speeches and appearances into a SplashCast widget. Now his supporters can embed that widget on their MySpace pages and blogs. The candidate ends up being syndicated broadly by his own supporters, and their friends can add it to their blogs and profiles as well. This is the social potential of widgets.

HOW THEY THREATEN INSTITUTIONAL POWER. By themselves, RSS and widgets don't threaten institutional power. But since they accelerate the consumption of other groundswell material, they intensify the threat to institutions. RSS consumers can read more blogs, including blogs that may be critical of your company (and they may see a trend as blogs refer to and reinforce each other). And people with a cause against—or for—a company may develop widgets and spread them. Imagine a "Boycott [your company name here]" widget shared and posted by people who think your company inappropriately uses sweatshop labor in Asia, for example.

HOW YOU CAN USE THEM. RSS and widgets can be excellent marketing tools, especially when it comes to pushing out regularly updated content to your customers. This means your blog, press releases, product catalogs, and anything else you update regularly should be available through RSS feeds. Most blogging tools already support RSS.

As for widgets, they're beginning to catch on with marketers. UPS built an advertising campaign in the United Kingdom, France, and Germany around a character—called, of course, Widget—that makes you more efficient. Download the character-shaped widget to your desktop, and it not only tells you where your packages are but also delivers a subtle UPS branding message.[19] In the United States, the Discovery Channel created a Shark Week widget[20] so that viewers who love its shark-related programs (and there are plenty—Shark Week is one of Discovery's most popular features) can put a continually updated feed of videos and promotions on their blogs or personal profile pages. Web-based widgets, like YouTube videos, have the potential to spread virally as your fans e-mail them around and embed them on social networking profile pages and in blog posts.

evaluating new technologies

The groundswell doesn't stand still. Master the tools we described in the last dozen pages or so, and you're still not done with the groundswell's rapidly evolving technology base.

Case in point: Twitter.

Twitter is a tool that lets members sign up free (of course) and then send short messages anytime they want. The prompt from Twitter is "What are you doing?" The person using Twitter types in a message of no more than 140 characters, either on the Web or as a text message on a mobile phone. That message is then sent out to all the person's "followers"—basically, everyone who's interested in that person's musings. As a follower, you could see a friend's "tweets" on a Web page or a mobile phone.

In March 2007, we began to get a lot of questions about Twitter. Twitter was intriguing for several reasons. One, it had caught fire in the previous two weeks, with tens of thousands of new people using it. One of those was presidential candidate John Edwards, who was regularly offering short updates from the campaign trail. Second, because it connected to mobile phones on both the writing and receiving ends, it had the potential to become a pervasive element of the groundswell. After all, people have their mobile phones with them nearly all the time, in many places where they don't necessarily have a computer.

On the other hand, some people were using Twitter in some pretty silly ways. Some people were giving hourly updates on what they had for lunch or what meeting they had just entered. Even if you're getting tweets just from your friends, that gets pretty insipid after a very short while.

As our clients began to ask us about Twitter, we asked ourselves the broader question—how can you evaluate new technologies as they enter the groundswell? Which ones will catch on, and which will fizzle? And which ones do you need to pay attention to, and which ones can you safely ignore? So based on our experience of new social technology adoption around the world in the past five years, we came up with the groundswell technology test.

the groundswell technology test

When we started this chapter, we said you should concentrate on the relationships, not the technologies. So when it comes to a new technology, again, the relationships are paramount. A tool that enables new relationships in new ways will catch on faster than one that doesn't. "Faster" on the Internet means weeks and months, not years.

So when evaluating a new technology, ask yourself the following questions:

- *Does it enable people to connect with each other in new ways?* The groundswell is about making connections. If a tool makes those connections more interesting, more varied, or more frequent, it has good potential for adoption—because that's what the groundswell is looking for. Furthermore, such technologies spread virally, as existing participants recruit new people to join them. For example, Facebook opened its social network to anybody in September 2006 (before that, it was mostly for college students) and grew rapidly thereafter. YouTube enabled a new form of communication—easily broadcast, universally available video. Twitter doesn't add media to existing forms of communication like blogging and texting, but it permits people to broadcast and subscribe to a constant stream of content in a new place: the mobile phone.

- *Is it effortless to sign up for?* Most groundswell technologies are free. The ones that succeed are also easy to connect up to technologies people already have. For example, Twitter is free and is based on mobile phone texting and a simple Web interface, both of which are commonplace. A technology that requires consumers to buy and carry a new piece of mobile hardware, like a smart phone, would need to be incredibly compelling and would grow very slowly—at least until those smart phones became more broadly available.

- *Does it shift power from institutions to people?* Technologies that mostly benefit companies don't tend to catch on. Those that benefit people do. Facebook gave people power to connect without corporate supervision; Wikipedia allowed them to create without expert approval. Twitter, similarly, lets people connect. One of the first applications that got people's attention was audience members twittering back and forth at a music and technology conference called SXSW. This may have drawn some attention away from the planned events on stage, but it made the audience members more connected.

- *Does the community generate enough content to sustain itself?* All the successful technologies listed in this chapter, from blogs to tagging, make it easy for people to create content and to benefit from each others' content. Twitter fits the same description. Use it, and you create value for your followers. (Of course, all the tools in the groundswell can be used to create garbage, too. But the fact that your tweets are boring doesn't mean Twitter is a failure—it just means your followers will give up reading your tweets.)

- *Is it an open platform that invites partnerships?* This determines whether a product will wither or flourish. Closed platforms like Digg don't evolve as fast because they don't tap into the well of innovation that is the Web 2.0 development community.[21] Open platforms like Facebook, which opened up its interfaces to application developers in 2007, get continual new functionality without so much work on the part of the founders. As for Twitter, it's easy to tap into from either end—other applications can generate tweets or display them. For example, a developer at Olin College in Massachusetts built an application that automatically generates tweets (text messages, if your phone is set up to read them) about the availability of washers and dryers in the dorm laundry room so students don't have to waste a trip to see if a washer is free.[22]

Of course, a lot more goes into analyzing new technologies—do the privacy policies make people feel secure, for example, or can these technologies get a boost from existing big players like Apple, Google, Microsoft, Nokia, or Comcast? But in general, technologies that get a yes on all the questions we just described are the ones mostly likely to take off. And based on this test, Twitter is likely to find its place among other groundswell technologies, and companies should pay attention to it.

The groundswell has two key ingredients: technology and people. We ran down the technologies; now it's time to talk about the people—specifically, your customers and what they're doing (and not doing) online. The answer to this question is different for every company, which is why we created the Social Technographics Profile, the topic of chapter 3.

3. the social technographics profile

How do people participate in the groundswell? Consider a tale of three AFOLs.

AFOLs are adult fans of Lego. Lego bricks, of course, are a favorite building toy of children everywhere. According to Tormod Askildsen, senior director of business development at the Lego Group, 5 to 10 percent of the company's sales—at least $50 million—goes to AFOLs. And unlike children, AFOLs don't age out of the target market. They just get more enthusiastic and buy more. So it turns out that selling Lego bricks to grown-ups is an important business. Furthermore, AFOLs tend to congregate online, so the groundswell is a great way to reach them. But not all AFOLs participate equally.

Among the most active and creative adult Lego fans is Eric Kingsley. Eric posts frequently and uploads photos to LUGNET, the Lego User Group Network, a support forum for AFOLs. In fact, Kingsley was the eighteenth person to join the network. In addition to his many contributions there, he maintains three separate Web sites—one for his family, one for the local Lego group in New England, and a far more detailed page dedicated specifically to Lego trains, his passion, with dozens of photos and blog posts about his efforts to get the Lego company to preserve its line of 9-volt Lego trains. From Lego's perspective,

Eric Kingsley is an active contributor to the Lego culture. As you'll see in chapter 7, in fact, Lego has singled him out for special attention, energizing his Lego enthusiasm to reach out to others.

One of those others is Joe Comeau. Joe is just as enthusiastic as Eric but tends not to work as much on creating Web sites. Instead, he mostly makes his contribution by responding and reacting to the ideas of others. He participates in ongoing activity online—he has been a frequent poster on LUGNET's forums, contributing to discussions about everything from Lego trains to BrikWars, a Lego fantasy war game. He also buys around $4,000 of Lego toys a year, so he's an important customer for the company. His contribution to Lego lore on the Web is just as important as Eric's but qualitatively different. "When someone comes up with a new idea, you build upon it," he says. "Before you know it, you are building at a level far surpassing what you ever thought of." The groundswell is filled with people like Joe—in fact, there are many more of them than there are people like Eric.

Finally, consider Linda Nee. In comparison to Eric and Joe, she's more inclined to participate in group projects like trying to set the world speed record for assembling one of Lego's most complex kits, the Imperial Star Destroyer. But like Eric and Joe, she's hooked on building with Lego, spending, as she puts it, "an unhealthy percentage" of her income on Lego kits. "My participation in forums is light," she says, "but I read almost everything other people write."

Eric Kingsley, Joe Comeau, and Linda Nee are all active members of the AFOL community, but their roles are different. Eric is creating, Joe is reacting, and Linda is reading. In fact, it's the interactions among them—Eric's creative activities, Joe's reactions, and their effect on thousands of people like Linda—that makes this community so dynamic. It's the same with any community on the Internet—the interactions among different contributors make it all fly.

To truly understand the groundswell, you need to dissect and quantify the dynamics that separate different participants. Why? Because a strategy that treats everyone alike.will spell failure—people aren't alike and won't respond in the same way. Your strategy must also account for how groups differ—how the groundswell is different for South Koreans and Canadians, or for Target and RadioShack shoppers. That is the goal of

the Social Technographics Profile, the tool we introduce in this chapter—
to allow people in business to examine and then create strategies based
on the groundswell tendencies of any group of people, anywhere.

a new way to look at participation in the groundswell

In chapter 2 we looked at all the different activities and applications in
the groundswell. Each section began with some statistics. Let's collect
them all here in one place, in figure 3-1.[1]

There's a lot of information in figure 3-1—too much information.
Certain things are clear—for example, far more people join social networks than contribute to blogs. But this chart raises as many questions
as it answers. Are these figures different for women and men, for example? How do they vary by age? And finally, how do you make sense of
all this?

In chapter 2 we said it pays to concentrate on the relationships, not
the technologies. That is the purpose of the Social Technographics
Profile. "Social" refers to the people-to-people activities in the groundswell. "Technographics" refers to Forrester Research's methodology for
surveying consumers—it's similar to demographics and psychographics
but focuses on technology behaviors. And like any other profile, this
profile is designed to allow you to compare any two groups of people—
Gen Y versus Gen X, for example, or Ford owners versus GM owners.

At the core of the Social Technographics Profile is a way to group
people based on the groundswell activities in which they participate.
Think of these groups of people and their activities as rungs on a ladder, as shown in figure 3-2. The ladder shows how we can classify consumers according to their involvement in the groundswell, placing them
into one or more of six groups.[2] Figure 3-3 shows the relative sizes of
these groups among online U.S. adults. Notice that these groups overlap—most Creators are also Spectators, for example.

The Social Technographics Profile includes the following groups:

- *Creators,* at the top of the ladder, are online consumers who at
  least once a month publish a blog or article online, maintain a
  Web page, or upload videos or audio to sites like YouTube. Eric

FIGURE 3-1

Participation in groundswell activities

These statistics were collected in an online survey of over ten thousand U.S. consumers. Bars reflect participation in the indicated activities at least monthly.

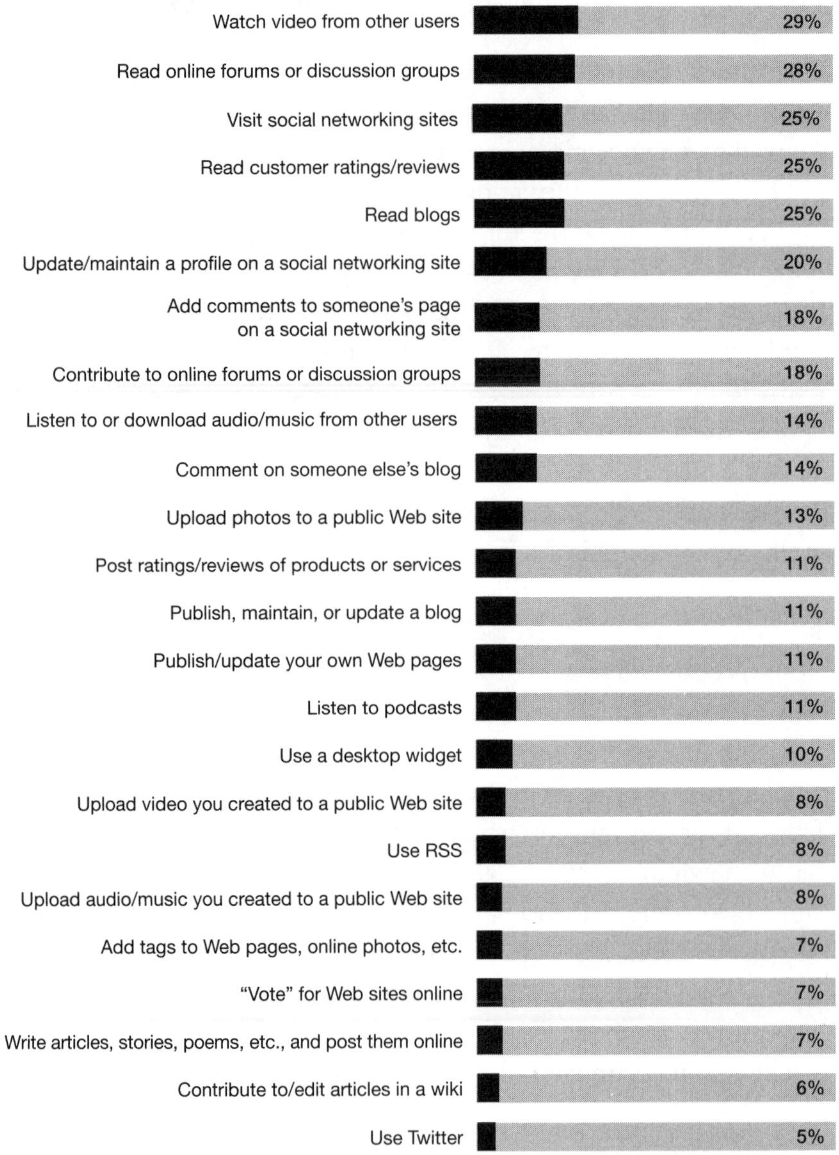

Activity	Percentage
Watch video from other users	29%
Read online forums or discussion groups	28%
Visit social networking sites	25%
Read customer ratings/reviews	25%
Read blogs	25%
Update/maintain a profile on a social networking site	20%
Add comments to someone's page on a social networking site	18%
Contribute to online forums or discussion groups	18%
Listen to or download audio/music from other users	14%
Comment on someone else's blog	14%
Upload photos to a public Web site	13%
Post ratings/reviews of products or services	11%
Publish, maintain, or update a blog	11%
Publish/update your own Web pages	11%
Listen to podcasts	11%
Use a desktop widget	10%
Upload video you created to a public Web site	8%
Use RSS	8%
Upload audio/music you created to a public Web site	8%
Add tags to Web pages, online photos, etc.	7%
"Vote" for Web sites online	7%
Write articles, stories, poems, etc., and post them online	7%
Contribute to/edit articles in a wiki	6%
Use Twitter	5%

Figures represent percentage of online U.S. adults participating at least monthly (over 10,000 consumers surveyed).

Source: Forrester s North American Social Technographics Online Survey, Q2 2007.

Kingsley is a good example. Based on a 2007 survey, in the United States, Creators represent 18 percent of the online adult population; in Europe, they're only 10 percent. South Korea, which has an extremely active blogging population, includes an amazing 38 percent Creators.

- *Critics* react to other content online, posting comments on blogs or online forums, posting ratings or reviews, or editing wikis. Joe Comeau is a typical Critic in the Lego world. Since it's easier to react than to create, it's no surprise that there are more Critics than Creators. One in four online American adults is a Critic, as

FIGURE 3-2

The Social Technographics ladder

Each step on the ladder represents a group of consumers more involved in the groundswell than the previous steps. To join the group on a step, a consumer need only participate in one of the listed activities at least monthly.

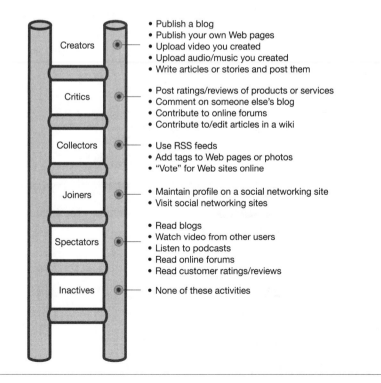

Creators
- Publish a blog
- Publish your own Web pages
- Upload video you created
- Upload audio/music you created
- Write articles or stories and post them

Critics
- Post ratings/reviews of products or services
- Comment on someone else's blog
- Contribute to online forums
- Contribute to/edit articles in a wiki

Collectors
- Use RSS feeds
- Add tags to Web pages or photos
- "Vote" for Web sites online

Joiners
- Maintain profile on a social networking site
- Visit social networking sites

Spectators
- Read blogs
- Watch video from other users
- Listen to podcasts
- Read online forums
- Read customer ratings/reviews

Inactives
- None of these activities

are one in five online Europeans and 36 percent of Japan's online population.

- *Collectors* save URLs and tags on a social-bookmarking service like del.icio.us, vote for sites on a service like Digg, or use RSS feeds on services like Bloglines. This act of collecting and aggregating information plays a vital role in organizing the tremendous amount of content being produced by Creators and Critics. For example, anyone who searches for "MauiHotel" will come upon the collected sites with that tag on del.icio.us. Similarly, visitors to digg.com see the top stories recommended by the Collectors on that site. Collectors are an elite group, including only around 10 percent of online Americans and Europeans, but should grow as more sites build in diverse types of Collector-type activities. Collecting is more popular in Hong Kong and South Korea than in the United States, but it is actually less popular in Japan, where only 6 percent of online adults are Collectors.

- *Joiners* participate in or maintain profiles on a social networking site like MySpace. In the United States, where Facebook is growing rapidly among adults, Joiners have already reached 25 percent of the online population; in South Korea, where Cyworld is pop-

FIGURE 3-3

The Social Technographics Profile of online U.S. adults

Note the percentages add to more than 100% because the groups overlap.

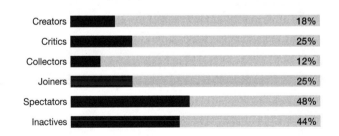

Creators	18%
Critics	25%
Collectors	12%
Joiners	25%
Spectators	48%
Inactives	44%

Base: Online U.S. adults.

Source: Forrester's North American Social Technographics Online Survey, Q2 2007.

ular, it's nearly 40 percent. Right now Europe is behind on social networking activity, with Joiners only half as common as in the United States.

- *Spectators* consume what the rest produce—blogs, online videos, podcasts, forums, and reviews. For example, Linda Nee is a Spectator in the adult Lego community. Since being a Spectator requires so much less effort than the other activities in the groundswell, it's no surprise that this is the largest group, with 48 percent of online adult Americans, 37 percent of online adult Europeans, and two-thirds of the online adults of Japan and of the large Chinese cities where we conduct surveys.

- *Inactives*—nonparticipants—still remain. Among those online in 2007, 41 percent of Americans, 53 percent of Europeans, and only 37 percent of South Koreans are untouched by the groundswell. Of course, this is just the online population. Offline consumers can't participate at all.

the social technographics profile: an example

Classifications are fine. But the real power in the Social Technographics Profile is this: with it we can understand how social technologies are being adopted by any group of people. If that group happens to be your customers, you can use their Social Technographics Profile to build an appropriate social strategy.

For example, suppose you are a marketer at the television network MTV, and you want to build a groundswell strategy for people ages eighteen to twenty-seven. You'd also like to know whether the young men in your audience behave differently from the women.

Figure 3-4 shows the Social Technographics Profile of online Americans in Generation Y, ages eighteen to twenty-seven. This single graphic, based on the Social Technographics groups, provides a complete and actionable profile of the people MTV is trying to reach.

On the left, the bars show how young men and women compare to average online Americans. On the right, the index reflects those differences numerically. An index above 100 means higher participation than

FIGURE 3-4

The Social Technographics Profile of young men and women

Note the very high level of Joiner activity. Young men are more active Creators, Critics, and Collectors than young women, but they join social networks at almost the same rate.

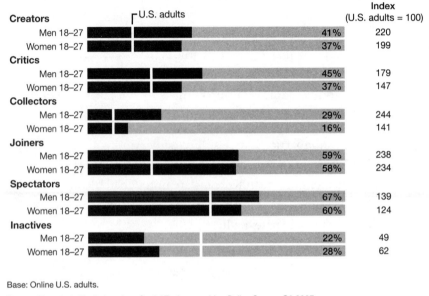

		U.S. adults		Index (U.S. adults = 100)
Creators				
Men 18–27			41%	220
Women 18–27			37%	199
Critics				
Men 18–27			45%	179
Women 18–27			37%	147
Collectors				
Men 18–27			29%	244
Women 18–27			16%	141
Joiners				
Men 18–27			59%	238
Women 18–27			58%	234
Spectators				
Men 18–27			67%	139
Women 18–27			60%	124
Inactives				
Men 18–27			22%	49
Women 18–27			28%	62

Base: Online U.S. adults.

Source: Forrester's North American Social Technographics Online Survey, Q2 2007.

the average for all online U.S. adults, while an index below 100 indicates lower participation.

Right away you can see that young people are more active in the groundswell than the average consumer, which is no surprise if you've ever met any. But now we can *quantify* those insights.

One statistic that jumps out is that young men and women are very likely to be Joiners, with around 60 percent participation in social networks, more than twice the level of participation of average adults (index greater than 200). Sure enough, there are over five hundred Facebook groups and over eight hundred MySpace groups with the keyword MTV. MTV needs a presence on these sites.

It's also clear that youth overindexes on Creators, Critics, and Collectors, especially for young men. MTV needs to recognize that any blogging, video uploading, discussion forum, or RSS-based initiatives it pursues are more likely to attract men than women. Women in Gen Y are still significantly more likely to participate than the average American, just not as much as their male counterparts.

To see how profiles work in practice, here's a real example from a client who had identified a new kind of woman to reach out to: the Alpha Mom.

CASE STUDY

targeting alpha moms

A new segment of consumers is emerging. They're called Alpha Moms, and at least at the moment of this writing in 2007, they're hot.

The term *Alpha Mom* was coined by Constance Van Flandern, who used it to identify the target for the video-on-demand mommy channel she is working on. Alpha Moms are comfortable with technology, interested in parenting, and have above-average incomes. An article in *USA Today* describes them this way:

> Alpha Moms are educated, tech-savvy, Type A moms with a common goal: mommy excellence. She is a multitasker. She is kidcentric. She is hands-on. She may or may not work outside the home, but at home, she views motherhood as a job that can be mastered with diligent research.[3]

According to the article, companies like Nintendo, Cadillac, and Kimberly-Clark are targeting Alpha Moms. Where marketers want to go, media is sure to follow. Which is why, in mid-2007, a media company came to us with plans to build a social networking site for Alpha Moms. This client was interested in learning what Alpha Moms want from the groundswell.

To answer this question, we needed first to define Alpha Moms clearly with identifiable survey answers. Using our Social Technographics survey, we defined Alpha Moms as mothers who have an optimistic attitude toward technology and are family motivated,[4] have a household income

of at least $55,000, and have some college education. The resulting seg-
ment included around 2.5 percent of online American adults.

So much for who the Alpha Moms are. But what do they want?

Figure 3-5 shows the Social Technographics Profile of Alpha Moms.
And if you're designing a site for them, certain things become abundantly clear.

First of all, Alpha Moms are far less likely to be Creators; only 11
percent of them are in this group that creates blogs, maintains Web
sites, and uploads video. On the other hand, one in four of them likes to
react to content—Alpha Moms include proportionally more Critics than
the rest of the population. And well over half are Spectators, consuming groundswell content at a greater rate than average online adult consumers in the United States.

Our client, a director at the media company, saw the profile and
rethought the company's strategy, shifting the focus from Creator to
Critic activities. "We had always thought that blogging would be a part
of the service. But looking at the data, I'm thinking that we should hold
off on that feature for the time being." Instead, she and her team began

FIGURE 3-5

The Social Technographics Profile of Alpha Moms

*This highly active group of mothers ($55,000 household income and up, with some college
education and favorable attitudes toward family and technology) overindexes on Critic
activities.*

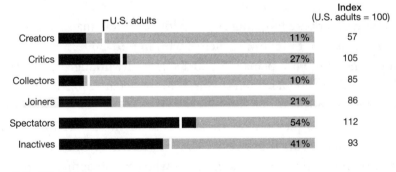

Base: Online U.S. adults.

Source: Forrester's North American Social Technographics Online Survey, Q2 2007.

---

to think about technologies including forums, ratings, and reviews—reactive forms of groundswell content.

It's too soon to know whether this service will be successful, but the people creating it took the time to determine where their target customers fit into the equation. That saved them from a potentially fatal emphasis on the wrong features.

the global power of social technographics profiles

The world is not completely flat. People in India don't use the same social networks as people in Germany. In France, Dailymotion is more popular than YouTube. But the fundamental emotions that drive people to the groundswell—the desire to connect, to create, to stay in touch, and to help each other—are universal. As a result, we can use the same Social Technographics Profile groups, applying them by demographic variables, or behaviors, anywhere in the world that we've done a survey.

Table 3-1 shows how participation in these groups varies in six Asia Pacific countries and seven European countries. (Note that because of differences in survey methodology, these tables aren't strictly comparable to each other or to the U.S. numbers. Also: in China and India, we survey affluent people in large cities only.)

Studying these charts, it's clear that companies with customers in these Asian countries can move much more aggressively in the groundswell, confident that large numbers of consumers are there to meet them. Japan, for example, has a very high level of participation in the groundswell with 70 percent Spectators and only 26 percent Inactives. Participation in South Korea is similar, but with a much broader focus on Joiners, partly because of the popular Cyworld social networking site. And while we can't see the whole population in China, among the affluent consumers we survey, Creator activity—especially blogging—is popular.

Europeans' participation is more similar to Americans', but with variations by country. Swedish and Dutch companies can count on engaging with their highly active customers in the groundswell. There are comparatively more Critics in Germany than in the rest of Europe, so forums and ratings make the most sense there. The French are far less likely to belong to social networks, although that may indicate a hole in the market that a good social network could fill. Italian and Spanish consumers are lower on many measures of participation, partly because of scarcer broadband connections.

But unless you're selling to a completely general audience, these numbers are just the start of the analysis. To see how the Social Technograph-

TABLE 3-1

The Social Technographics Profile of Asian and European countries

In Europe participation is highest in Sweden. Asian countries participate in groundswell activities at the highest rates in the world.

	Metro China	Hong Kong	Metro India	Japan	South Korea	Australia
Creators	36%	34%	24%	22%	38%	11%
Critics	44%	46%	24%	36%	27%	23%
Collectors	18%	17%	12%	6%	14%	5%
Joiners	32%	26%	42%	22%	41%	14%
Spectators	71%	67%	39%	70%	39%	38%
Inactives	25%	27%	31%	26%	36%	56%

Base: Online adults.

Source: Forrester's Asia Pacific Technographics Benchmark Survey, Q1 2007.

	France	Germany	Italy	Spain	United Kingdom	Netherlands	Sweden
Creators	10%	8%	19%	8%	9%	17%	12%
Critics	18%	22%	19%	18%	16%	17%	19%
Collectors	12%	12%	4%	6%	5%	6%	27%
Joiners	4%	12%	10%	5%	21%	26%	25%
Spectators	38%	44%	39%	41%	37%	41%	45%
Inactives	57%	49%	57%	56%	54%	46%	42%

Base: Online adults.

Source: Forrester's European Technographics Benchmark Survey, Q2 2007.

ics Profile applies in practice, we'll analyze some specific challenges—selling PCs in Japan, getting elected in the United States, and developing social strategy for retailers and health care companies in North America.

japanese pc buyers: fujitsu owners are more active than nec owners

To see how the Social Technographics Profile applies in markets outside the United States, let's look at PC owners in Japan. Figure 3-6 shows the Social Technographics Profile of two top brands: NEC and Fujitsu. Notice that in this case, we compare these groups to online Japanese adults, a group that's generally more active than Americans in most groundswell activities.

FIGURE 3-6

The Social Technographics Profile of Japanese PC owners

Fujitsu owners participate at a higher level than NEC owners in all activities.

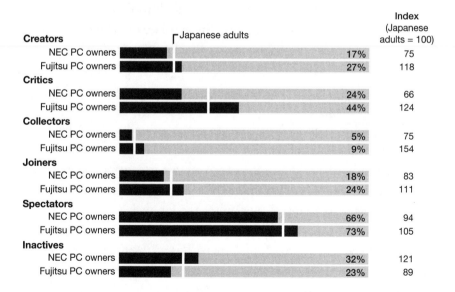

	Japanese adults	Index (Japanese adults = 100)
Creators		
NEC PC owners	17%	75
Fujitsu PC owners	27%	118
Critics		
NEC PC owners	24%	66
Fujitsu PC owners	44%	124
Collectors		
NEC PC owners	5%	75
Fujitsu PC owners	9%	154
Joiners		
NEC PC owners	18%	83
Fujitsu PC owners	24%	111
Spectators		
NEC PC owners	66%	94
Fujitsu PC owners	73%	105
Inactives		
NEC PC owners	32%	121
Fujitsu PC owners	23%	89

Base: Online Japanese adults.

Source: Forrester's Asia Pacific Technographics Benchmark Survey, Q1 2007.

Of the two, NEC has a slightly higher market share than Fujitsu. But NEC owners participate in all groundswell activities less than the average Japanese person online. In fact, they're 15 percent less likely to be Creators and 17 percent less likely to be Joiners than their fellow Japanese citizens.

By contrast, the Fujitsu owners are 18 percent *more* likely than average to be Creators and 24 percent more likely to be Critics. Fujitsu has focused on a stylish variety of notebook computers under its Lifebooks brand, including some of the smallest full-function PCs available in Japan. Its advertising features pop star Takuya Kimura.[5] Based on the profile, it appears Fujitsu's younger owners are also more active in the groundswell.

Examining the profile, you should always note the absolute magnitude of these activities, not just the index. Despite their less participatory profile, NEC owners are still 24 percent Critics and 66 percent Spectators. As a result, if NEC's objective was research, for example, it would make sense to monitor forums, online reviews, and blogs, since many of the company's customers are viewing this information. If Fujitsu, on the other hand, had an objective focused on marketing, the company could set up blogs or forums of its own to reach its owners. Despite the index of 154 on Collectors for Fujitsu, the absolute number of Collectors is still only 9 percent—probably not worth a lot of extra effort.

older adults: participation is lower, but there are still opportunities

Are there groups that don't participate in the groundswell? What if one of those is your target market?

For example, earlier in this chapter, you saw the incredible participation levels of Gen Y Americans. Is the converse also true: that older Americans *don't* participate? Not quite. See figure 3-7.

As you might expect, people over fifty aren't present in the groundswell at the levels of younger consumers. *But many of them are there.* For example, 39 percent of Americans ages fifty-two to sixty-two and 30 percent of those sixty-three or older are Spectators. Sure, those boomers are less than half as likely as an average adult to be Creators, but at an 8 percent penetration, there are still millions of people over fifty blogging and maintaining Web sites.

FIGURE 3-7

The Social Technographics Profile of older Americans

Americans over 52 still participate in many groundswell activities, just at a lower rate.

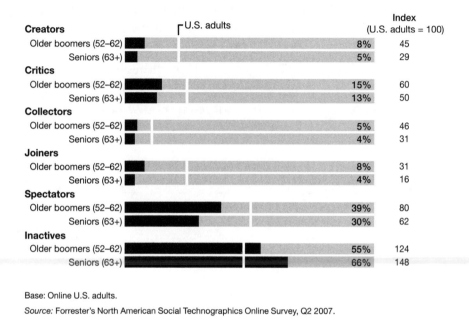

		Index
	U.S. adults	(U.S. adults = 100)
Creators		
Older boomers (52–62)	8%	45
Seniors (63+)	5%	29
Critics		
Older boomers (52–62)	15%	60
Seniors (63+)	13%	50
Collectors		
Older boomers (52–62)	5%	46
Seniors (63+)	4%	31
Joiners		
Older boomers (52–62)	8%	31
Seniors (63+)	4%	16
Spectators		
Older boomers (52–62)	39%	80
Seniors (63+)	30%	62
Inactives		
Older boomers (52–62)	55%	124
Seniors (63+)	66%	148

Base: Online U.S. adults.

Source: Forrester's North American Social Technographics Online Survey, Q2 2007.

If you're selling slots in retirement communities, should you give up on the groundswell? Not necessarily. In this case, the profile tells you that you'll reach an active subset, not nearly your whole market. If your objective is marketing, this tells you that the slice of your budget appropriate for the groundswell needs to be smaller. And with those lower levels of activity, you may be better off reaching older groundswell denizens where they are already hanging out—like the social networking sites Eons and Gather—rather than trying to build your own.

american politics: democrats participate more, but republicans can't sit on the sidelines

Imagine for a moment that you are a Web strategist for a candidate in a U.S. presidential election. Your objective is simple—reach more people with your messages and energize your base. What Web strategies are appropriate to mobilize your supporters?

To answer these questions, we examined the Social Technographics Profiles of Democrats, Republicans, and independents. (For the purposes of this analysis, we included independents who usually vote for Democrats in the Democrats column and those who usually vote for Republicans in the Republicans column. The independents in the chart don't have a party preference at all.) Figure 3-8 shows the results.

Unlike the other profiles we've seen in this section, this one shows that Democrats, Republicans, and independents are all close to the av-

FIGURE 3-8

The Social Technographics Profile by political party

Democrats have slightly above-average participation in all social technologies; Republicans are below average.

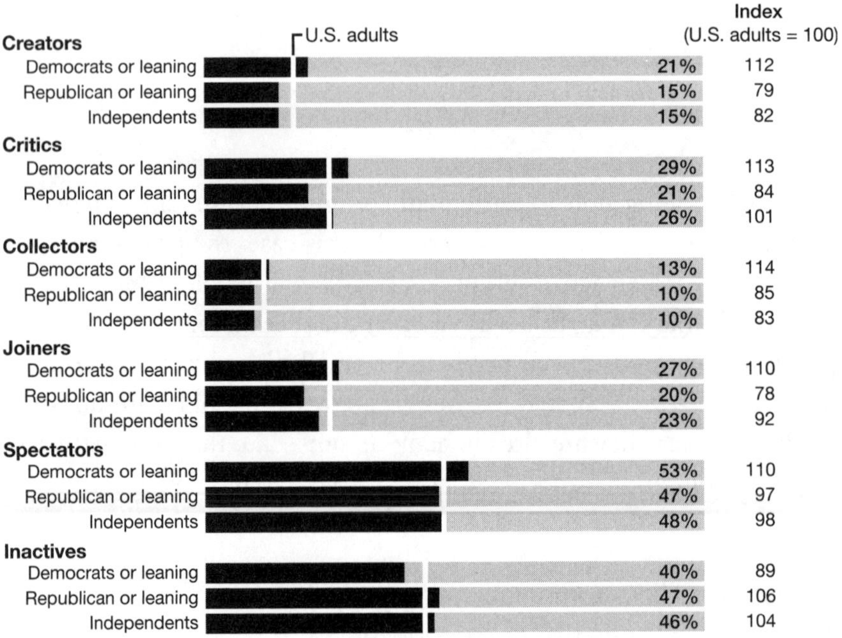

	U.S. adults	%	Index (U.S. adults = 100)
Creators			
Democrats or leaning		21%	112
Republican or leaning		15%	79
Independents		15%	82
Critics			
Democrats or leaning		29%	113
Republican or leaning		21%	84
Independents		26%	101
Collectors			
Democrats or leaning		13%	114
Republican or leaning		10%	85
Independents		10%	83
Joiners			
Democrats or leaning		27%	110
Republican or leaning		20%	78
Independents		23%	92
Spectators			
Democrats or leaning		53%	110
Republican or leaning		47%	97
Independents		48%	98
Inactives			
Democrats or leaning		40%	89
Republican or leaning		47%	106
Independents		46%	104

Base: Online U.S. adults.

Source: Forrester's North American Social Technographics Online Survey, Q2 2007.

erage in their participation in social technologies. But as a strategist, you're trained to exploit differences.

In this case, the message for Democrats is that their base is about 10 percent more likely to participate in any element of the groundswell. Given this profile, if your objective as a Democratic strategist is to spread your messages to the base of democrats, you would be well served to connect with the 27 percent of the base that are Joiners. This is the strategy that candidate Barack Obama pursued throughout the primary season with his own social network, my.barackobama.com.

As for Republicans, their participation tends to run about 20 percent *below* average. This doesn't mean that Republicans should ignore the groundswell, but they are better off spending scarce resources on other ways to reach people. Note that nearly half of Republicans are Spectators, so even if they're not contributing to the discourse on blogs, on YouTube, and in discussion groups, they're observing it. For this reason alone, Republican strategists must still pay attention to their image in the groundswell. For example, Rudy Giuliani finally did create a profile on Facebook, fixing an absence that had been a big mistake. And we'd recommend that all the candidates invest in some of the monitoring technologies we describe in chapter 5.

But perhaps the most interesting lesson in this profile comes from the independents. These voters, who will probably decide the election, approach the United States average in the concentration of Critics, Joiners, and Spectators. Many *do* participate, and of those who don't, many are watching. The party that energizes its own base in the groundswell could well win some of this group over. As is often the case in the groundswell, the key is to reach the Creators and Critics—if candidates were Lego sets, the Creators and Critics would be enthusiasts like Eric Kingsley and Joe Comeau—and charge them up to influence the rest of your potential supporters, especially the independents who are likely to be Joiners and Spectators.

shoppers: toys "r" us and l. l. bean should reach out
based on customers' profiles

Suppose you're a retailer. Should your store create a shopper community? A blog? Should it be active on MySpace? In figure 3-9 we show the profile of customers of two stores, the toy store Toys "R" Us and the outdoor equipment and clothing retailer L. L. Bean, which does most of its business through its catalog and Web site. If you work at one of these companies, you're in luck—your customers are surprisingly active in the groundswell.

Toys "R" Us shoppers were the third most active in groundswell participation among the twenty-seven retailers we studied, just behind the online-only retailers Amazon and eBay. Why? We're not sure. But as of now, the Toys "R" Us Web site hasn't yet tapped into any of these behaviors. Toys "R" Us shoppers are close to 50 percent more likely to be Joiners, Critics, and Creators as the U.S. average. While toysrus.com includes ratings and reviews, content is pretty thin on these features, likely because they haven't been promoted to online customers. Toys "R" Us needs to focus its groundswell energy around a specific goal—in this case, placing

---

FIGURE 3-9

The Social Technographics Profile of Toys "R" Us and L. L. Bean shoppers

Toys "R" Us and L. L. Bean both have highly active shoppers in the groundswell, but there are far more Joiners among Toys "R" Us customers.

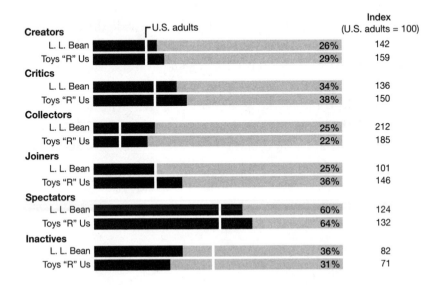

	U.S. adults	Index (U.S. adults = 100)
Creators		
L. L. Bean	26%	142
Toys "R" Us	29%	159
Critics		
L. L. Bean	34%	136
Toys "R" Us	38%	150
Collectors		
L. L. Bean	25%	212
Toys "R" Us	22%	185
Joiners		
L. L. Bean	25%	101
Toys "R" Us	36%	146
Spectators		
L. L. Bean	60%	124
Toys "R" Us	64%	132
Inactives		
L. L. Bean	36%	82
Toys "R" Us	31%	71

Base: Online U.S. adults.

Source: Forrester's North American Social Technographics Online Survey, Q2 2007.

the ratings tools in prominent locations and e-mailing online buyers to re-mind them to write a review a few weeks after they buy. Or the company could support the Joiner tendencies of Gen X parents to create an online community centered around kids and age-appropriate toys and activities.

As for L. L. Bean, despite its preponderance of online shoppers and sophisticated Web site, its customers aren't quite as at home in the groundswell as the customers of Toys "R" Us. But its meticulous shop-pers apparently love the Collector impulse—25 percent of them are Collectors, higher than any other retailer we asked about. Based on this, we'd recommend that the company enable the Collectors among its cus-tomers to create packing lists of their favorite products around activities like family camping or fishing trips. It could also create customized RSS feeds and widgets around those specific interests. (Check for yourself—they may have added these features since we wrote this.) The high number of Creators might be served by allowing members to easily post pictures of their camping and fishing trips, as Dick's Sporting Goods does.

We also took a look at Wal-Mart shoppers' profile, which isn't shown here, but with more than half of America shopping at Wal-Mart, you won't be surprised to find that its profile is pretty much the same as average on-line adults. Wal-Mart would be best served to segment its customers and profile the segments, just as we're sure it does with traditional marketing. With the youth segment so active on social networks, Wal-Mart ought to be on social networking sites (and in fact, it started a Facebook group for college students in 2007). Wal-Mart needs to analyze its own Alpha Moms, boomers, seniors, and so on to determine what they need. It would also make sense to profile Wal-Mart customers geographically—strategies that would work in California may be more problematic in Kansas.

disease sufferers: obesity treatments have an opportunity in the groundswell

Health care companies have a couple of big challenges working in the groundswell. First, their target customers are typically older—and older people participate in the groundswell at lower rates, although as we saw earlier, some are definitely participating. And second, they're part of heavily regulated industries that put the brakes on the kind of free in-novation in marketing that most ordinary manufacturers can employ.

Despite their age, people with health problems often identify with others in similar situations, sharing information and coping strategies—a perfect application for communities, wikis, and support forums. So is the groundswell good for you if you have a health problem or not? Depends on what's wrong with you.

Figure 3-10 shows the different profiles of people with two chronic health problems—cancer and obesity.

Based on these numbers, you might think a community of cancer patients wouldn't fly. In fact, the American Cancer Society's Cancer Survivors Network (www.acscsn.org) is a vibrant source of support for cancer sufferers across the nation. The lesson here is this: lower scores on a Social Technographics Profile don't doom a community strategy.

FIGURE 3-10

The Social Technographics Profile of cancer patients and obese people

Because of their age, most people with chronic health problems are less likely to participate in groundswell technologies. Obesity is the exception—obese people are often Critics and Joiners.

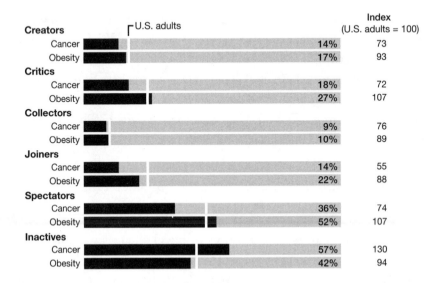

	U.S. adults	Index (U.S. adults = 100)
Creators		
Cancer	14%	73
Obesity	17%	93
Critics		
Cancer	18%	72
Obesity	27%	107
Collectors		
Cancer	9%	76
Obesity	10%	89
Joiners		
Cancer	14%	55
Obesity	22%	88
Spectators		
Cancer	36%	74
Obesity	52%	107
Inactives		
Cancer	57%	130
Obesity	42%	94

Base: Online U.S. adults.

Source: Forrester's North American Social Technographics Online Survey, Q2 2007.

The people at the American Cancer Society have an objective of support: helping patients help each other. They found their community attracted a small but growing and passionate subset of cancer patients. These discussions can also reach Spectators who may benefit, even if they don't participate.

Another thing we find interesting in this chart is the opportunity that exists for treating obesity. Obesity treatment and weight loss depend heavily on support, which is why groups like Weight Watchers and Jenny Craig exist. Now this activity is moving online. When GlaxoSmithKline launched its alli drug, its objective was support, to increase the success of its customers. It launched a dedicated site, myalli .com, featuring discussion boards with participation by a dietitian—perfect not just for the Critics, but for the Spectators who observe what others have written. While it's tricky to do this and maintain regulatory compliance, it makes good marketing sense in light of the relatively high numbers of groundswell participants among the obese.

profiling your own customers

If you have access to a data source like Forrester's surveys, great—you're on your way to learning about your customers. If not, you can still make a reasonable estimate of the social activity of your customer base. Survey your customers on your Web site or with a custom survey—ask them what technologies they use. To help you get started, we've provided a free tool at groundswell.forrester.com. Enter the country where you want to do business and the age and gender of your customer base, and we'll show you the Social Technographics Profile of the group you've specified.

the final question: why do people participate in the groundswell?

Having reached this point, and looking back on all the analysis of people and their levels of participation in the groundswell, there's still one fundamental question unanswered. And it's an important one because it determines the future of this social trend.

Why do people participate in the first place?

What's their *emotional* motivation? What do they get out of it?

The reason this question is so difficult is that there are so many different possible answers—*and they're all right.* Clearly, Creators like Lego enthusiast Eric Kingsley aren't after the same thing as Spectators like Linda Nee. In fact, the same person may have different motivations depending on where she's participating, what day it is, and her current mood or objectives. And yet there is something fundamental behind this drive to be social—something that touches, or will touch, all of us. It's a need to connect.

Going beyond that, we've been collecting reasons for participation as we interview both businesspeople and ordinary groundswell participants. We've come up with this list. It's surely not complete—in some sense there are at least as many reasons as there are people—but it's a start:

- *Keeping up friendships.* Facebook is about connecting with people you know. If you care how Jill's date went or whether Rafe passed the exam, you'll check in. And Jill and Rafe will let you know on their page because they know you care.

- *Making new friends.* We've all heard stories of people hooking up on social networks. One in five online singles has viewed or participated in online dating in the past year.[6] And it's not just young people; the singles areas on sites like Eons, which caters to the fifty-plus crowd, are hopping, too.

- *Succumbing to social pressure from existing friends.* People in the groundswell want their friends there, too. Even if you're not a Joiner, your friends, your daughter, or your drinking buddies might be. Whoever it is, that person is e-mailing you right now, asking you to join him or her in the groundswell. Sooner or later, you'll give in.

- *Paying it forward.* Having seen that a site is useful, you may be moved to contribute. If you read a review on a Web site and it helped you out, then when an email reminds you to submit a review yourself, you might say "what the heck" and add your own, especially since sites make it really easy to participate, whether you want to write something or just click a button to indicate a star rating. If you're going to use a site in the future, then it makes sense to contribute now and hope everyone else behaves similarly.

- *The altruistic impulse.* People give blood because they think they should. They risk their lives as volunteer firefighters to serve their communities. In the stories you'll read in the rest of this book, you'll find amazing examples of people who put in hundreds or thousands of hours just because they think social sites are worthwhile. Wikipedia became the largest encyclopedia in the world, fueled by this impulse. On a popular site, if even 1 percent are contributing content, that's often enough to serve the rest of the site's visitors.

- *The prurient impulse.* People are fascinating. Some of them are sexy, some are entertaining, and some, frankly, are stupid. All that is on display in an endless parade of exhibitionism. Watching beats what's on TV most nights!

- *The creative impulse.* Not everybody is a photographer, a writer, or a videographer, but for those who are, the Web is the perfect place to show off their work on (respectively) Flickr, a blog, or YouTube. Even if you're not a professional, the ability to express yourself—and to get positive and constructive feedback—is, in a way, payment for the creative psyche.

- *The validation impulse.* People who post information on Yahoo! Answers and Intuit's tax wiki would like to be seen as knowledgeable experts. Validation is a powerful driver for social networks, and it's a huge force driving bloggers. People put themselves out there, and the community reassures them about their place in the world.

- *The affinity impulse.* If your bowling league, your PTA, or your fellow Red Sox fans have connected online—and no matter what your interest is, some start-up company is surely targeting it—then you can join and connect with people who share your interests and concerns. You have a common base of experience with these people, and it makes sense to join up with them online.

Many impulses drive people to participate. The key isn't trying to psych out all those motivations but to find the levers that you can pull to get your customers and employees to participate *with you*. It's one thing to understand what drives the groundswell—it's quite another to dive into it and turn those forces to your advantage.

———————————

The biggest challenge in the groundswell isn't whether you master the technology or whether you annoy or delight your customers. It's whether you're accomplishing a useful business goal and, on top of that, how you'll measure that success and then prove that the groundswell effort was worth it.

The next part of this book is designed to help you with that. You may decide to enter the groundswell to conduct research. You may be pursuing marketing goals or boosting sales. Or you may want to save money in technical support or invite customers into your innovation processes.

Regardless of what you are after, to get there, you need not only the kind of data we've shown in this chapter but also a clear strategy—a framework for groundswell thinking. That's exactly what we'll provide in chapter 4.

part two.

tapping the
groundswell

4. strategies for tapping the groundswell

In early 2007, we received a call from one of the largest retailers in America. Our client, a strategist at the company, had noticed that Sears, a competitor, had started an online community for survey and research purposes. The client, whom we'll call Charlie, wanted to know how his company should respond. When we got on the phone with him, the conversation went something like this:

"Hi, Charlie, how can we help you today?"

"I saw that Sears has started this community, and I wondered if we should do one, too."

"OK. So what's your objective, Charlie?"

Long silence, stammering.

"Are you more interested in a community for listening to what your customers are saying or for influencing them?"

"Well, I'm really not sure. But if Sears is doing it, I'm sure we need to be looking into it."

"Have you seen what Victoria's Secret has done by creating a profile on Facebook and reaching out to other Facebook members to create relationships?"

"No, I haven't seen that. I just want to know if Sears is onto something here."

The conversation went on in that vein for some time. Now, before you begin to think that Charlie hadn't done his homework and is just not paying enough attention, we should mention that his company has one of the most advanced commerce sites on the Web. It *seems* to have its act together. And yet, when it comes to the groundswell, Charlie knows his company has to be there, but he doesn't know *why*.

We have this conversation with clients all the time. There was the IT strategist at a fast-food company who wanted to know how her company could "become part of the social networking space." The CIO at a furniture company who wanted to know best practices for starting a blog. And dozens of others.

Now, these people know they need to get involved, but they're nervous about moving forward. To us, they seem to have developed a sort of low-grade fever. In fact, this problem is so common we have a name for it: *groundswell approach-avoidance syndrome.* Look for these symptoms in yourself or your coworkers:

- Strong, and in some cases obsessive, interest in the blogosphere and in online doings at sites like Facebook and YouTube. Repeated forwarding of articles on said topics to fellow sufferers.

- Excessive salivation upon hearing much-repeated stories of corporations that have developed partnerships with social networking sites, started online communities, or otherwise managed to get held up as winners in news reports and at marketing conferences.

- Checking the megablogs techcrunch.com and gigaom.com multiple times per day to make sure you are as up to date as possible on all social media and Web 2.0 developments, rumors, stray thoughts, and buzz. After a few hours of doing this, you feel as if you have run a half marathon while never getting anywhere at all.

- Increasing nervousness about answering superiors' and subordinates' questions about the company's "online strategy in the Web 2.0 era."

- Asking your teenage kids, "What's up with this MySpace thing?" and listening intently for ideas you can use at work.

- Anxiety at the thought of actually participating in social technologies, balanced by similar anxiety at the thought of missing out.

Should you or any of your colleagues be experiencing these symptoms, please don't despair. You're not alone. We can identify the causes and suggest a treatment, which is to clarify your objectives first. That's what this chapter is about.

The problem with Charlie—and so many of our clients—is that they're going about their strategy backward. They start by thinking about technology. But technology is shifting so quickly—chasing it is like trying to jump on a speeding merry-go-round. The resulting dizziness is what causes groundswell approach-avoidance syndrome.

There's a cure. It's this: take a step back and ask yourself, "What are my customers ready for?" and then "What are my objectives?" Once you know that, *then* you can start planning.

We've created an acronym for the four-step planning process, starting with these questions, that you should use to build your groundswell strategy. We call it the POST method, for *people, objectives, strategy,* and *technology.*[1] POST is the foundation of groundswell thinking—a systematic framework for assembling your plan. Let's walk through the four steps in a little more detail:

- *People.* What are your customers ready for? The Social Technographics Profile we described in the last chapter is designed to answer this question (remember, you can also generate your own customer profiles with the tool at groundswell.forrester.com). What's important is to assess how your customers will engage, based on what they're already doing. Skipping this step and making guesses about your customers might work, but you might also build a whole social networking strategy only to find that your customers are more likely to write reviews than join social networks.

- *Objectives.* What are your goals? Are you more interested in talking with the groundswell for marketing, for example, or in generating sales by energizing your best customers? Or are you interested in tapping the groundswell internally to help your employees work together more efficiently? We lay out five of the most powerful objectives in the next section.

- *Strategy.* How do you want relationships with your customers to change? Do you want customers to help carry messages to others in your market? Do you want them to become more engaged with your company? By answering this question, not only can you plan for the desired changes up front, but you can also figure out how to measure them once the strategy is under way. You'll also need to prepare and get buy-in from people within your company who may be threatened by changes in these customer relationships.

- *Technology.* What applications should you build? *After* having decided on the people, objectives, and strategy, you can move on to pick appropriate technologies, including the ones we described in chapter 2—blogs, wikis, social networks, and so forth.

five objectives that companies can pursue in the groundswell

The clarity of your objectives will make or break your strategy. Success depends on a beacon to go toward—a reason to enter the groundswell.

Based on our observation of hundreds of companies pursuing groundswell strategies, we've identified five primary objectives that companies successfully pursue in the groundswell. You should pick the one that best matches the objectives of your company as a whole:

1. *Listening.* Use the groundswell for research and to better understand your customers. This goal is best suited for companies that are seeking customer insights for use in marketing and development.

2. *Talking.* Use the groundswell to spread messages about your company. Choose this goal if you're ready to extend your current digital marketing initiatives (banner ads, search ads, email) to a more interactive channel.

3. *Energizing.* Find your most enthusiastic customers, and use the groundswell to supercharge the power of their word of mouth.

This works best for companies that know that they have brand enthusiasts to energize.

4. *Supporting.* Set up groundswell tools to help your customers support each other. This is effective for companies with significant support costs and customers who have a natural affinity for each other.

5. *Embracing.* Integrate your customers into the way your business works, including using their help to design your products. This is the most challenging of the five goals, and it's best suited to companies that have succeeded with one of the other four goals already.

In fact, these five objectives are linked to the familiar business functions in your company, except that they're far more engaged with customers and include more communication—especially communication that happens between customers. Table 4-1 shows the relationship.

Some groundswell thinkers will tell you that these objectives are too narrow. Baloney. Each one can make a powerful impact on your company.

TABLE 4-1

Existing business functions and their groundswell alternatives

You already have this business function	Now you can pursue this groundswell objective	How things are different in the groundswell
Research	Listening	Ongoing monitoring of your customers' conversations with *each other*, instead of occasional surveys and focus groups
Marketing	Talking	Participating in and stimulating two-way conversations your customers have with *each other*, not just outbound communications to your customers
Sales	Energizing	Making it possible for your enthusiastic customers to help sell *each other*
Support	Supporting	Enabling your customers to support *each other*
Development	Embracing	Helping your customers work with *each other* to come up with ideas to improve your products and services

But if you don't enter the groundswell with a specific goal, you *will* fail. It is true that once you get started, you can accomplish more than you set out to do. Corporate bloggers, who typically start thinking about *talking*, find they end up *listening* more. Companies that set up communities for *supporting* find their customers have great product ideas and end up *embracing* them. But your strategy should be designed from the start to focus on a primary objective, and it is progress toward that objective that you should measure. Then you will be able to measure the return on your groundswell investment. And that, based on our experience, is the path most likely to lead to success.

In the next five chapters, we examine case studies for each of these objectives and show how to follow through from people and objectives to strategy and technology choices. (And in chapter 11 we'll show how you can accomplish these same objectives with an internal groundswell—your employees.)

what about business-to-business?

The groundswell is not just for consumers. Companies that sell to businesses frequently ask us questions about their own potential involvement, just like consumer companies. In many ways, it seems harder for business-to-business companies to make progress in groundswell thinking, just because there are so few role models—most of the big, highly visible applications out there are geared toward consumers.

Our advice for companies aiming at businesses is simple but fundamental: *businesspeople are people, too.* There is no such thing as a social network for businesses or a business commenting on a blog. Businesses don't interact. People do.

For example, we've seen successful applications aimed at franchisees of McDonald's restaurants, at people in small businesses who use email marketing services (see chapter 7), and at businesspeople using customer relationship management software. All were very different. But all had applied the same lessons—and the same POST process—that applies to engaging with consumers.

In applications for business, the people side is even more important. The people you want to engage in your application typically have a parallel role within their companies—they're salespeople, or IT professionals, or buyers of office supplies. They have their job in common, just as much as consumers who shop at Target or who own pets have a common interest.

In business-to-business settings, picking an objective first is still the best practice. You can listen to, talk to, energize, support, or embrace your business customers—business*people*—just as you would consumers. And if you don't start with a clear objective, you're just as likely to go wrong.

thinking through a strategy

We recently helped a clothing company with its entry into the groundswell. The company's customers were already active with social technologies, and the company culture encouraged reaching out to customers in new and innovative ways—but very few social initiatives were under way already. That is, the company strategists *knew* they had to connect with their customers in the groundswell; they just didn't know *how*.

To get the company kick-started, the executives planned a multiday retreat with multiple outside speakers. By the time we saw these executives on the third day of their off-site, they were already buzzing about ways they could use the new technologies, from setting up a MySpace page to creating a viral campaign that leveraged a podcast. As we began our presentation and discussion, it became clear that they were heading into a dangerous place. By becoming more comfortable with the groundswell, they felt they had the tools and knowledge to act, but they had not yet thought through the consequences.

The key exercise we led them through was to envision how their relationship with customers would be different and better in three years, and to raise the key questions that follow from any groundswell engagement. For example, the president of one division asked, if we allow people to review our products in discussion groups, will we allow negative reviews to appear? If so, how will our manufacturing partners react? How will our employees react? And once we've been doing this for a year or two, how will we expand and use the information? Now the company was thinking things through. And the strategy, which began with little ideas like "let's start a blog" and "let's implement ratings," began to move toward the real question: how will we engage our customers, and how will that engagement grow over time?

The company's executives had acquired the right focus—thinking about the relationships they would build. They were well along in the POST process. Now they needed to hear some of the general advice that applies to every project, based on our experience with how groundswell projects affect companies, managers, technology vendors, and their relationships. As you'll see, these suggestions come up over and over again, regardless of the objective you're pursuing.

- *Create a plan that starts small but has room to grow.* Companies that try to map out their whole strategy over the course of a year will find their planning is obsolete by the time they finish it. But conversely, companies that quickly launch one technology and then jump to another aren't necessarily helping themselves. Instead, you should create a rough plan—what you will do first; how you will measure success; and if you do succeed, how you will build on that success. Then be ready to revise that plan every six to twelve months. Imagine where engaging with the groundswell might take you, but don't lock yourself in right away.

- *Think through the consequences of your strategy.* As with the clothing company we just described, your plan should include how engaging the groundswell will change your company. Consider what the endgame is going to be—a very different relationship with your customers. Imagine how the groundswell will change the way you run your business over the next few years. How will it change your traditional marketing, advertising, and PR functions? What are the consequences for your suppliers and distributors? Who will talk to them about it? Will it change your cost structure or the way you compensate salespeople? What are the legal consequences? All these issues need to be considered before the plan is complete.

- *Put somebody important in charge of it.* You're about to transform your relationship with your customers. Is this a job for some mid-level IT or marketing person? The ultimate responsibility for this plan should rest with an executive who reports up quite high in the organization. Which one depends on your goals—if you're listening, it might be the head of research, for example; if you're talking, the CMO would be a better choice. In many companies the CIO or other high-level IT staff are key advisors based on their technology knowledge. But in the end whoever is in charge of the plan must regularly brief the CEO on how it is transforming the way the company does business with customers. Groundswell projects routinely stir up people well above the part of the organization where they started.

- *Use great care in selecting your technology and agency partners.* Companies don't generally have the resources to build social applications by themselves. As a result, they work with partners—these could be technology vendors like Leverage Software that specialize in communities, agencies like Avenue A/Razorfish that build applications, or large portal companies like Yahoo! that can host applications or communities. Regardless, the choice of partner is critical. You'll want to be sure you're working with people who've built multiple applications before and understand your brand and your company. Crucially important is that they understand your objectives—or else you'll be constantly explaining why you want things to be one way versus another. Ask them not just about current capabilities but—since the technology is shifting quickly—how they perceive the one- to two-year future of the types of technologies they are building. This is no time to go with the lowest bidder or even the company with the most features. If you're not comfortable that your partner understands what you're trying to accomplish and how that could change, *walk away*. Find one who does.

what could go wrong?

Creating and implementing a social strategy is hard, primarily because there are few precedents and role models to follow. This means you need to be constantly aware of the challenges and prepared to fix them. While there are many sources of failure, the most common relate to the four elements of the POST process—failures in assessing people's tendencies, a weak definition of objectives, failure to think through strategy, and poor technology implementation.

For example, if your application isn't attracting the participation you hoped for, you may have a profile mismatch. This occurs when companies build strategies that are ill suited to the capabilities of their customers—for instance, a customer blogging site for retirement savings plans. This is the mistake that the media company targeting Alpha Moms was about to make in chapter 3. To avoid this problem, consider your customers' Social Technographics Profile, and be sure you're choosing applications in which they'll participate, rather than focusing on what you and your fellow planners think are the coolest applications.

If you find your initiatives floundering or changing direction frequently, you need to reexamine your choice of objectives. For example, we recently spoke with a retailer who had a highly active community on his site that was contributing nothing to his business, and he wanted to know how to shut it down. His company had expended a lot of energy but had failed to align the community's objective with business goals that mattered to him. Now he would have to spend more to undo the mistake. If an executive is pushing for rapid deployment of a social technology, push back; insist that the effort cannot move forward until you've agreed on a clear objective tied to business goals.

What if your customers engage but not in the ways you expected? An unwillingness to assess and address the way that social technologies change customer relationships dooms many a project. Wal-Mart's application for college students on Facebook ran afoul of this problem. While Wal-Mart picked the right people strategy (using Facebook to target college students) and had a clear objective (promoting dorm decor), it failed to think through the consequences of opening up an uncontrolled dialogue in Facebook. Result: the company's Facebook application became a magnet for negative comments about Wal-Mart's business practices. By thinking through possible consequences and recruiting an executive sponsor who won't bolt at the first sign of trouble, you can minimize your chances of falling into this strategic trap.

Finally, there are dozens of ways to doom a project with poor technology implementation. The Web is filled with lightly trafficked communities, for example, where poor usability prevented the community from attracting an active set of participants. Because technologies change so quickly, you should plan on quick, simple, and staged deployments that provide flexibility. And measure success as you go along, making changes as you see what's working best.

Things *will* go wrong. The groundswell is not under your control, and you've probably never done this before. When problems arise, go back to POST. Diagnosing *how* a social initiative is failing is the first step on the road to fixing the problem.

there's no going back

You're about to fundamentally change how your company relates to its customers. This will require not only fortitude on your part but difficult negotiations with other people throughout your company. We've identified some mistakes you may make, and you'll probably find a few we haven't thought of. At this point you might ask yourself, "Why should I bother?"

Here's why.

You cannot ignore this trend. You cannot sit this one out. Unless you are retiring in the next six months, it's too late to quit and let somebody else handle it. The groundswell trend is unstoppable, and your customers are there. You may go a little slower or a little faster, but *you have to move forward.* There is no going back.

We will leave you with this: *there is no one "right way" to engage with the groundswell.*

While there are plenty of wrong ways to join the groundswell—not listening, for example, or trying to fool people—there are also many effective strategies. Each company must adopt the tactics that are right for its customers and its way of doing business and adapt as the technologies change. Copying others doesn't work because your company, your customers, and your goals are not the same as anybody else's.

So it's time to engage with the groundswell. Your company will be better for it.

In this chapter we've assembled the basic elements you need to build a groundswell strategy. Once you've chosen your primary objective—listening, talking, energizing, supporting, or embracing—we've got the cases and tools you need to really understand how the groundswell can help in the next five chapters. We'll start with listening in chapter 5.

5. **listening to the groundswell**

Lynn Perry has cancer. In fact, he has had three forms of terminal cancer: prostate cancer, which spread to the bones; lung cancer; and cancer of the epiglottis. The treatments to his throat give him a hoarse, smoky voice like a country singer, which fits pretty well since he's a Harley-riding, keyboard-playing ex-engineer from Plano, Texas.

Perry (everybody calls him Perry) has an engineering background that makes him a pretty analytical guy, in his own down-home country philosopher way. He doesn't sound sad about his cancer—he's lived with it for six years and will keep going until he can't anymore. He's sixty-six, and he reserves his sympathy for people he feels are worse off than him—children he's met while waiting for treatment, for example. Although he doesn't waste too much time on emotional "cancer talk," as he puts it, he does have a fair amount to say about cancer treatment and the way it's delivered. With the analytical mind-set he brings to it, you listen and realize his perspective is well worth hearing.

"There are things that make me question M. D. Anderson," says Perry. (M. D. Anderson is the major cancer treatment center in Houston, where he goes for treatment.) "They give you this little document; they're very insistent on patient promptness. I am there right on the button. I sit there, wait an hour, an hour and a half, two hours. There is something wrong with this picture. My time is more precious than theirs." (At this point Perry reveals that if the doctors are right, he'll be dead in less than six months.)[1] "Patients complain if the wait is too long, so they won't go to that [cancer treatment center]. I don't care if they have a faith healer in there, a mundane reason like the wait will stop 'em. 'I had to sit there for four hours,' they say, and they won't go again. The best hospitals and the best rankings [he means the published rankings from *U.S. News & World Report*] don't faze those type patients at all."

M. D. Anderson, Perry's cancer center, prides itself on its reputation. *U.S. News & World Report* ranks it tops in the nation.[2] It just spent $125 million on a proton therapy cancer treatment center, the most advanced treatment technology there is.[3] If a cancer can be treated, M. D. Anderson can treat it.

But that's all for naught if, as Lynn Perry points out, the patients give up and walk out.

As it turns out, though, M. D. Anderson has made listening to patients like Lynn Perry a priority. M. D. Anderson is investing major efforts in improving its scheduling. Why? Because it's put a priority on listening—and because it's figured out ways to integrate opinions like Lynn Perry's into its research, every bit as much as it pays attention to medical research. Which is a good thing since, according to Perry, those impatient patients may prefer to go to their local community hospital instead of M. D. Anderson—and it's going to need a lot of patients and a lot of treatments to pay for that proton therapy center.

your brand is what your customers say it is

Marketers tell us they define and manage brands. Some spend millions, or hundreds of millions, of dollars on advertising. They carefully extend brand names, putting *Scope* on a tube of toothpaste to see what happens. We bought this brand, they say. We spent on it. We own it.

Bull.

Your brand is whatever your customers say it is. And in the groundswell where they communicate with each other, they decide.

One of the most brilliant brand theorists we've ever met is Ricardo Guimarães, founder of Thymus Branding, in São Paulo, Brazil. After running a big Brazilian ad agency for a long time, Guimarães started his consultancy to spread a new way of thinking. He says brands belong to customers, not companies. In his words:[4]

The value of a brand belongs to the market, and not to the company. The company in this sense is a tool to create value for the brand . . . Brand in this sense—it lives outside the company, not in the company. When I say that the management is not prepared for dealing with the brand, it is because in their mind-set they are managing a closed structure that is the company. The brand is an open structure—they don't know how to manage an open structure.

For example, M. D. Anderson thinks its brand is defined by a shiny new $125 million proton therapy center. But Lynn Perry thinks part of the M. D. Anderson brand is about making him wait. What do your customers think *your* brand is about?

There's one way to find out. You have to listen.

If you were in charge of marketing for M. D. Anderson, you'd probably like some way to put Lynn Perry and three hundred other cancer patients on call, ask them how they make treatment decisions, ask them what's on their minds. If you were smart, you would listen in as they talk to each other and learn how they think. This is *listening to the groundswell*, and it's exactly what several cancer centers around the United States (including M. D. Anderson) did. They hired a company called Communispace to recruit and manage a private community of cancer patients, and those patients are now revealing how they think, every day. That's current, continuous insight on demand, and it's the topic of this chapter.

what do we mean by listening?

Cynics will tell you that companies never listen to their customers. That's completely untrue. They not only listen to their customers; they pay large amounts of money to do so, very, very carefully. They just don't call it listening. They call it market research. Market research is very good at finding answers to questions. It's just not so effective at generating insights.

Companies pay over $15 billion annually for market research.[5] For example, marketers paid Nielsen over $3.7 billion in 2006 for information about which products were selling in stores; what television programs people were watching; and what music, books, and Web sites people were consuming. In the same year, health care companies paid over $2 billion to IMS Health, which reports information about what conditions doctors are diagnosing and which drugs are prescribed to whom. It's safe to say that Lynn Perry's complaints about scheduling were not included in those IMS Health reports.

Companies pay money for syndicated research sources like Nielsen and IMS Health because they all want answers to similar questions (for example, how many people are watching *Heroes*, or how well is Viagra selling?). Syndicated research is a valuable tool for mapping trends, but it can't tell you what people are thinking.

Marketers also pay handsomely for their own surveys. A mail, phone, or Internet survey of a thousand consumers will tell you what those thousand consumers are thinking about the questions you ask them. Those surveys typically cost at least $10,000 and, with expert analysis, can easily cost over $100,000, especially if the people you'd like to survey are hard to find, like people with cancer. Designed cleverly enough, these surveys will answer any question you can think up. But they can't tell you what you never thought to ask. And what you never thought to ask might be the most important question for your business.

Finally, there are focus groups. For $7,000 to $15,000, you can listen to ten or fifteen people for a couple of hours as they react to whatever you throw at them. Here, finally, you can get a spontaneous reaction, and you may hear something that surprises you—that is, if you get lucky and happen to get someone as thoughtful as Lynn Perry in your focus group.

Come to think of it, the most thoughtful people among your target customers don't want to take your surveys or be in your focus groups. The thoughtful people may not be on those survey panels, and they may not show up for your focus groups; even if they are, those research methods are designed to answer questions, not to tap into consumer insights.

listening to the groundswell reveals new insights

If only there were some way to observe your customers in their natural habitats, as it were, you could get beyond the bias of surveys and the limitations of focus groups. Ideally, you could observe hundreds, if not thousands, of the people you'd like to know more about. You'd watch them as they interacted with your company, your competitors, and each other in the course of their normal day-to-day business. It would be even better if they'd take notes about their own behavior so that you'd have a record of what they were thinking.

Thanks to the groundswell, this kind of insight is available. Consumers in the groundswell are leaving clues about their opinions, positive and negative, on a daily or hourly basis. If you have a retail store, they're blogging about your store experience, your selection, and their favorite products. If you make TV sets, shoes, or tires—just about anything—they're on discussion forums dissecting the pros and cons of your product's features, your prices, and your customer support. They're rating your products and services on Yelp and TripAdvisor. And it's all there for you to listen to.

By itself, analyzing this activity has problems. To begin with, you won't hear from everybody; you'll only hear from people willing to talk. So listening to the groundswell comes with a huge caveat—you'll gain new insights, but don't assume that the people you hear from are representative.

Even so, the very volume of comments out there is a vast source of information. And that's the second problem. Volume. There's so much information flowing out of the groundswell, it's like watching a thousand television channels at once. To make sense of it, you need to apply some technology, boiling down the chatter to a manageable stream of insights.

As you might imagine, a bunch of technology companies have sprung up to solve these problems. In the rest of this chapter, we'll show you how to use their services to gain insights from the groundswell— groundswell thinking applied to research.

two listening strategies

There are lots of ways to listen to the groundswell. Google your product name along with the word *sucks* or *awesome*, for example. Do a blog search on Technorati. Or check out what the people who have tagged your company or your products on del.icio.us are saying. But in working with clients, we've seen that these homegrown monitoring methods don't scale. To gain real insight, you're better off working with vendors that provide professional tools. There are two basic ways to do this:

1. *Set up your own private community.* That's how cancer centers like M. D. Anderson were able to learn about the insights from Lynn Perry. A private community is like a continuously running, huge, engaged focus group—a natural interaction in a setting where you can listen in. One primary supplier of private communities is Communispace, although the category is growing rapidly with similar products from the vendors MarketTools and Networked Insights. We'll describe how private communities work in the first case in this chapter.

2. *Begin brand monitoring.* Hire a company to listen to the Internet—blogs, discussion forums, YouTube, and everything else—on your behalf. Then have it deliver to you neat summary reports about what's happening or push the results out to departments, like customer service, that can address pressing customer issues. There are dozens of companies that will do this, starting with two that were acquired by a couple of the largest research companies on the planet: Nielsen's BuzzMetrics and TNS's Cymfony. We'll show the power of blog monitoring in the second case in this chapter, which looks at the car company Mini.

One more thing: listening by itself is sterile. Those neat reports that come from Communispace and BuzzMetrics are a waste of cash if they sit on the shelf. To profit from listening, you need a plan to *act* on what you learn. That's what you'll see in these cases from the National Comprehensive Cancer Network and Mini, and it's why their listening strategies paid off.

CASE STUDY

national comprehensive cancer network: listening with a private community

Ellen Sonet, VP of marketing for New York's Memorial Sloan-Kettering Cancer Center, is passionate about customers' insights. "To me as a marketing person, it's most important that I understand what it feels like to be my consumer," she told us.

Now, anybody can say that, but based on what Ellen told us about her background, we believe her.

Earlier in her career, when she was marketing over-the-counter pharmaceutical products, she would hang out in drugstores and observe customers. "Why did he pick up that other nasal spray and not mine?" she would think. Hours and hours of this sort of observation went into plans for everything from advertising to packaging.

In the past ten years, as the top marketer at Memorial Sloan-Kettering, she's had to develop new methods. As you might imagine, marketers aren't powerful in the hospital world—doctors are. Doctors interact with patients. Doctors know best. Doctors are in charge. Memorial Sloan-Kettering has nine thousand employees. Counting Ellen, three and a half of those work in marketing.

Ellen regularly volunteers to deliver flowers to patients, just to get a feel for what's going on with her customers. But there's only so much to be learned from that, since she can't really interact with the patients in any meaningful way. Which is why, when Ellen Sonet met Diane Hessan at a marketing event in 2003, she became certain they needed to work together.

Diane Hessan is the CEO of Communispace, one of the most rapidly growing vendors in the groundswell. Communispace has set up hundreds of private communities for its clients, which include over seventy-five companies, ranging from hair care and breakfast cereal to financial services and IT advice. Communispace's service is relatively simple to describe. The company recruits three hundred to five hundred people in the client's target market—young men for Axe body spray, or people trying to lose weight for GlaxoSmithKline's alli weight control drug. Those recruits form a community that looks like any other online social network, with profiles, discussion forums, online chat, and uploaded photos. But this network is a *research* network. No one can see it except the members, the moderators from Communispace, and the client.

A Communispace community is a listening machine that generates insight. It's a miniature groundswell in a box. The members typically are thanked with inexpensive Amazon gift certificates. They look just like groundswell participants out in the real world, except that they promise to spend an hour a week on the site. Communispace has duplicated the features that make other communities so interactive, and as a result, the participants behave in a very natural way—not at all like the stilted one-time interactions in a focus group, for example.

Of course, there was the little problem of money—a Communispace community costs at least $180,000 for a six-month trial and about $20,000 per month after that, and Ellen had very little budget. But Memorial Sloan-Kettering is part of the National Comprehensive Cancer Network (NCCN), a group of twenty-one dedicated cancer centers around the country. All the NCCN centers had a similar need to learn about their patients. It took two years, but Ellen convinced several of the NCCN cancer centers to go in with her on a Communispace community. Both Communispace and the cancer centers invited cancer patients to join the community and recruited over three hundred of them. Then Ellen began listening.

research information versus community insights

Research goes where you expect it to go. You find out whether people will spend an extra $100 if the TV is six inches bigger. You see whether Hispanics really respond to your new TV commercial.

Ellen Sonet started with this same approach, but right away she got a surprise. The first question the NCCN members asked the community was the most important: how did you decide where to get treated?

The prevailing wisdom among the doctors at Memorial Sloan-Kettering was that patients choose their treatment center based on reputation. Since patients want the best chance for a successful outcome, they would choose to go to a world-renowned cancer center like Memorial Sloan-Kettering. So the most important thing was to make sure the public recognized the cancer center's outstanding expertise.

Wrong.

A cancer patient does not make decisions like a business executive choosing what supplier to work with. Imagine it. You've just been diagnosed with cancer. It's shocking and terrifying, and you're ignorant. You're meeting new doctors for the first time, and now you have a crucial decision to make: where to go for treatment.

Want to know how this feels? Here's a comment from "Tracy D" in the Communispace forum:[6]

> As I'm sure you know, when you hear a diagnosis of cancer, you go into a tailspin. You are coping with so many fears and emotions, yet you want to know as much as you can. The Web has been invaluable for that, but I really appreciated [my doctor] taking charge and telling me where he thought I should go. There was really no discussion about it. I was not capable of discussion at the time.

Like Tracy, more than half of patients cite *their primary care physician* as important in the recommendation on where to get treatment. The primary care physician is typically a trusted professional the patient has been seeing for years. So in the stressful days after a cancer diagnosis, many a patient falls back on the familiar, regardless of the lofty reputation a cancer center may have made for itself.

Already the community had proved its worth. Memorial Sloan-Kettering still prides itself on its outstanding reputation among consumers and uses marketing to maintain that image. But Ellen Sonet now had the proof she needed to change the way a 9,000-employee cancer center markets itself. "We have not historically had the best relationships with community docs, yet they are an important source of referrals for us," she said. So she began to change things. "I . . . instituted many programs to improve our relationships with community [primary care physicians], urologists, and ob-gyns," she points out. Change had begun.

People who fill out surveys don't really care what happens next. Cancer patients in an ongoing community do. Seven out of ten visit the community every week. And it's not the gift certificates that drive them—two out of three community members said they received greater value from the community itself. Here's a typical comment: "If there is ANYTHING I have learned it is that the more connections we make with folks with the same kind of cancer the better the information we can learn about how to deal with it." Research is one-way. A community, even a research community like this one, offers a more lasting value. Of seventy-six discussions in the NCCN community, only eighteen were initiated by the moderators—the rest were started by the members themselves.

We mentioned that listening does no good unless you act on it. Here's a perfect example. NCCN asked cancer patients, "Where do you get information about your diagnosis and treatment?" Out of 81 respondents, 78 looked for information on the Internet. Out of 114 respondents, 106 said they were likely to recommend the Internet as a source of information. These results were overwhelmingly clear, but any survey could have revealed them (although getting cancer patients into a survey would be challenging). In fact, given that these respondents were already members of an Internet community, there is clearly some online bias present here.

But the community allowed people to converse and tell *what* they looked for and *how* they used it in ways that no survey could. Here, in part, is what Lynn Perry, the Harley-riding engineer we met at the start of the chapter, said about how he uses online resources:

(2) What sources of information did/do you use to learn about treatment options?

I spent hours and hours on the Internet, looking for info I was totally unfamiliar [with] at the time. I was on numerous sites that included [the American Cancer Society], NCCN, [the National Cancer Institute], and a dozen or so sites of the top U.S. Clinics. Although much information I found on one site would be redundantly duplicated on another, it was all helpful. As I recall, the ACS site was the most helpful because it had numerous resource links as well as a diagnostic tool . . . I also downloaded M.D. Anderson's treatment guidelines . . .

(3) Where did you/do you go to find out about long-term effects of your treatment, side-effects of treatment, etc.?

(a) Although much of this type [of] info was also found in sites described in (2), above, I relied more heavily on info I downloaded from the drug or chemo manufacturers' website whose product I was researching. I also used info published on professional oncology sites, oncology journals, and European oncology sites.

(4) Throughout this process, which sources have been especially helpful? Which have not? Who are they?

(a) . . . Those that have been especially helpful include the ACS,

NCCN, NCI, the "search" feature on M.D. Anderson's website, and
M.D. Anderson's downloadable PDF files of their guidelines.

No survey could get to this—Lynn Perry's personal guide to cancer
resources on the Internet. Groundswell thinking applied to research
had yielded a far more detailed set of insights.

Many doctors hate the Internet because it lets patients get their own
information, some of which is of dubious quality. (One patient reported
that when she brought up information she found online, her doctor responded, "Stay off the Internet!") But it's now abundantly clear to doctors at NCCN cancer centers that they must have an Internet strategy,
and the Communispace community is helping them figure it out.

Ellen Sonet is helping build Web resources for her cancer center right
now. She knows that patients go to cancer organizations like the American Cancer Society more, WebMD a little less, and cancer center Web
sites even less than that. She even knows (since Communispace asked)
which search terms people use—you could guess that it makes sense for
her to buy "breast cancer" keywords on Google, but would you have
guessed that lots of people search on "metastatic"? From this, she can
populate Memorial Sloan-Kettering's site with information and make it
both a jumping-off point and a search destination for cancer patients.
And that will improve patients' affinity for her cancer center.

the real power of listening

Ellen Sonet started from a position of weakness, a marketer in a doctor's
world. Now she has insights. This has a side effect. It's called respect.

"What started as a marketing project has a quasi-clinical halo," she
told us. She presented a poster session of her research findings at a
medical meeting, a role nearly always filled before this by clinicians and
medical researchers.

Because she's tapped into Communispace's private cancer community, Ellen has become a part of more decisions at her organization. She
described how a nurse was looking to do research on compliance with
oral chemotherapy: "She was talking about doing focus groups. By the
time you get them budgeted, set up, and recruited . . . it could take six

months. Or we could turn it around in two weeks and spend nothing incremental [that is, no additional cost in surveying the Communispace community]." Own the resource that generates the insights, and you have clout.

This change isn't unusual; it's typical. For example, at Unilever, Alison Zelen is in charge of consumer and market insights for deodorants in North America. She set up a private community to study young guys, the target market for Axe bodyspray. Like Ellen Sonet, Alison is keen to know everything about her customers—to get inside their heads. She had the young men in her community upload pictures of their rooms, use the language that comes naturally, and talk about their attitudes about everything from music to girls. Girls, as you might expect, are central. And the result of Alison's research is that Axe was positioned dead-on as attracting the opposite sex, with ads that spoke to young men in the terminology and settings they find familiar. Alison had acted on her insights. Those ads rang true because she knows an awful lot about how young men think.

The other effect, as with Ellen Sonet, is that Alison Zelen's profile has risen. She got quoted in publications ranging from the *Boston Globe* to *Advertising Age*, which published an interview with her titled "For Axe Star, It Sure Helps to Think Like Guy."[7] It pays to have your own community on call for insights.

The popularity of private communities has spread because they deliver not just insights but actionable insights. Charles Schwab used private communities to get inside the heads of Generation X investors, discovered that these consumers start their investment thinking at their checking accounts, and then launched a high-yield checking account and redesigned its site. Payoff: 32 percent more Generation X investors over the previous year.[8] Network Solutions, which sells domain names and Web design solutions to small businesses, built a small-business owners community and learned that the language in its marketing pages didn't match the way that these business owners talk. It also made its Web design tool far more flexible and easy to use by implementing changes it piloted with the private community. Payoff: a 10 percent increase in some attributes of customer satisfaction, an important measure for a service that charges tight-fisted business owners by the month.

As we've shown, having your own community has significant advantages—you can ask members whatever you want. But that's only one way to listen to the groundswell. Another is just to put your ear to the ground and see what people everywhere are talking about. That's brand monitoring, and it's the subject of our next case.

CASE STUDY

mini usa: listening through brand monitoring

Trudy Hardy faced an interesting challenge in 2006. As head of marketing for Mini USA, the American arm of BMW's Mini Cooper brand, she had to keep her cute little car relevant. Competitors like Volkswagen and Honda were releasing new models in the small-car segment. In the car business, everything revolves around new models—they generate press, which generates buzz, which generates sales. Mini had . . . well, the same cars it had the previous year. Mini had grown significantly since Trudy launched the brand five years earlier, but how could she keep it on a growth path?

As the brand's steward since its inception, Trudy had confidence in the cars. She knew Mini owners loved their vehicles. But what did they love, and how could Mini take advantage of that? To understand and answer this question, Mini decided to monitor online chatter about its cars—to listen in on the natural conversation. This had two benefits. First, it helped reveal how Mini owners felt. And second, it enabled Mini to measure the effects of its own marketing efforts by monitoring buzz before and after.

monitoring spawns a radical idea—marketing to existing customers

First of all, are enough Mini owners likely to be interacting online to make the buzz worth monitoring? Figure 5-1 shows the Social Technographics Profile of owners of Minis and two competing brands: Honda and Volkswagen. As you can see, these people rate above average on Creator and Critic activities, so it's well worth listening to what they have to say.

FIGURE 5-1

The Social Technographics Profile of Mini, Honda, and Volkswagen owners

These consumers score above average on Creator and Critic activities. We combine the three groups because there aren't enough Mini owners in our sample to draw conclusions and because Honda and Volkswagen are among Mini's self-identified competitors.

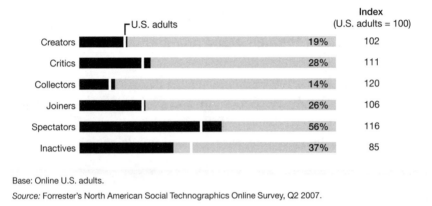

		Index (U.S. adults = 100)
Creators	19%	102
Critics	28%	111
Collectors	14%	120
Joiners	26%	106
Spectators	56%	116
Inactives	37%	85

Base: Online U.S. adults.

Source: Forrester's North American Social Technographics Online Survey, Q2 2007.

Mini and its agency—Butler, Shine, Stern & Partners—selected MotiveQuest to monitor the brand's online buzz. MotiveQuest is one of half a dozen companies, including Nielsen's BuzzMetrics and TNS's Cymfony, that offer brand-monitoring services. All these companies have moved to automatic monitoring, not just of blogs, but of the entire online chatter associated with a brand: discussion groups, forums, MySpace pages, and so on. Some cost more, some cost less; MotiveQuest is among the most expensive, typically charging $70,000 per project. While its competitors also track positive and negative sentiment in thousands of online comments and blog posts, MotiveQuest goes further, tracking responses by analyzing five hundred expressions of emotional sentiment with names like "inspiration," "anger," "hatred," "relaxation," and "excitement," developed in conjunction with the marketing whizzes at Northwestern University's Kellogg School of Management.

At the start of MotiveQuest's analysis in mid-2006, the Mini brand was generating more online discussion than any of the competing brands MotiveQuest was tracking, with the exception of the Volkswagen Jetta.

And the Mini comments were four times more likely to be positive than negative. But MotiveQuest and Mini had to look deeper to see what was really going on. Mini owners scored well above average on community activities, like sharing pictures and joining local clubs. Here's a typical comment:[9]

> I have never been involved in another car culture. Friends who are tell me when they meet MINI owners that our culture is in some ways very familiar—complete obsession with the MINIs—and in some ways very different—it seems to transcend the car. We get to know each other on a much more personal level.

So where Camaro owners might talk about their car's power and Lexus owners about their car's luxurious styling, Mini owners would rather see themselves as members of an exclusive club of people who belonged together. As the first buyers of this odd little car, they bonded with each other. They identified themselves—and each other—*as* Mini owners.

Here, then, was the key to making sure Mini was not another Chrysler PT Cruiser or Volkswagen Beetle—a car that's fashionable for a few years and then falls out of favor. Mini USA needed to strengthen the community, which would itself go out and proselytize others to the brand. (We discuss this technique, which we call energizing, in more detail in chapter 7.) According to J.D. Power and Associates, in 2006 Mini outranked every other brand in owners' likelihood to recommend the car to others.[10]

This insight led Trudy and her agency to a radical conclusion: it was time to market to Mini *owners*, not prospective Mini *buyers*. Think of that. Every car company in the world spends its marketing dollars trying to convince people to buy a new car. Once you've bought, you generate cost, not revenue, as you consume warranty service. And Mini now proposed to spend its money on people who've already bought the car? That took guts. But marketing to your own owners in hopes of spreading word of mouth—that's groundswell thinking.

At Mini, Trudy Hardy said, "I had the ability to be brave and try new things . . . At Jaguar [her previous company], it was difficult to be brave, I couldn't get people to try new things, let alone buy into a brave approach." The result was a completely radical ad campaign that mystified the advertising community even as it captivated the Mini owners. Mini sent owners a decoder package and then created ads with coded messages that only they could read. The company created "Mini Takes the States," a series of rallies for Mini owners all across America. And it worked, at least from the buzz perspective. In a year in which Mini sold thirty-eight thousand cars, over three thousand owners came to Mini events, spawning over twenty-one hundred photos posted on Flickr and eight You-Tube videos. Here's what one owner said about the secret decoder:

> lol [laughing out loud] I like that. It just takes some brains to figure it out! Most MINI owners are pretty smart, so . . . lol Nice find. Thanks for sharing!

Buzz measurement by MotiveQuest revealed that the idea of targeting existing owners was working—they were talking. But did this translate into sales?

the relationship between buzz and sales

There's no proof—yet—that online buzz leads directly to sales in every industry. But vendors like MotiveQuest and academics are finding more and more evidence that with the right measurements, online word of mouth is a leading indicator for sales.

From working with mobile phone makers, MotiveQuest CEO David Rabjohns had already seen evidence that an increase in positive comments about a handset typically appeared a month or two before an increase in market share for that handset. MotiveQuest began working with a team at Northwestern University, including marketing professor Jacquelyn Thomas, on metrics that could nail down this correlation across multiple industries.

Analyzing monthly sales data for Mini, David saw the same pattern. MotiveQuest and Northwestern created an indicator they called the "online promoter score"—an estimate of the online chatter likely to lead to a recommendation. For seven months between February and August 2006, the pattern was clear—when the online promoter activity went up, sales went up in the following month. When the activity went down, sales went down.

After August the dynamic changed, in part because Mini's word of mouth began spiking as a result of its earlier marketing focused on the customer community. At the same time word leaked out that a new Mini model was coming, which can depress current-month sales as people wait for the new car. But overall Mini's sales in 2006 were down only 4 percent from 2005, a decline that Trudy attributes to production constraints. In a year with no new models, this is excellent performance. Mini had saved 2006, in part because of marketing to its own customers and listening as the groundswell responded.

listening to the groundswell: what it means to you

Listening is perhaps the most essential neglected skill in business. Part of the reason is that it's always been so hard. The result was the narrowest form of listening—market research. But in the era of the groundswell, listening is easy. Not listening, on the other hand, is criminal.

Whether you choose to start a private community, engage a company for brand monitoring, or just use the available tools to do rudimentary listening on your own, your organization must get started. Here are six reasons why:

1. *Find out what your brand stands for.* You know the message you're trying to get across. How is that different from what people are talking about? Mini thought its brand was about a snappy, cool way to deliver an experience they called *motoring*. The company was right, but needed brand monitoring to realize its brand was also about a community. If Brazilian brand theorist Ricardo Guimarães is right, then your brand is whatever people say it is. You'd better find out what they're saying. This applies not just to traditional media but to how you talk to the groundswell—a topic we cover in detail in the next chapter.

2. *Understand how buzz is shifting.* Start listening, and you have a baseline. Keep listening, and you understand change. Is your competitor getting all the talk? Are people talking less about your style and more about your high prices? Surveys can find this out at a coarse degree of resolution. Listening to the groundswell gives you the answer in high definition, on a weekly or

even daily basis. And as more evidence accumulates that buzz is a leading indicator for sales, you'd better be paying attention. This tracking also enables you to find people with problems and connect with them to address their problems directly. In fact, Dell is using this technique with Visible Technologies to head off support issues with squeaky wheels on blogs and forums. We talk more about using the groundswell for supporting customers in chapter 8.

3. *Save research money; increase research responsiveness.* If you do a survey once in a while, listening is more expensive. But if your company has a regular research budget, some of it should go to listening. A private community like the ones offered by Communispace, once it's up and running, can deliver survey results far more quickly than a custom survey. And it allows you to ask "why," which ordinary surveys don't do so well. Brand monitoring is no substitute for traditional research, but it can fill in the details once you've identified a trend.

4. *Find the sources of influence in your market.* Who's talking about your product? Are the bloggers more influential, or are the discussion forums? Are thousands of people watching videos about it on YouTube? Has somebody scooped up your identity on MySpace or started a community around it on Facebook? Monitoring vendors like BuzzLogic specialize in identifying who has influence. Once you find the influencers, you can cultivate them. This is *energizing the groundswell*, and we discuss it in detail in chapter 7.

5. *Manage PR crises.* If your company is going to suffer an assault from the groundswell—a negative YouTube video, a rapidly spreading blog post, bad buzz on forums—you'll hear about it earlier if you're listening. Brand monitoring can function as an early-warning system, allowing your organization to respond before things get out of hand. In these situations, hours can count.

6. *Generate new product and marketing ideas.* Your customers use your products and services all the time. They generate lots of in-

telligent ideas about those products and services, and they will offer those ideas to you—*for free*. Is there a Lynn Perry in your market, describing how your service should be made more efficient? Is there a blogger suggesting new features or packaging for your products? Maybe a discussion group has figured out what your new marketing message should be or a new type of store you should sell through. You can get access to all these ideas, but only if you listen. For more on how customers can collaborate with you on products and marketing, see chapter 9.

your listening plan

So if you've decided to start listening, what should you do? From our experience working with companies, listening generally starts in the research or marketing department. Over time, though, listening will become a responsibility that is spread throughout an organization (we show some examples of this in chapter 10). Here are some practical suggestions that will help you succeed with listening to the groundswell:

- *Check the Social Technographics Profile of your customers.* Listening is most effective if your customers are *in* the groundswell to begin with. Check, in particular, the number of Creators and Critics in your customer base. If those numbers are high—at least 15 percent of your customers—then you can use brand monitoring effectively to listen to your market (this applies to most car brands, for example). If they're very high—30 percent or more—then brand monitoring becomes an imperative (as with most technology products and services). Less than 15 percent means you'll be listening to a narrower slice of your audience, which may still be worthwhile but won't be remotely representative (this will happen if your audience skews older, for example). In that case, you may want to consider a private community instead.

- *Start small, think big.* For large companies with many brands, undertaking an overall brand-monitoring program can escalate into the million-dollar price range rapidly. Instead, start with a single brand and monitor that. Private communities also work best on a single brand or customer segment, like Alison Zelen's young men for Unilever's deodorant brands. But over and over again, we've seen these programs spread, based on their utility to the company. Imagine for a moment that your listening program spreads to five or ten times the cost and complexity you start with. Who will manage that, and how? Can your vendors grow with you? It's best to think these questions through before you begin so you'll be prepared.

- *Make sure your listening vendor has dedicated an experienced team to your effort.* Monitoring and community companies are new enough that it's likely to be the CEO, head of marketing, or head of sales who pitches you. They're smart. Are their staffs as well? "You need to focus specifically on the team you will be getting, the analysts at the vendor," says analyst Peter Kim, Forrester's expert on brand monitoring.[11] Since this is a new world you'll be navigating, you'll want an experienced team to help you create and manage the information coming in and to understand the results.

- *Choose a senior person to interpret the information and integrate it with other sources.* Paying hundreds of thousands of dollars for a community or monitoring service and failing to exploit the information is like buying a private jet and forgetting where you parked it. Listening generates insights, but they won't sneak up and shout in your ears—you need to manage this resource. One staffer needs to dedicate time to reading the reports, interfacing with the vendors, and suggesting new information to retrieve. This staffer should be able to integrate the insights from listening to the groundswell with other syndicated research, surveys, and focus groups to create a complete market picture. If this is your job, be prepared—you'll be interfacing with marketing, product development, and other brands before long, which should boost your status, as it did for Ellen Sonet at Memorial Sloan-Kettering.

how listening will change your organization

So even as you get smarter by listening to the groundswell, you should prepare for some of the ways it will change your organization. Once you begin to listen and act on that information, your company will never be the same.

First, it's likely to change the power structure of your organization. Market research departments tend to be sequestered off to the side, a resource used by marketers and development teams. Whatever department takes charge of listening to the groundswell—whether it's research or marketing—will soon become far more central to how decisions are made. As happened with Ellen Sonet at Memorial Sloan-Kettering, expect marketing and research to exert a more powerful influence on development. Of course, this can lead to conflict with powerful development groups. That's why it's so important to package up the results of listening in ways that other groups in your organization can understand. Your job becomes to communicate what you've learned—to turn insight into change.

Second, the instant availability of information from customers can become like a drug that companies can become addicted to. Organizations that are used to near-real-time feedback (like ratings in the TV industry and point-of-sale data in retail) have learned to balance the short-term scorekeeping with the long-term strategy. But unlike simple scorekeeping, listening to the groundswell is richer and applies to far more industries. As listening becomes a bigger part of your company, you should integrate the results into corporate decision making. For example, at a retailer, the executive in charge of listening should become a regular part of buying and merchandising decisions; in a brand company, she should become a regular fixture in advertising strategy meetings.

Third is what we call the no-more-being-stupid factor. Every company has stupid products, policies, and organizational quirks. These corporate elements persist because a top executive is biased toward them, or because they're baked into corporate processes and systems, or just because of tradition. Maybe every transaction gets a legal review that delays it a day but hasn't revealed a problem in the past two years. Maybe your promises that the service technician will show up during a particular four-hour window are right only 75 percent of the time. Listening to the groundswell will relentlessly reveal your stupidity. When customers can complain, bitterly and accurately, about the way you do business and you can *measure and quantify* their complaints, it's hard to deny your own flaws. The constituency for stupid policies and products will evaporate in the face of highly visible customer feedback.

Finally, you may think that listening is the easiest way to engage with the groundswell because it's low risk—it doesn't require you to put yourself into the conversation. But while listening is part of a conversation, every conversation includes talking as well. Listening to the groundswell and then speaking through traditional media and advertising is like responding to a friend's whispered confidence with a bullhorn. Listeners inevitably feel the temptation to respond by talking *within* the groundswell, by publishing blogs, contributing to user-generated content sites, and setting up communities. So if you're listening now, expect to be talking soon, too.

Talking—the other side of the conversation—is the topic of the next chapter. In it we describe a variety of techniques for entering the groundswell as a speaker, not just a listener.

6. talking with the groundswell

Steve Ogborn is a management consultant with three teenage kids in a suburb of Chicago. One day in the summer of 2007, he was reading one of his favorite blogs—Engadget, which is aimed at lovers of personal technology—when he saw the unthinkable.

Some nut had put an Apple iPhone—the hottest technology product out there, just released—into a blender.[1] The online video on Engadget featured a geeky-looking guy in a lab coat and safety goggles. The iPhone, in a matter of less than a minute, was reduced to dust (or "iSmoke" as the geeky-looking guy put it).

After this, Steve did two things.

First, he went to the Web site mentioned in the video—willitblend .com—and watched videos of the same blender destroying hockey pucks, cubic zirconia, and similar objects rarely seen in the average kitchen.

And second, somewhere in the back of his mind, an idea formed. Steve Ogborn's children love smoothies. "They eat their weight in fruit," he told us. His current blender just wasn't cutting it. So he checked out the blender in the videos, which was described in detail on willitblend.com.

The blender that had reduced the iPhone to dust cost $399. "My first reaction was 'boy, that's a lot for that blender,'" says Steve. But his extensive online investigation showed that Blendtec's $399 blender wasn't available anywhere else, either at that price or lower. So, thinking of his fruit-loving teenagers, he placed the order for the most expensive blender he'd ever owned.

It turns out, there are a lot of people like Steve Ogborn. Sales at Blendtec are up 20 percent since Blendtec's "Will It Blend?" series started appearing on sites like YouTube. Who's the genius who conceived this marketing program?

George Wright, marketing director for Blendtec, was an unlikely hero for the groundswell, having had no background in consumer marketing (or video) before joining Blendtec.

He conceived the idea of marketing with YouTube the day after he noticed sawdust all over the floor of the testing room—his techs had been grinding up two-by-two lumber as a way to test their heavy-duty blenders. Incredible, thought George. People have got to see this. And with that, he conceived the idea of putting extreme blending videos on the Internet. The first five videos cost a total of $50 to create. But with a little boost—Blendtec's Web expert, Ray Hansen, posted a link on Digg after setting up the videos on Blendtec's site—the videos caught fire, scoring 6 million views in the first week. (When George Wright told the CEO, Tom Dickson—the geeky-looking guy who starred in the videos—that he was now a hit on YouTube, his response was "Who-Tube?" Tom knew the videos were going up on Blendtec's own site, but he had no idea that the video-sharing site even existed.) This was rapidly followed with appearances on VH1 and *The Today Show*. Later Jay Leno featured Tom Dickson on *The Tonight Show* (after blending a rake handle to splinters, Jay remarked, "[If] you need to get some fiber in your diet, this is perfect"[2]). Soon people had viewed Blendtec's videos a total of 60 million times.

George Wright and Blendtec had created a consumer brand, basically, from a video camera and a few dollars' worth of goodies (true, destroying the iPod must have cost a few bucks, but nowhere near what it typically costs to film and place a TV commercial). Blendtec had exploited the groundswell's viral potential for marketing messages. George had cracked the code, in his own unique way, for talking with the groundswell.

how talking with the groundswell differs from marketing

Companies already spend a lot of effort speaking to customers. This is the job of the marketing department. Two of the main—and expensive—methods they use are advertising and public relations.

Worldwide, marketers spent more than $400 billion on advertising in 2006, according to PricewaterhouseCoopers.[3] Much of this money is spent on television commercials. This is not talking, this is *shouting*. Advertising thrives on repetition. The two main measures are reach (the gross number of individuals screamed at) and frequency (the number of times each one hears the shout). Advertising is about mass. "Advertise on the football game to reach more men" is as personal as it usually gets.

Public relations aims at exposures in free media. PR firms (still!) broadcast press releases about their clients' every deal and accomplishment—that McDonald's is trying to reduce trans fats, or that sales were up 3 percent at Toyota—to every reporter and "influencer" who might conceivably want to write about such stories. They hope these facts will get mentioned in the *Wall Street Journal* or featured on CNN or in a trade magazine.

Something's broken here, and you can see what it is in figure 6-1. It's the marketing funnel, a venerable metaphor that describes how consumers

FIGURE 6-1

The marketing funnel

In traditional marketing theory, consumers are driven into the big end through awareness activities like advertising. They proceed through stages—including consideration, preference, and action—to become buyers. Marketers have little control over what happens in the middle stages, but the influence of the groundswell is heaviest there.

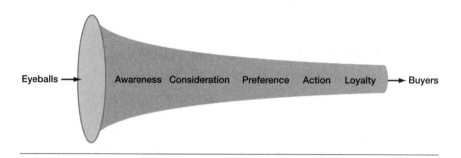

Eyeballs → Awareness Consideration Preference Action Loyalty → Buyers

march down the path from awareness to purchase and loyalty. Shouting—advertising—herds them in the big end. Activities in the middle try
to pull them down to that purchase, and if you're lucky, they come out the
other end as customers.

With so many products trying to get people's attention, shouting at
them isn't nearly as effective as it used to be. And once they reach the middle of the funnel, shouting hardly works at all. In analyzing this in a 2007
report, Forrester marketing analyst Brian Haven put it this way: "The funnel has outlived its usefulness as a metaphor. Face it: marketers no longer
dictate the path people take, nor do they lead the dialogue."[4] Once people
are aware of your product, a new dynamic kicks in: people learning from
each other. Social technologies have revved up that word-of-mouth dynamic, increasing the influence of regular people while diluting the value
of traditional marketing. When we surveyed online consumers at the end
of 2006, 83 percent said they trusted recommendations from friends and
acquaintances, and more than half trusted online reviews from strangers.
At the same time, trust in ads continued to plummet.[5]

Customers in the middle of the funnel are engaged in conversations on
blogs, in discussion forums, and in social networks. Your company can
participate in these places, but shouting doesn't work. Conversations do. If
your company creates a presence on a social network like Facebook, people
will post comments and expect you to respond. If you put up a blog, they
will comment and expect you to pay attention to those comments. These
conversations require work, but they do influence people in the middle of
the funnel—and not just those who comment, but those who read those
comments, even if those readers never comment themselves.

Blendtec understands this. On the "Will It Blog" area of willitblend
.com, George Wright tells you when and where you can see a blender
demonstration in your town, and he invites visitors to suggest new things
to blend. (That's how he got the idea to pulverize an iPod.) George
Wright isn't just shouting; he's talking *with* his customers and listening as
they talk back to him.

techniques for talking with the groundswell

There are lots of ways to talk with the groundswell. But for simplicity,
we've narrowed them down to the ones that are the most common and

most effective. Here are the four that we will explore in more detail in this chapter:

1. *Post a viral video.* Put a video online, and let people share it. That's what Blendtec did with its extreme blending videos.

2. *Engage in social networks and user-generated content sites.* Creating a personality within social networking sites like MySpace is one of the simplest ways to extend your brand reach. Turning it into a conversation is harder.

3. *Join the blogosphere.* Empower your executives or staff to write blogs. Integral to this strategy is listening to and responding to other blogs in the blogosphere—and that's one way talking with blogs is different from issuing press releases. In this chapter we show how HP uses blogs to its advantage.

4. *Create a community.* Communities are a powerful way to engage with your customers and deliver value to them. They're also effective at delivering marketing messages, as long as you listen, not just shout. We'll show this through the example of Procter & Gamble's beinggirl.com, a site for adolescent girls.

turning viral videos into a conversation

For George Wright and Blendtec, "Will It Blend?" started out to be about awareness. It was, basically, a substitute for an advertising campaign. It was focused at the big end of the funnel.

Solving awareness problems with viral videos doesn't just work for consumer products—it can work in a business-to-business setting, too. Consider "Greg the Architect," an extremely cheesy video series from Tibco about service-oriented architecture (SOA) solutions[6]—a service that appeals to information technology professionals who integrate applications. The "Greg the Architect" videos on YouTube follow the trials of a young and heroic software architect (played by an action figure) as he tries to make sense of technology strategy, dealing with his company's CIO and acronym-slinging technology vendors (played, of course, by other action figures, including Barbie, who makes a cameo). This is funny stuff, but it's for an extremely narrow audience—the series has racked up sixty thousand views on YouTube, far fewer than "Will It Blend?"

But as Tibco's head of worldwide direct marketing, Dan Ziman, explained to us, he's not trying to reach everybody—he's just trying to start a dialogue with big IT buyers. The typical Tibco SOA deal generates over $500,000 and may take six months or more to negotiate. So instead of pursuing sales, like Blendtec's George Wright, he's pursuing relationships. Since "Greg the Architect" started running, subscriptions to Tibco's SOA newsletter are up fourfold, which promotes the relationships the company needs. Faced with an awareness problem and well-funded competitors like IBM and Oracle, Dan found a cheap way to elbow his way in front of customers by treating them as people—people with needs that his videos portray in an empathetic, if satirical, way.

If you pursue this strategy, keep your objective in mind. Videos like Dan's and George's can get people's attention. What will you do once you have that attention?

Blendtec maintains, at willitblend.com, a site that makes it easy to learn more about the blenders and possibly order one. Tibco's videos create relationships through its newsletter. If your YouTube video doesn't create at least the beginning of a relationship, it's just another way of shouting.

To be most effective, these videos must allow people to interact. They should direct people to a social network, a blog, or a community where they can form further relationships with each other or with the company. These are the mechanisms that can help people in the middle of the funnel, and we discuss them in the rest of this chapter.

CASE STUDY

ernst & young: talking in social networks

Social networks are popular. For example, 25 percent of online adults in North America, 21 percent of Europeans, and 35 percent of South Koreans have joined them. Your customers are there. Where are you?

For example, consider Ernst & Young's problem. To keep up with its clients' needs, the global accounting firm has to hire thirty-five hundred new college grads every year. And since 74 percent of college students are Joiners[7]—members of social networks—Ernst & Young (E&Y)

meets them there, where they live. As Dan Black, director of campus recruiting for the Americas, told us, "Facebook stood out to us—at the time [we started], they told us that 85 percent of all college students have a profile."

On the day in 2007 that we looked, E&Y's careers group on Facebook had 8,469 members, of which 68 had joined that day.[8] What sets E&Y apart, though, is the dialogue it creates within the site. Dan demonstrates real groundswell thinking by realizing that it's student-to-student communication that sets this medium apart. "This generation puts a lot of stock in the opinion and advice and direction of their peers," he says, an argument he used to justify the Facebook effort to the firm's executive management. And while he's extremely busy with all that hiring, he still makes time to answer questions posted on the "wall" for Ernst & Young's Facebook page because he knows his target students are reading the results. Here's a typical dialogue:

DJ: Hello, I am completing my MBA . . . next summer double majoring in Accounting and Finance from UMass Boston. What do you suggest to apply for an internship or fulltime entry level positions ? . . . Thank you, DJ

Dan: . . . Please send a message via Facebook directly to Julia De-Wolfe . . . [S]he is our Boston recruiter and will be best able to assess your candidacy.

DJ: Thanks Dan. I have one more question. Do you consider [a] candidate for only that particular location he has applied or [do] you consider [an] application for openings nationwide?

Dan: To answer your question, we interview each candidate once during the process. If you do well, you certainly have the option to discuss different locations. However, if you do not do well in the interview we do not permit you to interview with someone else in another location. This is because our interview model is such that the first interview will cover the same information regardless of who is doing the interviewing from EY.

Let's tie this back to the funnel. Through advertising on campus and on Facebook, Ernst & Young makes its target audience—college students—aware of the company. E&Y's career's page on Facebook is also filled with information, videos, and other traditional advertising elements.

But *beyond* awareness, E&Y uses Facebook to draw students into the process further at their own pace and answers questions individually. E&Y is talking *with* these candidates, rather than just shouting at them. And while you might think this is a lot of trouble for each candidate, remember that others visiting E&Y's page can see this dialogue. Any of the college students who has "friended" Ernst & Young's careers page—made friends with it, as they would a person—can get notices of these updates. Students can also interact with each other there. For a decision as big as where to take that first job, this type of connection is powerful. And since an Ernst & Young staffer could easily generate millions of dollars in audit, tax, or similar services over the course of her career, the efforts on this site are well worth it.

ways to use—and measure—the results of participation in social networks

The key to succeeding in social networks is to help people spread your message and to measure the result.

To understand how these efforts work, consider what Adidas and its agencies, Isobar and Carat, did with its soccer shoes. Visitors to www .myspace.com/adidassoccer are invited to choose between two philosophies of soccer and two types of shoes; they choose the Predator if their approach is team oriented and precise or F50 Tunit if they're more about showmanship. Adidas knows its audience and their passions—of more than fifty thousand MySpace members who made friends with Adidas soccer, the split between Predator and F50 Tunit was nearly even. The site is filled with opportunities to taunt the other side and to change your own MySpace profile with wallpaper and graphics from Adidas—interactions that go way beyond shouting by engaging visitors.

Engagement pays off. According to Market Evolution—a consultancy that analyzed the campaign for MySpace and Carat in a 2007 report called "Never Ending Friending"[9]—every $100,000 spent in advertising drove twenty-six thousand people to become more likely to buy, based on their exposure to Adidas's MySpace page. But beyond that, many of those passed along the brand to their friends, resulting in thousands of more pages featuring Adidas soccer graphics and eighteen thousand additional people whose likelihood to buy had increased. And beyond *that*, over 4 million people were exposed to the brand on those members' pages. This is the effect that makes talking through social networks so powerful. (We talk more about the power of energizing your customers in chapter 7.)

Even more compelling are examples from South Korea, where the Cyworld social network dominates. Pizza Hut launched a new Italian-style pizza with an ad campaign driving people to its "mini-hompy" (mini homepage) in Cyworld. In eight weeks the campaign generated 5 million visits to the page, fifty thousand "friends," and over fifty thousand pizza orders placed through the mini-hompy. Other brands have had similar success: Motorola got sixty-one thousand people to clip images of the pink Razr phone for use on their own pages, and almost half a million did the same for the South Korean film *Typhoon*, an action thriller that draws its drama from the tension between North and South Korea.

when brands should use social networks

As compelling as these examples are, branding on social networks isn't for everyone. This is only one way to connect with people who've entered the murky center of the funnel. Should *you* use social networking sites to talk with your prospective customers? Here's our advice:

- *Use the Social Technographics Profile to verify that your customers are in social networks.* If half of them are Joiners, then marketing through social networks makes sense. Age makes all the difference here. Brands that appeal to consumers ages thirteen to twenty-three *must* engage in social networks because their customers are already there, while those with a market between twenty-four to thirty-five are likely to be successful with this strategy. As networks like Facebook reach out to embrace older people, other brands can begin to pursue this strategy, too.

- *Move forward if people love your brand.* Brands like Victoria's Secret, Adidas, Jeep, Target, and Apple have loyal followers who will friend them. A company like Sears without such avid brand enthusiasts will have to think and work a little harder—focusing on its Craftsman tools brand, for example.

- *See what's out there already.* Popular brands inevitably spawn friend pages and networks even before the company gets involved. For example, the Mountain Dew addicts group on MySpace, not authorized by the company, has almost five thousand members. The existence of groups like this shouldn't discourage brands—making friends with them will help you get your own group off the ground. We think Barack Obama's campaign, for example, missed an opportunity when it insisted on shutting down Joe Anthony's Barack Obama profile on MySpace,[10] which had garnered over thirty thousand friends, rather than finding a way to work with him.

- *Create a presence that encourages interaction.* Your fans on MySpace or Facebook want to connect with you. How will you enable that? How will you respond to wall postings? And what interactive elements—wallpaper, badges, widgets—will you provide so people can spread your brand and its messages? Visitors to your page already have some relationship with your brand—how will you help them go deeper into the funnel and influence others? You'll need staff responsible for programming the page and responding to comments, just as if it were part of your Web site. Then prime the pump with a little advertising to your targeted audience, and watch people spread your messages.

Many messages are not quite so easy to spread as the ones marketers are putting on Facebook and MySpace. If you're ready to make a longer-term commitment to your customers—and especially if your brand isn't quite as catchy as a *Typhoon* trailer—then it may be time to look at another way to talk with the groundswell: blogging.

CASE STUDY

hp: talking with customers through blogging

HP has a marketing problem. It sells hundreds of different products. Dozens of types of printers. Cameras. Flat-panel TVs. Every kind of computer, from low-cost notebooks for consumers to huge enterprise-class servers. Lots and lots of software. And billons of dollars' worth of services. All these products are sold to a diverse set of customers—from the largest corporations, to small businesses, to millions of individual consumers around the world.

Many of HP's products are complex, and buyers need help as they reach the middle of the funnel. Advertising or press releases are futile when selling these types of products. Buyers need product details with a human face to help them along. That's why blogging fills a need at HP.

HP decided not to have a single corporate blog, like GM's FastLane, but a variety from all over the company. As the number of bloggers grew, however, HP needed to harness the enthusiasm without allowing chaos to rein. This job of herding the cats fell to Alison Watterson, editor in chief of HP's rich and information-packed Web site. The result was a short, straightforward blogging policy and a course that would-be bloggers could take to keep them within the guardrails. HP's blogging policy includes such commonsensical but better-not-violate gems as "Include your name and position [in blogs and comments] . . . and write in the first person" and this one that made the lawyers happy: "Your blog must comply with financial disclosure laws, regulations and requirements."

Ironically, these rules made blogging spread because now the corporation had blessed it. And HP began to reap the benefits.

hp's blogging paid off

HP now has nearly fifty executive blogs, on topics from storage and mobility to small businesses. If you're interested in specific types of products or HP's approach to a particular market, there's probably a blog for you.

While the blogs generate traffic, awareness is not the most important benefit. The benefit is that HP can now *respond* to its customers in the middle of the funnel. The dialogue is frequent and diverse with lots of updates, as bloggers respond to what they hear from their own customers, or from comments on the blog. These blogs generate trust because they're personal statements from the executives. And they stimulate discussion among other buyers and bloggers because HP is an active participant in the blogosphere. The total effect is to influence the mass of HP's customers who are blog readers, many of whom are in the Spectators group shown in figure 6-2.

A typical example is what happened when Microsoft released Windows Vista. Many customers began to experience printing problems—reports began to circulate on the Web that Vista printer drivers were not working. Then Vince Ferraro, an HP vice president who heads worldwide marketing for HP's LaserJet printers, explained how to solve the Vista problems on his blog.[11] This really opened up communication. Twenty-six blog readers posted comments and questions (sample: "Does this also work for inkjet printers?"). Ferraro responded to these comments, both with comments on his own original post and with a second blog post with lots more detail. As other bloggers linked to the Vista LaserJet post, it rose to become the top result on Google in a search for "HP Vista printer problems." Imagine the hundreds of support calls and unhappy customer complaints nipped in the bud when they read the blog post. Imagine, also, the amount of ink and toner HP sold by keeping those printers humming on the new operating system. By talking with a few customers, Vince Ferraro had responded to thousands of others with similar problems.

FIGURE 6-2

The Social Technographics Profile of HP computer owners

HP owners are almost a perfect match to the online population in America.

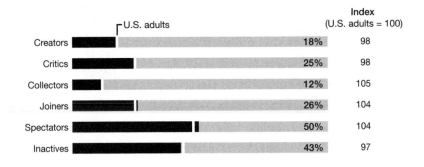

	U.S. adults		Index (U.S. adults = 100)
Creators		18%	98
Critics		25%	98
Collectors		12%	105
Joiners		26%	104
Spectators		50%	104
Inactives		43%	97

Base: Online U.S. adults.

Source: Forrester's North American Social Technographics Online Survey, Q2 2007.

Eric Kintz, a thirty-eight-year-old marketing VP and blogger at HP, who was named one of the top ten next-generation marketers by *Brandweek*, explains the value this way: "A lot of our customers look at how much we 'get' this new space. *Fortune* 500 companies need to adapt to this world, and they look to technology partners to help them drive this transformation. If HP impresses just one decision maker at a company this size, the result could unlock tens of millions of dollars of consulting and IT services revenue."

Blogs also allow companies like HP to react appropriately to the blogosphere itself. For example, in August 2006, Sun Microsystems CEO Jonathan Schwartz put this post on his blog after buying cardboard cutouts of HP's founders:[12]

> When presented with the opportunity to purchase the likeness of Bill Hewlett and Dave Packard, it having made the trek from the printer ink section of a San Jose Office Depot, our friends at HP elected not to honor their founders. So out of respect for HP's legacy, the fine folks in Sun's marketing team decided to acquire the artwork. Bill and Dave are absolute legends, held in the deepest respect by all of us at Sun. We were honored at the opportunity . . .
>
> With nearly 25% of Solaris downloads requested onto HP's servers, we know their customers really want the partnership, and we're happy to oblige.

Solaris is Sun's operating system. The post was accompanied by a photo of the HP founders wearing a "Sun Solaris" T-shirt. Now this kind of trash talking is silly, admittedly, but it creates a problem. HP's CEO can't respond without looking petty. A press release would seem totally defensive. But in the catty world of Silicon Valley gossip, some response was necessary. So Eric Kintz responded with this blog post:[13]

> We strongly value our humble beginnings and the vision of our innovative founders. You can find portraits of Bill and Dave in our lobby; we retained their offices in the condition they were in when they left them and keep them open to everyone here at HP (in the middle of the labs). We also embarked in the last years on a significant effort to preserve the

garage on Addison Avenue, where it all began for us and for Silicon Valley. I never met Bill or Dave, but I bet neither of them would have approved paying thousands for representations of themselves.

As for . . . comments on HP-UX, I thought I would share the real story [the last two words are hyperlinked information about the success of HP-UX, HP's system that competes with Sun's Solaris].

Result: the news stories that followed quoted this response and were balanced; Sun's little PR gibe didn't blow up into a full-fledged PR distraction. Decision makers—buyers making decisions about Solaris versus HP-UX—would have had only Sun's CEO's comments about how HP had lost its edge. Now Eric Kintz had presented the other side of the dialogue, by talking *with* his customers.

Companies often ask us about the ROI of blogging. After studying blogs for years, we came up with the model in table 6-1,[14] based on a high-end blog like GM's FastLane (described at the end of chapter 1). Technology is *not* the main source of costs; executive education and time are. And the payoff comes down the road, after the blog has developed a following. But because blogs generate high visibility, answer customers' questions, head off PR problems, and eventually lead to insight through customer feedback, they *do* generate significant ROI.

should you blog?

We get more questions about blogging than any other groundswell technology. And it's not just in America—on a recent trip to Brazil, nearly every CEO we met with was asking about blogging. No matter

TABLE 6-1

ROI of an executive's blog

In this analysis we assume a single high-level executive blog for a large company, similar to GM's FastLane. Costs include technology, training, and content. Content and training costs account for executives' time. Costs are typical estimates for a large company; many would be lower for smaller companies with a lower profile. All numbers rounded to the nearest thousand.

Start-up costs	Costs
Planning and development	$25K
Training for blogging executive	10K
Ongoing costs (annual)	
Blogging platform	25K
Brand-monitoring service	50K
IT support	3K
Content production, including executive time	150K
Review and redirection	20K
Total costs, year one	*$283K*

Again, for benefits we assume a large company blog. Estimates are taken from the FastLane blog. Benefits do not directly account for sales decisions driven from blog readership.

Benefit analysis (annual)	Value of benefit
Advertising value: visibility/traffic (estimate 7,500 daily page views at a $2.50 cost per thousand)	$7K
PR value; press stories about/driven from blog content (estimate 24 stories at value of $10K each)	240K
Word-of-mouth value: referring posts on other medium- to high-profile blogs (estimate 370 posts at value of $100 each)	37K
Support value: support calls avoided because of information on blog (estimate 50 daily support calls avoided at $5.50 per call)	69K
Research value: customer insights (estimate comments/feedback equivalent to 5 focus groups at $8K each)	40K
Total benefits, year one	*$393K*

what your company does, whom it sells to, or what parts of the world you do business in, people are blogging about your product. As HP found out, your competitors are probably blogging or thinking about blogging. And as we showed in chapter 1, what starts on blogs can rapidly spread to mainstream media.

But before you dive into the blogosphere, ask yourself this question: do I really want to do this?

For example, we recently spoke with Carol Meyers, the CMO at Unica, a company that provides software and services that automate marketing processes. Unica put a lot of effort behind a blog that Carol launched with high hopes in August 2006. In an attempt to reach out as broadly as possible to its marketing customers, Unica tapped a number of guest writer-moderators from inside and outside the company. "We would focus on a topic within marketing every month; we had a little editorial calendar," she explains. "But it got to the point, every month we had to spin somebody up," that is, explain the system to a new contributor. The blog lacked a consistent voice, which we believe made it harder to build an audience, even as it created management challenges for Carol. So the company shut the effort down after a little more than one full year, with a very honest last post in which Carol owned up to fact that the investment needed to maintain the blog wasn't paying off.[15]

Contrast this story with another business-to-business blog from a company called Emerson Process Management, which makes automation systems for manufacturers. Jim Cahill, in Emerson's marketing communications group, is the company's chief blogger at www .emersonprocessxperts.com. Unless you're a plant manager and automation buyer, we're sure you'll find most of Jim's posts pretty boring. But for process automation buyers, these tales from the front lines of process automation are war stories—they can relate, and the stories prove Emerson knows what it's doing. And while Jim frequently features experts from Emerson as guest bloggers, the blog is a big part of his job, and filling it up two or three times a week takes about 30 percent of his time. And it's working—Jim gets three to five contacts a week through the blog, contacts representing early leads that can be worth millions of dollars to his salespeople as they sell huge process automation systems.

What accounts for the difference in these two stories? A couple of things. First of all, Jim was excited to blog and enjoyed the attention, while Carol was continually managing others to contribute; her guest authors didn't really own the blog. This lack of ownership shows through— remember, your readers are *people*, even in a business-to-business setting, and they want to connect with another person.

Also, it's important to note that Jim knew his audience—people who buy and use process automation systems. Carol's audience—marketers— was probably too broad. One important product at Unica is in marketing analytics—if the company starts a new blog with that focus, it could be more successful the second time around.

tips for successful blogging

The prerequisite for starting a blog is to *want* to engage in dialogue with your customers. Some companies have a CEO or senior executive who is aching to say what's on his or her mind—those are good candidates. Like Rick Clancy, Sony's EVP of communications whom you met in the introduction, they may be nervous, but they have the drive. Nobody can be forced to do this. Blogging is too personal, and requires too much effort, to be crammed down anybody's throat. The result of that, inevitably, will look and feel lame, and it's worse than not having a blog at all.

If you or your company is ready to seriously consider entering the blogosphere, remember to start with *people* and *objectives*—the *p* and the *o* in the POST method from chapter 4. If you know whom you want to reach and exactly what you want to accomplish, then you're far more likely to succeed. What remains is to implement the strategy and technology appropriately to accomplish your objectives. Here are ten suggestions for beginning the dialogue, based on our experience:

1. *Start by listening.* A small knot of people at a cocktail party are conversing. Would you walk up to them and just start talking? Or would you listen, first, and see how you can join their conversation? The blogosphere is the same. Listen to what's being said out there before you dive in. Monitor the blogs in your industry, from competitors, pundits, and other influencers. For a more comprehensive view, hire a brand-monitoring service like Nielsen BuzzMetrics or TNS Cymfony (see chapter 5).

2. *Determine a goal for the blog.* Will you focus on announcing new products? Supporting existing customers? Responding to news stories? Making your executives seem more human? Choose goals so you know where you are going.

3. *Estimate the ROI.* Using a spreadsheet like table 6-1, determine how you think the blog will pay off and what it will cost. This is especially helpful in gaining buy-in from other functions throughout the company and in disciplining your thinking.

4. *Develop a plan.* Some blogs—like Jonathan Schwartz's at Sun—have one author. Others, like GM's FastLane, feature several. (If one person doesn't have enough time or content to post every week or so, this is a good idea.) You'll also need to determine whether you'll have a single company blog, like George Wright's at Blendtec, or a policy that enables blogging to spread to many employees and many different blogs, like HP's.

5. *Rehearse.* Write five or ten posts *before* allowing them to go live. This is your spring training—when you find out what it's going to be like without all the flashbulbs going off. It also allows you to explore what sorts of topics you'll cover. If you can't write five practice posts, you're not ready for the big leagues.

6. *Develop an editorial process.* Who, if anyone, needs to review posts? (The general counsel? The CMO? A copy editor?) Who's your backup if these people aren't available? This process needs to be built lightweight for speed because you'll sometimes want to post quickly to respond to events and news items.

7. *Design the blog and its connection to your site.* You'll have to decide how—and even whether—to feature your blog on the company's home page, depending on how central you'd like it to be to the company's image. Your design and the way you link the blog to your site will communicate just how official this point of view is.

8. *Develop a marketing plan so people can find the blog.* Start with traditional methods—a press release to get coverage from trade

magazines in your area, for example, and emails to your customers introducing the blog. You may also want to buy words on search engines. But remember that the blogosphere is a conversation—you're talking with people, not shouting at them. You can leverage the traffic of the popular blogs you identified in step 1: include links to those blogs in your posts, and post comments on them to lead people back to you. The text of your posts will also help—by using the names of your company and your products in the titles and text of posts, you will make it easier for people to find your blog in search engines.

9. *Remember, blogging is more than writing.* To be a successful blogger, you should start by monitoring the blogosphere and responding to what else is out there, not behaving as if you are in a vacuum. And remember that your blog will have comments—if it doesn't, there's no dialogue, and you're no longer talking with people as they make decisions about your products—and that's the whole point. Finally, many corporate blogs use moderation, vetting comments to make sure offensive and off-topic chatter doesn't mar the blog. This takes time, too, but you should do it. You can delegate the tasks of monitoring other blogs and responding to and moderating comments, but someone has to do them, or your blog won't be part of the dialogue.

10. *Final advice: be honest.* People expect a blog to be a genuine statement of a person's opinion. This doesn't mean you can't be positive about your company, but you need to respond as a real person. Sometimes bad things happen to good people and good companies—like Dell's laptop batteries catching fire. Dell's first post on the topic actually linked to a picture of the "flaming notebook" and included this frank admission: "We . . . are still investigating the cause."[16] This was followed up by posts about how to get defective batteries replaced, once the company had decided to offer replacements. A company that responds honestly, even when thing go wrong, boosts its credibility.

Even with all the focus on blogging, it's a mistake to assume this is the only way, or even the best way, to talk with the groundswell. George

Wright of Blendtec found another way. And Procter & Gamble, as you'll see in the next case, found a unique way to use communities to talk to a very challenging collection of customers.

procter's & gamble's beinggirl.com: talking with a community

Let's talk about tampons.

What's that you say? You don't *want* to talk about tampons? Well, now you can understand the challenge Bob Arnold has at Procter & Gamble (P&G).

Bob is part of the team tasked with marketing feminine care products to young girls. At age thirty, he's had only one employer, P&G, and had previously worked on Internet sites for P&G's cleaning products aimed at women. But feminine care products are a whole other level of difficulty.

The consumers in this case are utterly resistant to messages about the product category. (Even more than you don't want to talk about tampons, an eleven-year old girl *really* doesn't want to talk about them—or listen to a commercial when her brother is in the room.) The consumers are surrounded by parents who object to marketing messages directed at their children. In fact, these consumers and their parents are often making decisions based on discussions that P&G can't be a part of. And in this market, once a consumer makes a choice, she probably sticks with it for a long time.

Bob Arnold and the team at Procter & Gamble's femcare group needed a new way to speak to their consumers. Traditional advertising was problematic—shouting doesn't work so well when people are embarrassed to listen. So Bob and his team conceived a new approach—solve the girls' problems, instead of marketing to them. This was the genesis of beinggirl.com.

what's beinggirl.com?

Beinggirl.com is not a community site about tampons. (Who would visit that?) It's about *everything* that young girls deal with. Nearly half of girls ages twelve to fifteen are community-loving Joiners, as you can see from figure 6-3, and three out of ten are Critics that react to content in, for example, discussion forums. So Bob set out to create a site that had categories girls would be interested in, as opposed to those that would sell product. "We own this sort of growing-up part that people are too scared to touch," he told us. "We've really tried to create a community around that."

What does this mean? It means girls can share their most embarrassing experiences, like this one:[17]

"Have you ever done it?"

I was taking a walk with my crush and we were talking about a lot of different things. Eventually he started talking about sports, but I wasn't listening because I was too busy checking him out. Then I heard him say, "Have you ever done it?" I responded with, "No, not yet, because I want to find and fall in love with the right person first." He looked at me and said, "I was talking about snowboarding, remember?!" I thought he had asked if I'd ever had sex before!

FIGURE 6-3

The Social Technographics Profile of young girls, ages 12–18

Young girls include many Creators, Critics, Joiners, and Spectators, although somewhat fewer proportionally to U.S. youth, ages 12–18, overall.

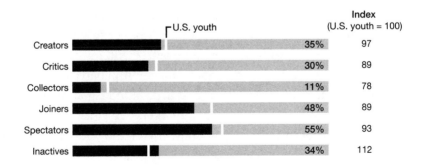

Base: Online U.S. youth.

Source: Forrester's North American Social Technographics Retail and Marketing Online Youth Survey, Q4 2007.

What does this have to do with tampons? Nothing. What does it have to do with being a young girl? Everything! This entry, by the way, got 19,331 votes from other girls on the site, making it the top submission in the "Laugh out loud" section.

Another popular part of the site features a psychologist, Dr. Iris Prager, who will answer your questions, no matter how embarrassing. Here's a typical example from "Ask Iris."[18]

How should you react when you get your first period

Hey, Iris,
  When you get your period for the first time, how should you react?
  Jody

Dear Jody,
  I think you should celebrate . . . this is a huge "rite of passage" in your life. You should tell your mom first and let her set the tone. It's a really important event in your life and you'll always remember just how it happened. You can also click here to find good information on what to expect when you get your period.
  Good Luck, Iris, for beinggirl.com, brought to you by Always pads & pantiliners and Tampax tampons

Notice how subtle the branding is. What's delivered here is big dose of sensitivity with a small dollop of information and a tiny brand message. This really is talking *with* your customers.

Iris also answers other favorites like "Will a shark attack me if I swim in the ocean during my period?" (answer: it's better to be careful and wear a tampon) and "How can I get along better with my mom?" (don't always try to have the last word). Some are about puberty and health, and some are not. But every post has that little brand tag at the end.

Bob Arnold and his team know their market. Beinggirl.com features music through a partnership with Sony BMG (no money changed hands—Sony likes the audience, and P&G likes the content). It includes sharing and games, the kind of stuff that girls connect with. It's carefully monitored to prevent people from exchanging phone numbers, real names, or email addresses, which keeps girls safe. And of course, it includes information about periods and feminine care products—in an environment where girls can check it out without officially going to a "tampon site."

Is it working? Well, Bob says beinggirl.com now attracts more than 2 million visitors a month worldwide. Traffic in 2007 was up over 150 percent versus the previous year. That's a record any media site would envy, and this is a site set up by a consumer packaged goods company!

How did beinggirl.com get there? Procter & Gamble cleverly gives the site a little boost. First of all, it's featured in the kits that the company distributes for health classes around the country. That's how a lot of girls hear about it. Secondly, once a week, P&G emails girls who sign up, to remind them about the site and bring them back. And finally, the company includes a free sample area—fill out a few questions, and P&G will figure out what you need and send you a few.

Take a look at what P&G did here. Because young girls resist messages about the company's products, its marketers were pretty much locked out of the funnel. To become part of the dialogue among young girls, Procter & Gamble created a social network. And because it solved customers' problems, instead of its own, the customers were willing to share. Add subtle brand messages and free samples, and P&G was able to become part of the dialogue from which it had previously been excluded.

measuring the payoff of beinggirl.com

Is there a company that understands the value of media better than P&G? This is the company that practically invented the soap opera and spends $7.9 billion per year to advertise its products worldwide.[19] But media is one thing. Community is another. Community is better.

According to P&G's internal math, beinggirl.com is four times as effective as advertising in reaching its target consumers. That's why P&G has expanded beinggirl.com to twenty-nine countries in Europe, Asia, and South America. "The world is getting smaller," Bob Arnold explains. "There are more similarities between girls then there are differences. The things that excite a girl in the U.S. are similar to [those that excite] a girl in China or Japan."

Let's do a little math on the value of beinggirl.com.

One purpose of beinggirl.com is to introduce girls to P&G products. Girls tend to stick with the same brand throughout their lives, so each of those girls could end up as a woman spending $5 a month for feminine care products for forty years or so. That's $2,400 per girl. Assume a profit margin of 20 percent, and each girl who picks Tampax and Always is worth $480 to the company.

We estimate that a site like this, now being run internationally, costs about $3 million a year to run. That means the site has to persuade only 6,250 girls to use its products to break even. Even a 1 percent conversion rate of beinggirl.com's traffic is three times higher than that break-even point.

Beinggirl.com has now expanded to include subtle messages about Herbal Essences shampoo and Venus razors—as long as the girls are there, might as well help 'em out with other personal care products. And based on the subtle approach, we doubt if the traffic will suffer.

Bob Arnold's success has had another side effect. P&G has instituted a "reverse mentoring" program. Internet whizzes like him now tutor the senior executives on how the groundswell will affect their brands. Not a bad spot for a thirty-year-old in a big, traditional company.

when communities make sense

Procter & Gamble took a big risk with beinggirl.com and reaped a big reward. Should your company do the same? Before deciding, you need to do a little risk-reward calculation on your own.

First, figure out whether your market really is a community—or could be one. Use the Social Technographics Profile to assess the community readiness of the target group—larger-than-average numbers of Joiners indicate a higher likelihood of a successful community. Then take the next step—ask yourself whether *your* customers really are a community.

Mini owners (see chapter 5) were pleased to join a community based on their affinity to a car. Other groups that might look to a community would include groups where people naturally support each other, like disease sufferers (see the cancer community examples in chapter 5) and adult Lego fans (see chapter 7). Fans of sports teams also form communities. But there's almost certainly no Grape-Nuts community and no cable subscriber community—these groups have little to bond over. Some companies will be able to think more broadly—as P&G did, creating a "young girl" community instead of a feminine care products site. But unless you can define a credible community around your customers' passions or pain points, you'll get nowhere.

Second, even if your customers are natural Joiners, they likely have already formed communities. P&G's beinggirl.com is actually in competition with other social networking sites aimed at young girls, like piczo.com and flip.com. It's always cheaper to sponsor such a site than to try to build your own, although you give up control. The key is, P&G defined a community around an issue that attracts girls' attention—the problems of growing up. Another generic girl community would have ended up competing with—and losing out to—Piczo, Barbie Girls, or other popular sites for young girls.

Third, once you've figured out whether you can form a community and what the central attraction will be, ask yourself these questions: What are we going to get out of this? How will talking with this community benefit us? With P&G's prospective lifetime value of each girl representing $2,400 worth of merchandise, the community makes sense. Unless you can do the math and generate a similarly positive outcome by advertising to your community, you'll be going to an awful lot of trouble for a dubious outcome.

Finally, do not continue unless you can support the community for the long term. Communities are cheap to create—you can create one for free at ning.com, for example—but to create an effective community, you must constantly support and maintain it. Communities need care and feeding—with content, new features, and redesigns—to stay relevant and successful. Pulling the plug will have a negative impact on your customers. So it's best not to proceed unless you're certain you'll get the benefits you're looking for.

talking with the groundswell: what it means to you

We've now seen four ways to talk with the groundswell—viral videos, social networks, blogs, and communities. Which will work for you?

Well, that depends on what your communications problem is. And that, in turn, depends on what your customers are doing in the middle of the funnel.

Do you have an *awareness* problem (people don't know about you)? Maybe you have a *word-of-mouth* problem (you need people to talk to each other). Or it could be that you have a *complexity* problem (you have complicated messages to communicate). Finally, if your customers are buried deep in the funnel where you can't reach them at all, you have an *accessibility* problem.

Each of the techniques we described in this chapter solves one of those problems.

Viral videos are best for punching through the noise—the awareness problem. They're great for unknowns like Blendtec. There's just one problem: you need a brilliant idea. Remember, people don't choose to watch commercials—while they *do* choose to watch (and recommend) videos like "Will It Blend?" and "Greg the Architect." Just remember that (if you succeed), you're about to enter into a conversation with hundreds of thousands of people who read the Web address at the end of your video (you did remember the Web address, didn't you?). You need to be ready, as Blendtec was, to convert all that interest into action and consideration as you suck those people into the funnel.

Social networks are the best solution for word-of-mouth problems. Word of mouth is critical for clothes, movies, TV shows—these are fashion products. It's also critical for cars. If you want to be hot, and have people talking about how hot you are, then MySpace and Facebook are for you—just don't forget to include the viral elements that your fans can share. These venues are also great for anything youth and campus focused, as Ernst & Young and Adidas have proved. The key is to be there—to respond to what your customers are saying—so you can help them through the funnel.

Big companies, technology companies, and lots of other companies have a complexity problem—they have multiple sets of customers, or they have high-consideration, complex products or services. Blogs help solve this problem. Complexity is a big issue in the middle of the funnel, since that's where decisions get made, and complexity hampers decisions. Financial services, technology, cars, home improvement, and fashion are all categories that involve consideration of complex options. Not only can blogs help with this consideration, but they can also reassure people before, during, and after the sale. And as an added bonus, blog posts often get featured in mainstream media and Web searches, improving awareness for complex products.

Finally, some customers are just stubbornly insistent on depending on each other, not on listening to you. For you, they represent an accessibility problem. If they insist on depending on each other, the best you can do is create an environment where they can do that. That's a community, and you should either create one for them or join one they've created for themselves. Just remember that maintaining a community is a long-term commitment.

how starting a conversation will change the way you think about marketing

The transition from shouting to conversation will challenge your marketing department. It's a fundamental change in attitude.

Marketers are used to shouting and then listening for the echo. This is an awareness tactic, and it's fine for the big end of the funnel. Awareness remains crucially important, so don't expect the groundswell to change that part of your marketing.

It's what comes next—the conversation—that marketers must prepare for.

You're about to become involved in the consideration process. This process is messy. It includes people, comments, and feedback. It's not a shout-once kind of a thing.

Marketing departments will need to develop new skills to listen, and then respond to, feedback from the groundswell. These are skills that companies have, but they're usually part of consultative selling or customer support. So prepare by getting the marketing people in your organization to know how to respond to customers as individuals. These people will be responding to posts on social networks, blog comments, community activity, and videos on user-generated sites. Think of them as moderators to the conversation.

These staff cost money, certainly. But remember that each response is visible on the Web. Your response to each individual is visible to many. Like Dan Black's answers for Ernst & Young employment queries, Eric Kintz's posts on HP server software, and Dr. Iris's advice to young girls, these responses will be read by hundreds of potential customers. That's the value that comes from talking with the groundswell.

Furthermore, remember that conversations require not just listening but responding. It's not about the big bang; it's about constant responsiveness, whether in a blog, a community, or a social network. HP's Vince Ferraro knew he needed a second post to solve his customers' LaserJet problems. You must adopt the same sort of thinking. Campaigns begin and end, but conversations go on forever.

Marketers must also prepare for changes in their agency relationships.

Shouting works well with traditional advertising agencies. One part of the agency creates the shout. Another places it in media. Then, if your agency is any good, you measure the results and see whether you made an impact.

Agencies aren't used to conversations, but some are learning. Carat's Isobar division has proved it can manage—and measure—campaigns on social networks. Edelman's Me2Revolution focuses on social technologies. Despite their early stumbles, we expect agencies to get better at helping clients with these activities. But ask for proof that an agency has managed—and measured—a campaign aimed at the murky social middle of the funnel.

Proof comes from measurement. But marketers and their agencies must now measure results that move well beyond reach and frequency to *engagement*—how far down the funnel your prospect has traveled. While engagement is trickier to measure, it includes tracking navigation paths on your own Web site and comments on your blogs. It also includes measures of buzz and sentiment about your products, metrics we explained in our description of listening in chapter 5.

If we can leave you with one thought about talking with the groundswell, it's this: the conversation will evolve continuously. Even as the technologies change, the basic conversational nature of those technologies will remain central. If you learn to talk, listen, and respond, you'll master the middle of the funnel.

All the marketing techniques we describe in this chapter tap into word of mouth: talking with the groundswell means stimulating conversation. Word of mouth is a powerful force in the groundswell. You can even use it to generate sales. That's the topic of chapter 7, where we describe how to use the groundswell to energize the sales potential of your best customers.

7. energizing the groundswell

Jim Noble is a hard-nosed computer security engineer from Georgia. He's a frequent traveler, a real "get-'er-done" kind of a guy, which is why it's so surprising to hear him talk with real enthusiasm about his luggage.

Sit next to him on a plane, and once he wedges his six-foot, three-inch, 300-pound frame into the seat, he'll tell you about his laptop bag. He calls it "an impromptu sales demo." First, you'll hear about how the "pumpkin-vomit-colored" interior (his words) makes it easy to see whether one of those dozens of little computer accessories has been left inside. "There isn't a wasted square centimeter on this bag," he says. And on and on until you ask him to stop.

How did Jim turn into a luggage evangelist? It's because the online store that sold the laptop bag to him, eBags, has figured out how to energize its customers.

Here's his story: after a long month of travel and on the way to a security conference in New York, a key zipper on Jim's laptop bag failed. The folks at eBags replaced it the next day. But that's not what turned Jim from a guy annoyed with his broken luggage into an eBags fan. What energized Jim is that people at eBags actually listened to the review he posted on their Web site, contacted him, and then improved the product, getting the factory in Hong Kong to change the design so the zipper wouldn't break anymore, even after constant punishment by road warriors like Jim.

As an engineer, Jim wants things to be built right. So a company that listens and fixes things, like eBags, gets his attention, his loyalty, and his copious word of mouth.

But eBags isn't just listening, and it's not just talking; it's energizing— finding enthusiast customers and turning them into word-of-mouth machines. And because most people, unlike Jim, don't talk all that much about luggage, eBags gives them the teeniest little push, encouraging them to write reviews on its site. This is energizing, the third level of groundswell thinking.

what is energizing?

In the late 1970s, Faberge Organics shampoo ran a commercial that sticks in the brain of any of us of a certain age. Heather Locklear (yes, it was her) enthused about how the shampoo was so great that "you'll tell two friends, and they'll tell two friends, and so on, and so on, and so on . . ."

It's a marketer's dream.

When political candidates get their supporters riled up and spreading the word, we call it "energizing the base." It's the same with companies and their customers. Energizing the base is a powerful way to use the groundswell to boost your business.

An energized customer like Jim Noble is a viral marketer, spreading brand benefits to his contacts without any cost to the company. Individually, no consumer can achieve the reach of mass media. But word of mouth is a powerful amplifier of brand marketing, achieving results no media campaign can achieve. Word of mouth succeeds because:

- *It's believable.* Testimonials from customers are far more credible than any media source.

- *It's self-reinforcing.* Hear it from one person, and it's intriguing. Hear it from five or ten, even if you didn't know them before, and it has to be true.

- *It's self-spreading.* Just as Heather Locklear said, if a product is worth using, its word of mouth generates more word of mouth in a cascade that's literally exponential.

According to the Word of Mouth Marketing Association (WOMMA), word of mouth "is the most honest form of marketing, building upon people's natural desire to share their experiences with family, friends, and colleagues."[1] It can't be faked, but it can be encouraged, which is why over five hundred marketers attend WOMMA's summit every year.

As we discussed in chapters 5 and 6, listening to the groundswell generates insights, and talking to the groundswell is effective, but marketers need not stop there. *Energizing* the groundswell means tapping into the power of word of mouth by connecting with, and turning on, your most committed customers, like Jim Noble with his improved laptop bag.

energizing the base and social technographics

In chapter 3 we laid out the Social Technographics ladder. Recall that 18 percent of online consumers in the United States are in the Creators group. This means that, on average, more than one out of six of your customers are blogging, uploading video, and maintaining Web sites. Are these people talking about your product? If they love your product, they *may* be. They're talking about something, in any case.

But the Creators are only part of the story. One in four are Critics, commenting on blogs or posting ratings and reviews. Nearly half are Spectators, reading the blogs and watching the videos created by the consumers further up the ladder.

Now suppose you could encourage those Creators to write about your product or to upload video about your product. All of a sudden, the people lower down on the ladder will start hearing about it. A little bit of effort could result in a lot of impact. And the impact will be more powerful because, as you can see from figure 7-1, people believe other *people* more than *media*.

the value of an energized customer

We told you this book would put ROI in the discussion of how to tap groundswell phenomena. Well, what's the value of an energized customer?

The definitive answer to this question comes from Fred Reichheld in his book *The Ultimate Question: Driving Good Profits and True Growth,*[2] one of the most influential business books of recent years. The ultimate question the book discusses is this: "How likely is it that you would recommend [company name/product name] to a friend or colleague?" Customers answer on a scale from 0 to 10. Subtract the detractors (those who answered 0 to 6) from the promoters (those who answered 9 or 10), and you get a Net Promoter Score (NPS). Fred Reichheld's exhaustive research proves that the NPS correlates with sustainable growth across many industries.

Jim Noble, the eBags' customer we met earlier, is a great example of a promoter. How much is a promoter like Jim worth? Well, that depends

FIGURE 7-1

How much online North American consumers trust sources of information about products or services

Note that friends' opinions rank higher than reviews in a newspaper, in a magazine, or on TV. Note also that 60% trust reviews on a retailer's site—reviews from people whom they have never met.

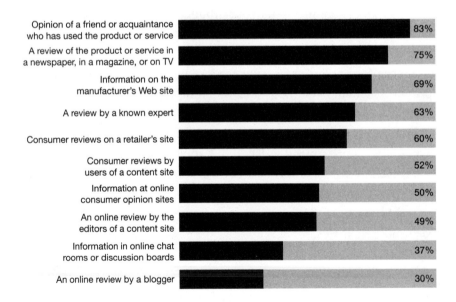

Figures include respondents who answered 4 or 5 on a scale of 1 (do not trust) to 5 (trust completely).

Base: Online North American consumers.

Source: Forrester s NACTAS Q3 2006 Media & Marketing Online Survey.

on how much of your business comes from word of mouth. For example, at Dell, 25 percent of new customers said they chose Dell from another customer's referral. Given the value of Dell's customers ($210 each), Fred Reichheld estimates the value of each promoter's positive word of mouth at $42.[3] Get that customer to generate twice as many positive contacts, and you double that return. That's the value of energizing.

There's one caveat. As Fred told us, "The value varies based on which customers come to you based on your reputation and referrals . . . and how much comes from advertising." But Fred is unequivocal about generating energized customers as being the best sign that a business is healthy and can grow. Assuming you have energized customers, amping up the word of mouth is definitely good business, with a value that increases for those with more business from referrals and a higher average purchase for those referred customers.

There's another measure of the value of word of mouth, and it's this: you can actually buy it.

A Massachusetts company, BzzAgent, will be happy to sell you a word-of-mouth program.[4] You sign up, and it sends some of its three hundred thousand "volunteer brand evangelists" your product or coupons for your product. If your product is poor, BzzAgents won't talk about it. But if they like it, they will.

In terms of the Social Technographics ladder, BzzAgent has recruited more than a quarter of a million Critics and put them on retainer, paid in coupons for coffee and the thrill of trying out new stuff. And those Critics talk to an average of sixty other people on each campaign.

How much does this cost? For a 10,000-agent campaign, the cost is $280,000. And while some find BzzAgent's tactics controversial, it does seem to work. (BzzAgent conducted over three hundred campaigns between 2005 and 2007.) So based on BzzAgent's math, an energized consumer will cost you $28.

This is great. But energizing your own customers can work even better than working with BzzAgents. BzzAgents only review what they're told to review. In contrast, your customers self-select because they like your products, and they keep talking about those products for years. That's why it's worth it to energize them.

techniques for energizing enthusiasts

So having absorbed the wisdom of Fred Reichheld and BzzAgent, let's say you've decided to take advantage of the passion of your most enthusiastic customers—the Jim Nobles in your customer base. You'd like to make it easy for them to spread the word about your product. You'd like to get them charged up so they'll tell everyone they know. What should you do?

Based on our interviews with companies that have succeeded in this endeavor, there are three basic techniques for connecting with your brand's enthusiasts:

1. *Tap into customers' enthusiasm with ratings and reviews.* This works best for retail companies and others with direct customer contact. Our first case study, eBags, shows how this works in detail.

2. *Create a community to energize your customers.* This works best if your customers are truly passionate about your product and have an affinity for each other, especially in business-to-business settings. Our second case study shows how this worked for email marketing service company Constant Contact.

3. *Participate in and energize online communities of your brand enthusiasts.* Our third case study examines how this worked for the Lego company as it energized its most enthusiastic adult customers.

CASE STUDY

ebags: energizing with ratings and reviews

The SVP of marketing at eBags, Peter Cobb, appears to be filled with boundless enthusiasm. Years ago he overcame cancer, and now he's dedicated his career to selling luggage. His company is an unalloyed success story, still posting a 30 percent annual growth rate after eight years of selling luggage, backpacks, and handbags on the Internet. But what's most interesting about eBags, and what Peter likes to talk about most, is how the company turns its customers into an incredibly power-ful asset. "We were just blown away by the level of detail people in-clude," says Peter, which is why their ratings and reviews are now front and center on the site.

For example, suppose you've decided to buy a carry-on that doubles as a backpack for that European vacation you've been planning. This purchase might be $50, $100, or $200, but it's far more important than that. If the bag fails to perform, you'll be suffering pain and frustration in a foreign country, which has to be one of the inner circles in Dante's vision of hell. So you'd better be sure it's right.

In three or four clicks on eBags, you learn not only that the eBags Week-ender Convertible, at $59.99, was a best seller but that "1151 of 1185 cus-tomers said they would buy this product again."[5] Wow! First of all, over a thousand customers took the time to give it a thumbs-up or a thumbs-down. And second, 97 percent of them gave it a thumbs-up. That's pretty reassuring, especially since those buyers rated it at least a 9 on a 10-point scale for features like appearance, durability, and price/value.

So who writes those reviews? Here's one, from a woman in Portland, Oregon, who doesn't travel much but used the bag to go on vacation:

> My husband purchased this bag first. It was very nice so I bought mine. Like someone reviewed, this is the bag to walk around European cobble roads since wheeled luggages are completely useless in such an envi-ronment. In my last trip, I used a regular carry-on wheeler for a check-in bag and took this bag as a carry-on. It fits in the compartment pretty nicely because it is very flexible without wheels. Since the airline com-panies more tightly restrict the weight of check-in luggages recently, it seems to be the best if you have two carry-on size bags. (Larger lug-gages may go over the weight limit once [they are] packed.) I recom-mend this bag especially if you are thinking of buying the second carry-on bag.

Thanks, whoever you are. That bit about the cobblestones is a good point—might not have thought of that. Two carry-on bags, good idea. And you bought a second one after your husband bought one; that's re-assuring. But what about the people who didn't like it? It takes only a second to sort those reviews from worst to best. Then you learn what David, from Jamaica Plain, Massachusetts, said:

> This is an excellent item, but it was too small for my needs so I returned it. I'm a big guy, so I need room for my big clothes. The quality of the material is excellent, the zippers seem very durable, and the tuck away straps and waist belt are of [superior] quality [compared] to many similar bags. There were a few aspects of the bag that I did not like: 1) It does not [expand] at all, so using it as a larger, checked bag is not an option. 2) The front pocket has zip pockets and pen holders which makes its storage ability less flexible. 3) It looks like a backpack even when the straps are zipped in. 4) The compression straps do not go around the entire bag. In the end I bought a Rick Steves bag for more money that is made of lower quality material but holds much more (and can still be checked). The weekender convertible is an exceptional bag if you are a talented packer able to bring only the necessities.

OK, so David didn't like it. But maybe he's just not a good packer; plus, his clothes are really big. If that's the worst that people can come up with, we're sold.

One click and we're happy. And eBags' Peter Cobb, who's clearly a hell of a salesman, didn't have to sell us at all. His *customers* did.

how ebags energized its customers

Buying luggage is a touchy-feely kind of purchase. This isn't like buying books on amazon.com; you don't have to see books to buy them. It's an intimate relationship we have with our luggage. Our *stuff* goes in there. You don't trust your stuff to just anything. So it would seem that an online seller of luggage would be at a disadvantage to a luggage store, where you can see the bag and talk to a salesperson. The people behind eBags knew this, so they implemented ratings and reviews on their site to make up for the insecurity that comes from not being able to touch the bag before you buy it.

Now, unlike some of the other examples in this book, there is no such thing as a luggage community. People don't get together over coffee and talk about luggage. There are no luggage enthusiasts (and if there are, you don't want to meet them). But people do care a lot about luggage, because that luggage holds their stuff. So when, twenty-one days after a bag ships, eBags sends an email suggesting that the customer review the product, 22 percent respond. On the Social Technographics ladder, eBags is tapping the Critics, which is far easier than trying to get luggage consumers to be Creators, blogging about their luggage experiences or uploading luggage videos to YouTube.

Take a quick look at the Social Technographics Profile of business travelers shown in figure 7-2. This is an upscale segment that overindexes in all the groups on the Social Technographics ladder. What's the right groundswell strategy for these folks? Energize their Critic activities, and use that to influence the Spectators. In other words, ratings and reviews are a perfect strategy for a company that targets business travelers.

What you see at eBags is the groundswell at work. People want to depend on other people. Peter Cobb knew that. All he had to do was to make it easy for them to talk, and they did. And like so many groundswell phenomena, the eBags site builds on itself. You read the reviews,

FIGURE 7-2

The Social Technographics Profile of business travelers

Business travelers are more likely than average consumers to be Critics and also overindex for Spectators. (This survey defines a business traveler as someone who has taken a business trip of 50 or more miles in the past 12 months.)

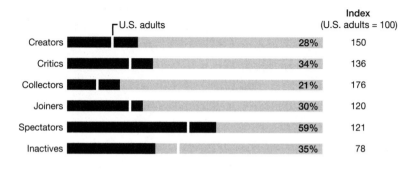

	U.S. adults	Index (U.S. adults = 100)
Creators	28%	150
Critics	34%	136
Collectors	21%	176
Joiners	30%	120
Spectators	59%	121
Inactives	35%	78

Base: Online U.S. adults.

Source: Forrester's North American Social Technographics Online Survey, Q2 2007.

you buy the product, you use it, and then you figure, "Hey, why don't I contribute to help the next guy?"

This is energizing the groundswell the easy way. There's no need to set up accounts, maintain profile pages, or weed out cyberstalkers. And it works.

benefits of ratings and reviews

At eBags, the return on ratings and reviews is highly measurable. Reviews increase the buy rate. It's hard to know just how much ratings improve the buy rate because there is no control case, no ebags.com without reviews. But our surveys show that 76 percent of customers use online reviews to help them make purchases.[6] In fact, even though only 25 percent of ecommerce sites have ratings and reviews, 96 percent of the sites that have them rate them as an effective merchandising tactic.[7] Sucharita Mulpuru, a Forrester analyst who concentrates on online retailing, recommends including reviews unequivocally: "Any site that allows the purchase of commodity products should collect and expose reviews."

Bazaarvoice, a company that makes ratings and reviews systems for Web sites, has done case studies with controls. Visitors to Petco's pet supplies site who browsed specifically by highest-rated products were 49 percent more likely to buy.[8] Although it's difficult to make direct comparisons (probably those who read reviews are generally more interested, which contributes to their willingness to purchase), it's clear that ratings and reviews generate more purchases.

Based on this, we can compute the ROI of ratings and reviews at a site like eBags (see table 7-1). Using very conservative estimates of increases in business, we estimate that a $200,000 investment in ratings will yield $400,000 in profit the first year, and more in subsequent years. That's double your investment back in one year. Not bad.

Web executives sometimes see this potential but worry about negative reviews. However, our research shows that about 80 percent of reviews tend to be positive.[9] And in fact, the negative reviews are essential to the credibility of the site—without them, the positive reviews just don't seem believable.

TABLE 7-1

ROI of ratings and reviews

Bazaarvoice charges about $25K a year for its system, with an up-front development cost of around $50K. Ratings are most effective with an employee in house analyzing what's coming back from the customers.

Cost analysis (first year)	Costs
Up-front development cost paid to technology vendor	$50K
Yearly ongoing costs paid to technology vendor	25K
Additional yearly ongoing costs at company	125K
Total costs, year one	*$200K*

Assume an online retailer that sells $25m a year, with 10m site visitors and 250K customers per year (a 2.5% conversion rate), and a $100 average transaction. We estimate that ratings increase the conversion rate by 20% and the transaction size for those customers by an average of 10% (many companies exceed this). Assume further that the reviews only boost sales on the top 20% of items, since those will get the most reviews in year one.

Profit analysis (first year)	After ratings and reviews
Site visitors	10m
Visitors seeing reviews (20% in year one)	2m
Sales at typical 2.5% conversion, $100 per transaction	$5m
Sales with ratings/reviews: 3% conversion, $110 per transaction	$6.6m
Net additional sales because of ratings/reviews	$1.6m
Net additional profit at 25% profit margin	*$400K*

But another reason ratings and reviews help, whether positive or negative, is leverage with suppliers. And eBags knows more about the products it sells than the people who manufacture them. It provides a report to every single one of its 370 brands every Monday, telling them not only what's selling but what people think of those products. What offline retailer could do that?

Reinforcing this last point, Peter Cobb told us an interesting story. His site sold a hard-sided bag called the International Traveler. It was popular because it looked sharp. But after getting great reviews for a while, something changed. "I started seeing thumbs-downs," Peter told us. At first, it was one a week, then three a week, and then six a week. People were saying, "I use this bag, and I love the looks. But the second time I used it, the outside cracked." Or "I threw it in a cab and it cracked." Peter decided the company must have changed something in the chemical process used to make the hard shell, and the new shell wasn't standing up to the beating that these bags take in the way that it used to.

The manufacturer denied it. Peter persisted. "No, we haven't changed anything," the manufacturer insisted.

As the negative comments mounted, the manufacturer reversed itself. "They came back and said, 'You were right; there was some type of manufacturing problem. We need to fix this,'" Peter reports. And that fix solved the cracking problem.

In traditional retail, the manufacturer is completely insulated from the end buyer. Returns go back up the supply chain. Macy's has no way to keep track of problems like this, and if it did, doing so could take months to figure out. But eBags has a powerful connection to its customers and knew within a few weeks that something went wrong. By aligning itself with the groundswell, eBags gained power over its suppliers, even as it became a hero to its own customers by fixing the problem.

CASE STUDY

constant contact: energizing by creating a community

What's the difference between spam and legitimate email?

Simple. Spam is email you don't want.

But on that simple question hangs the success of a company called Constant Contact. Constant Contact is an email marketing company. The focus at Constant Contact is on helping small businesses stay in touch with their own customers. If those customers have provided their email address, the small-business owner can drum up business by sending email newsletters, notes about what's on sale this month, and reminders for people to get their teeth or their chimneys cleaned. But by law (the CAN-SPAM Act), if people get annoyed, they can opt out of the email list. Legitimate email marketers comply with this rule. Spammers often don't.

As Gail Goodman, Constant Contact's CEO, explains, the lion's share of growth at Constant Contact comes from word of mouth. The company encourages this with a referral program—get a friend to sign up, and you get a $30 credit and he gets a $30 credit. Satisfaction is crucial because customers can stop paying the monthly fees at any time and opt out.

So when Gail's head of customer experience, Maureen Royal, proposed creating a community forum where customers could encourage each other, Gail was intrigued. Maureen had already proved that Constant Contact's customers loved to schmooze by assembling them, a dozen or so at a time, at dinners in various cities. Why not let them connect online? As you can see from figure 7-3, small-business owners are active participants in the groundswell.

Constant Contact's "ConnectUp!" community launched in 2005, and it worked. ConnectUp! now gets participation from thirteen thousand people, 10 percent of its customers. It's highly active, with over six thousand posts in thirty-nine forums.[10] People are answering each others' questions, encouraging new sign-ups to stick with it, and generating referrals. Constant Contact's forum is, basically, a home for energized customers.

Thirty percent of community members generate referrals. Constant Contact estimates that each referral that turns into a customer generates a lifetime revenue of almost $1,500 (the cost is the $60 credit). Constant Contact's revenues grew 88 percent between 2005 and 2006, beating the previous year's 82 percent growth.[11] This company is on a roll, and energizing its customers in a community is stoking the growth.

To understand why community works to drive revenue for Constant Contact, look first at its customer base—the people at the start of the

FIGURE 7-3

The Social Technographics Profile of small-business owners

While small-business owners aren't particularly likely to be Joiners, they do index high on Creator and Critic activities. Constant Contact customers, because they do business online through email, would likely have an even higher affinity for groundswell activities. (Small-business owners in this context are people who say they or their spouse owns a business with fewer than 50 employees.)

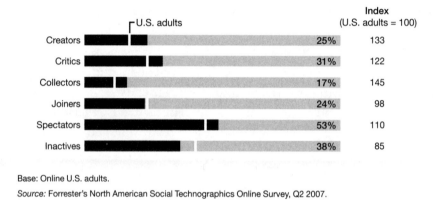

Base: Online U.S. adults.

Source: Forrester's North American Social Technographics Online Survey, Q2 2007.

POST process. Obviously, they're all online. But small-business people are a perfect target for community. They share common problems—running a company is tough, whether you're a restaurateur or a plumbing supplier. They're mostly not technical or marketing whizzes, so they can use help from those who've puzzled out the right ways to do email. And they like to brag about their successes to each other. So when Constant Contact encouraged them to join the community as they logged into their email marketing tools, many did.

Constant Contact's customers also shared another critical interest: *they didn't want to be seen as spammers.*

The first heated discussion on Constant Contact's newly minted forum concerned spam. And it threatened to get out of hand. Some respondents complained about how the company put their accounts on hold based on too many spam complaints. Others defended Constant Contact, pointing out that its reputation as a legitimate email marketer—not a spammer—depended on this activity. In the end Gail put on a Web seminar explaining the company's policy, and that settled the issue. The Constant Contact community raised an issue, the company responded, and its members went back to sending emails and referring new customers.

Even now the community has a self-supporting feeling. The altruism and "pay-it-forward" motivations we described in chapter 3 are powerful forces here. Kelly Rusk (known in the Constant Contact community as "cardcommunications"), a twenty-three-year-old Canadian woman working as an emarketing specialist, feels good when she gets to answer posts like this:[12]

BadAndy 80

That's me, the bad bad spammer . . . I had 6 spam reports out of 2000 emails, which is over the 1/1000 that they consider normal.

I waited on hold for 20 minutes to unfreeze my account and some guy acted like I was a bad guy for having 6. He genuinely sounded MAD at me. I couldn't believe my ears when he threatened me with "one last chance" before I was booted off the Constant Contact system.

cardcommunications

There's no excuse for the person on the phone to be rude to you.

HOWEVER, Constant Contact is just protecting their integrity—because . . . every spam complaint to every account is potentially a blacklist from an ISP.

If you find another email service provider who isn't so concerned about spam complaints—I would worry about them—because it's possible their mail is ending up in spam folders everywhere or just downright blocked by ISPs.

I would suggest [fine-tuning] your permission reminder and [writing] it as specifically as possible (i.e., you are receiving this email because you filled out a request for info form on our website and asked to receive email communications from us).

If you gained permission in a shady way (i.e., not explicitly asking for permission) then you should re-think your email marketing strategy!

Take a look at what Kelly is doing for Constant Contact. If Bad-Andy 80 got his list without asking people's permission, he'll give up on Constant Contact, taking his bad reputation with him. If he's just made a mistake, she's educated him and he might change how he does business. And for anybody else who reads this exchange, she's educated *them*. She's helped Constant Contact improve the behavior and integrity of its customer base, an asset that helps *all* its customers prevent being perceived as spammers. And education in the community is a heck of a lot cheaper than shutting people off.

As Maureen says, "It's about making them feel like a stakeholder. If they really feel that way, they are a part of our success. Who would leave Constant Contact when they feel that way?"

lessons from energizing a community

What can you take away from Constant Contact's experience with its community?

First, business-to-business companies have an advantage in building communities. Businesspeople form communities around their roles—in this case, as email marketers in small businesses. In fact, all of a company's business customers are far more likely to feel they have something in common than a consumer company's customers—because they're all trying to get the same work done. Consumer companies' customers may feel this affinity (like the Mini owners in chapter 5), or they may not (like eBags' luggage customers).

Second, communities can get out of hand. Gail and Maureen watched the first spam discussions with increasing alarm. To their credit, they took action and turned the community's attitude around to their advantage. Don't start a community until you've thought through what you'll do if conflicts like this arise. (And shutting off community members who say negative things isn't an option—they may well set up camp in a private community where you've got no influence over them at all.)

Finally, be sure you know what your objectives are going in. Constant Contact's community was designed from the start to energize customers. All the activity in the community (like the "show off your best campaign" section that's just begun) is about reinforcing positive behaviors, encouraging new customers, and generating referrals. This means Gail and Maureen can measure their success—a critical element of real groundswell thinking.

lego: energizing an existing community

Some products develop such enthusiastic supporters that communities spring up naturally.

Ask Tormod Askildsen. We introduced you to him in chapter 3. He's the senior director of business development at the Lego Group, the sixth-largest toy manufacturer in the world. But his job is to help sell Lego sets to people who don't see Lego as a toy at all.

Tormod is aiming at Lego buyers who think it's a creative building material, not just a toy. These are the adult fans of Lego, or AFOLs, whom he says are responsible for 5 percent to 10 percent of Lego's billion-dollar-plus business.

For example, in 2005 Lego created a product that seemed a little crazy at the time. The Imperial Star Destroyer kit costs $299 and includes 3,104 pieces. And once launched, it started flying off the shelves, becoming one of the most popular Lego kits ever. Who was buying these huge kits? Mostly grown-ups.

Tormod Askildsen was well aware of the AFOLs' own vibrant community, LUGNET, the International Lego Users Group Network (www.lugnet.com), which is not owned or operated by Lego. LUGNET is a global community of thousands of Lego enthusiasts. For Lego, replicating LUGNET on its own site would be a prescription for failure. Remember, community is about people's needs to connect, not your need to control, so if they're already out there, respect that.

Instead, Lego created a program called Lego Ambassadors. The Lego Ambassadors program accomplishes two goals: it builds relationships with the most enthusiastic AFOLs, and it helps Lego learn what's going on out in the highly connected AFOL world. Lego Ambassadors get information from the company on products coming out and then spread that information to their own personal networks, both in person and online. And the Lego Ambassadors have an explicit responsibility to listen to other AFOLs, develop consensus, and highlight their desires to the Lego company.

Active Lego builders vie to become one of the twenty-five or so ambassadors chosen by Lego. By limiting the number of positions, the Lego company creates competition, energizing its fans to step up and become spokespeople for the company's message. And Lego Ambassadors aren't paid in cash; they're paid in Lego bricks! That kind of compensation is cheap for the company yet highly valued by the ambassadors.

In chapter 3 we introduced you to three AFOLs at different spots on the Social Technographics ladder: the Creator Eric Kingsley, the Critic Joe Comeau, and the Spectator Linda Nee. Now you can see just how important they all are to Lego. It's easy to get Creators like Eric Kingsley stirred up, and with so many Critics and Spectators listening, it's valuable to do so. That's why Lego has made Eric Kingsley a Lego Ambassador.

the roi of energizing a community

What's it worth to Tormod Askildsen to energize the existing community of Lego enthusiasts? A whole lot more than it costs, that's for sure.

Lego Ambassadors require only Internet coordination, staff time, some travel, and payment in Lego bricks. We'd estimate the cost of a program like this at around $200,000.

But Tormod's twenty-five Lego Ambassadors are in touch with around a hundred other people each, more if you count their interactions online. That's around twenty-five hundred AFOLs, each of whom might be buying $1,000 of Lego products a year. If that increases to $1,200 a year based on the ambassadors' efforts, the company has used a $200,000 investment to increase sales by $500,000.

As with eBags, there's another return that's more subtle. The ambassadors bring Lego feedback on its products. They represent the community to the company. Because the AFOL community is so tightly knit and interdependent, the Lego Ambassador program means that Tormod and the product designers at Lego have an immediate two-way connection to the most influential members of that community. And as you may have read in *Wired*, Lego has even included these active customers in product design discussions[13]—an element of the embracing strategy we describe in chapter 9. This has incalculable value in helping ensure that products designed for adult Lego buyers will actually succeed. In this case, energizing the base includes a strong element of listening as well.

how you energize depends on how you want relationships to change

The examples in this chapter show three good ways to energize your customers—with ratings and reviews, communities, and ambassador programs. But there are many more, depending on what your customer base is like—and how you hope to change your relationship with those customers.

For example, Fiskars, a company that makes scissors and scrapbooking supplies, worked with a consultancy called Brains On Fire to create an ambassador program like Lego's. The program includes a community like Constant Contact's at www.fiskateers.com. After an intensive search, Fiskars picked four ambassadors who have now become icons in the scrapbooking community. Fiskars pays its ambassadors, but they return far more value in getting women charged up about scrapbooking.

Carnival Cruise Lines developed a program that helps people plan cruises with friends. Once you sign up at www.carnivalconnections .com, you can use the tools there to connect with friends, invite them along, and coordinate activities. Given the sporadic nature of Carnival's customer base, this event-based energizing strategy makes sense.

These companies were smart—they considered the propensities of their customer bases first, then designed strategies and chose technologies that matched the relationships they already had, and provided ways for their customers to extend those relationships. Do this skillfully, and you can get your customers to sell each other, too.

advice for energizers

Energizing is both more powerful and riskier than the techniques we discussed in the previous two chapters on listening and talking. The reason? Now you're dealing with *people* who are going to talk about your brand. As much as companies say they're in touch with their customers' needs, dealing with actual customers creates challenges for which they're often not ready.

If you want to energize your customers, you must prepare for a new way of thinking. Here are five steps for applying the techniques of energizing to your own organization.

1. figure out if you *want* to energize the groundswell

Energizing works well for companies with customers who are, or could be, enthusiastic about the company and its products. It's not for everybody.

Some companies provide commodities like copier paper or memory chips to their customers, products that are available from multiple suppliers and don't have strong brands or emotional connections. If this is your business, fine, but don't assume your customers want to talk about your products. Other companies succeed despite a significant number of dissatisfied customers. If that's you, then energizing your customers will only make things worse. If you're in either of these situations, we recommend listening to the groundswell (see chapter 5) so you can learn more about your customers' attitudes.

Even for companies with enthusiastic customers, energizing the groundswell can be bracing. The good news is that you'll connect, directly, to what people are really thinking. That's the bad news, too. Think about Jim Noble and his laptop bag or Eric Kingsley with his Lego trains. Do you really want to hear from these folks? Do you want your other customers to hear from them? Unless you and your whole management team can answer with an unequivocal yes, then you might not be ready to energize the groundswell.

2. check the social technographics profile of your customers

You need research to determine how actively and in what numbers your customers are participating in the groundswell. If you're selling PDAs or baseball mitts—anything that skews young and technologically savvy— then your customers are already heavily into the groundswell, and you can expect them to take naturally to a collection of community and social features. If you're selling mattresses or estate planning, then rein in your expectations accordingly—it's no use starting a community if your best customers have the wrong profile and won't be participating.

3. ask yourself, "what is my customer's problem?"

Remember, except in rare cases like Lego's, communities don't form around your products. If you have trouble believing this, just remember Procter & Gamble's beinggirl.com community from chapter 6, which was built around girls' problems, not feminine care products. Even Lego's customers aren't really talking about Legos; they're talking about *building* with Legos, which isn't quite the same thing. As eBags takes the next step, it might learn that its customers' problems center around travel in general, not just luggage.

4. pick a strategy that fits your customers' social technographics profile and problems

For retailers and other direct sellers, ratings and reviews make sense and have a proven payoff. If there are a lot of Critics among your customers, this is a great place to start.

For other companies, communities make sense. But check first. If your customers already have communities, like Lego's, then it's best to participate in those communities rather than build your own.

But be prepared. Although there are free community tools available from companies like ning.com and KickApps, to make a community that's successful, you must consider the costs of design, moderation, and marketing, which can easily run into the hundreds of thousands of dollars.

5. don't start unless you can stick around for the long haul

A community is like a marriage; it requires constant adjustment to grow and become more rewarding. And if you're not in it for the long haul, well, maybe you should think about the ugly endings you've seen to marriages that lacked that long-term effort.

Think about eBags' ratings. If the company stopped them, or stopped supporting them, not only would the site become stale and less popular, but the energized customers would suffer a backlash. Jim Noble is not a guy you want to antagonize; he'll start telling people how great eBags *used* to be before it stopped listening to people like him. If Lego stopped connecting with its top AFOLs, their enthusiasm would fade and the community would shrink.

how energizing will transform your company

In energizing the groundswell, you'll find out that not all your customers are equal.

In this chapter we talk about energizing the base. The base includes your most enthusiastic customers. But just like the base that any politician depends on, the base expects something back. It expects you to listen.

Whether you're anointing brand ambassadors like Lego, inviting customers into a community like Constant Contact, or empowering people with reviews like eBags, you're going to unleash some powerful voices.

Lego explicitly acknowledges that its brand ambassador program goes both ways—it is dependent on the brand ambassadors for ideas about future products and ways of doing business. In a comparable way, eBags has put Jim Noble on its advisory panel and checks in with him on ideas for its products. And eBags also taps its best reviewers to be field testers, sending them bags for review to get a preview of how the larger audience might like—or reject—those bags.

What happens if community members turn against you? If the top poster on LUGNET started dissing Lego's management or a group of Constant Contact's community members insisted on a change in policy, these companies would have an imperative to listen. An energized community expects a response, and energized customers wield power within the community of customers. The message, for any company, is to listen and, whenever possible, to give customers what they desire most.

What they want is information about the company's present and future products. They also want to see evidence that they are making a difference. A company that starts by energizing the groundswell will end up with a whole bunch of unpaid R&D partners. So long as you're willing to engage with your enthusiasts, this is fine. But they're yours forever—you can't lay them off if they stop behaving the way you want.

This is why companies that start out by energizing their most enthusiastic customers often end up *embracing* them—that is, turning those customers into an integral part of the company's products and processes. Energizing leads to embracing. So if you're going to energize your customers, you should take a look at chapter 9 to see where you may end up. Including customers in the product development process and as extensions of your business is exciting, but once again, the groundswell leads you to a space where you're less and less in control of your own business and brand.

Many of the communities we described in this chapter have the potential to go beyond energizing customers. In a mature community, people solve each others' problems. This not only invigorates the community but also cuts support costs. This is the groundswell supporting itself, and it's the topic of the next chapter.

8. **helping the groundswell support itself**

TJ and Michelle Howley were a couple of twenty-nine-year-olds expecting for the first time—twins, actually—when Michelle found herself in the hospital. We'll let them pick up the story from here (what you're reading is an online posting):[1]

[1st entry] September 04, 2006 at 07:20 PM EDT

On Wednesday August 30 Michelle's water broke. We immediately went to Portsmouth Hospital where they gave Michelle meds to hold off the contractions. After being transported by ambulance to Mass General in Boston, we heard all the grim news we already knew.

It was only 22 weeks and 3 days at that point. Babies are considered viable at 24 weeks. We were advised to induce labor at that point to avoid any potential risks involved with waiting.

We decided to hold off and see how things would go if we just took things one day at a time. So far we have been 5½ days without labor. No signs of infection and praying to make it to minimally 24 weeks so that the medical staff will potentially intervene if Michelle is to go into labor.

This type of decision really shouldn't fall upon any person. The facts are as follows:

We have two boys in there. One is doing fantastic! His sac is full and sealed and he is growing and moving around like a gymnast.

The other one has about 1 cm of fluid. He is cramped and potentially will have long term effects from lack of fluid/sac space.

If we reach 24 weeks without labor, the chances of survival go from about zero to 50%. Each week we get through provides a slight increase in this percentage. We were also informed that having babies born so premature can carry with it amazing developmental disability and neurological problems.

So that sums up what we were presented with. The official diagnosis is PPPROM (previable, preterm, premature rupture of membranes).

Many people have asked if they can do anything. All we really can ask of anyone is to keep us in your thoughts and prayers. We are in this for the long haul! We will update the page as often as we can with changes. At this point, No news is Good news! :)

Wishing you all the best . . .

TJ & Michelle

If you or anyone you care about has ever been in the hospital for a while, you know how TJ and Michelle felt. They were in an emotional whirlwind. They had to deal with doctors and nurses and make difficult decisions about medical facts they had never faced before. But that's just the medical situation.

Each hospitalization brings with it a parallel problem. Patients have families and friends. Families and friends are concerned—they want to know what's happening. And even though the patients want to tell their families and friends about their situation, that communication can be a burden.

"I hated getting calls," Michelle told us. "I was in the hospital, telling the same story over and over again." Her husband, TJ, was also overburdened as he tried to juggle communications with relatives, his job at a mortgage company, supporting his wife in a hospital more than an hour from his home, and making crucial medical decisions. It was just too much for anyone to bear.

Luckily, Georgia Peirce had put in place a system to help.

Georgia, director of communications for patient care services at Massachusetts General Hospital (MGH), knew that hundreds of patients like the Howleys struggle with how to communicate with friends and families. So when the SVP for patient care and chief nurse at MGH asked her to look into CarePages—an online system to help patients manage communicating with their loved ones—she loved the concept and suggested that MGH should adopt it.

CarePages is a specialized sort of blogging system designed especially for patients. Patients get easy tools so they can log in and post updates. And unlike most blogs, these updates have an intensely interested audience: friends and family. The Howleys had CarePages automatically send emails to the people who care about them, directing those friends and family members to visit the page for updates. Anytime the Howleys posted a new update or photos on their CarePages, those folks received a message. CarePages also includes a space where friends and family can post their own best wishes, which can make a huge emotional difference for patients. The Howley twins' page includes 121 of these little support messages, including not just the usual hopes and prayers but a series of original poems from a friend named Liana.

"We wouldn't have made it without the CarePage," Michelle told us. Unable to sleep at times, she would go to her CarePage and see who had visited (CarePages logs visits even from those who don't add comments). "I cried when I read them; it helped me get through each day," she said. "It renewed my spirit." Michelle's mother learned to go online just so she could check the CarePage twice a day. TJ gave access to co-workers and found he had an unexpected support network of well-wishers at the office.

For Massachusetts General Hospital, CarePages allows patients to concentrate more on medical decisions and getting better—and transforms the love of family and friends into a support system that's far less of a burden on patients. In a study of cancer patients by the Kaiser Family Foundation and the Harvard School of Public Health,[2] more than one in four said that their doctor does not pay attention to factors outside of direct medical care, including the patient's support network for dealing with cancer. As much as we'd like doctors to pay more attention to these support issues, doctors today seem too maxed out just dealing with the medical aspects of a case.

The Howleys' story has a happy ending, partly because of the support they got through CarePages. Since you can't read their CarePage—it's by invitation only—we'll quote some entries for you:

[4th entry] September 10, 2006 at 08:16 AM EDT
We made it to the last day of week 24!!! At this point, every day we can hang on gives a little more hope for the babies' health and survival.
The heart beats are still great. I can feel them move around daily . . .
We are trying to stay positive and all the wonderful messages you guys post really help us get through each day. You have no idea what a difference each one makes. Thank you!!!

[18th entry, accompanied by many photos] October 24, 2006 at 02:31 PM EDT
Hello everyone! . . . We made it through a crazy night!
Midday I started having contractions and then my temp started to creep up. About 4 hours after I had mentioned that I felt contractions, we had two new baby boys!! :) They both came out crying!
Matthew Domenic (Doc) was 3 lbs 7 oz. . . . Mark Joseph (MJ) was 3 lbs 11 oz. . . . They are both in the NICU and being monitored closely. I got to see them, and tonight they'll remove my IV and other attachments, so we'll go down there and hold Mark (because he isn't hooked up to as many things).
Thank you all for everything! You helped us get as far as we did . . .

[23rd entry] November 01, 2006 at 12:29 AM EST
The rollercoaster has begun . . . and we're holding on for dear life!
Today was a day of setbacks.
Mark had to be put back on the vent because he was showing signs of infection and repetitious apnea spells . . . He is on a round of very strong antibiotics . . . Seeing your small helpless baby do so well and then go back to wires and tubes and clear discomfort . . . it is an indescribable pain.

Matthew was doing fairly well. They are going to wean him off the ventilator very slowly, so as not to upset him.

[42nd entry] December 08, 2006 at 10:00 PM EST

Mark's home!!!! We brought him home tonight! We would have posted pictures, but things are a bit hectic with the move and the new baby :) He is a stinky boy . . . and he goes through more clothes than a fashion show . . . but he's awfully cute and we are beyond psyched to have the little man home!

[75th entry] June 07, 2007 at 09:07 PM EDT

THEY ARE BOTH HOME!!!!!!!!!!!!!

We made it through a couple days having both little guys here! It's been a hectic few days and if you've ever seen Mark in his fit of energy . . . I can only imagine it'll get more hectic when they can actually move around!

Clearly, the groundswell is a fantastic support system. Enable people to connect with each other, and they will, making life easier for both themselves and you. This is the groundswell supporting itself, and it's the topic of this chapter.

traditional support versus groundswell support

Supporting customers is a burden.

Once you buy a typical consumer product, the company doesn't want to hear from you. If you call, it means something is going wrong. An average call to a company's call center costs $6 or $7 when you include all the costs, according to Elizabeth Herrell, Forrester's expert on contact centers. Technical support calls cost around twice that: $10 to $20.

This adds up. Companies that do telephone support spend billions of dollars to run those call centers.

The quest to reduce those support costs has driven two of the huge trends in corporate America in the past ten years.

First, starting in the late 1990s, companies recognized they could send people to their Web sites for information. The result was the Web self-service revolution, in which companies put massive amounts of product and problem-solving information online and encouraged customers to use it. This was a plus—people could consult the information on their own schedules. And it saved money—as Harley Manning, Forrester's expert on Web design, puts it, "You can replace dollars with pennies." If your question was "When do flights leave tonight for Seattle?" this worked great. But more complicated questions still typically generated a phone call.

The second trend was outsourcing—moving support calls overseas. If an English-speaking engineer in India or the Philippines could answer questions as well as an American or a Brit, why not send the calls there? As of this writing, compensation for overseas telephone staff runs about 40 percent lower than the same staff in the United States—and most of the costs of those calls are staff costs. Based on these cost savings, 3.4 million American jobs and 1.2 million European jobs are likely to go offshore by 2015, many of them jobs in call centers.[3]

But are those calls any better at helping people?

Don't you dread calling support on the phone and navigating those interactive voice response systems? The problem isn't whether the person on the other end is in India or Ireland; it's whether he or she can actually help. And as for Web self-service—sure, we all try it, but the results are hit or miss.

Even as companies pursued these shifts to save money, people frustrated with the long waits, hit-or-miss quality, and paperwork associated with support for their products developed a new source of information—*each other*. People are far more willing to trust each other than a company, as we described in chapter 7. And amazingly, people are willing to spend lots of time *helping* each other, if you just get out of the way.

That's what Massachusetts General Hospital found out with Care-Pages—that people were happy to support each other, online, given the chance. Of course, you'd expect that people would help out their friends and loved ones, as the Howleys' family did. But the amazing thing is this: people are quite willing to help out total strangers.

In this chapter we'll show you three applications that demonstrate this impulse: support forums with Dell, wikis with BearingPoint, and questions and answers with Yahoo! and Naver.

CASE STUDY

dell: answering questions with support forums

Jeff Stenski works for an electric power company as a design engineer. That's his day job.

He has another job he also spends time on, although he doesn't get paid for it. He posts answers on Dell's community support forum. On the support forum, Jeff is known as "Predator." His specialty is optical drives, the drives that play CDs and DVDs.

Whenever there is an optical drive question, you'll find an answer from Predator. Here's an example. Imagine for a moment you are Alex from New York City, and when attempting to install a CD drive on your new Dell Dimension computer, you get the mysterious "Error 39." You might post this query on Dell's community forum (www.dellcommunity.com).[4]

AlexNYC: Philips DVD + RW DVD 8701 and HL-DT-ST DVD ROM drives showing Error 39 code on my Dimension 4700.

Tried disabling and restarting, cannot locate any driver updates, cannot lose system data by reinstalling System Hardware. Can somebody help???

Thank you!!!

This is followed by back and forth with several other members of the community until our pal Predator steps in, within a couple of hours of the original question:

Predator: RE: Philips DVD + RW DVD 8701 and HL-DT-ST DVD ROM drives showing Error 39 code on my Dimension 4700.

Alex,

Take a peek at Dell's article on the same subject; click on the CD/RW link in my post and scroll to Section 12, article 10.

Also you must be logged-on with Admin rights.

Best Regards!

God, grant me the senility to forget the people I never liked anyway, the good fortune to run into the ones I do and the eyesight to tell the difference.

AlexNYC: Re: Philips DVD + RW DVD 8701 and HL-DT-ST DVD ROM drives showing Error 39 code on my Dimension 4700.

Dear Jeff,

Thank you so much, it worked!!!!
You are a gem, and I love the take on the serenity prayer!!!

OK, let's unpack what just happened here. Alex asked an obscure question but one that was desperately important to him. Jeff/Predator quickly solved the problem. Alex walked away happy. Dell saved at least $10 on a support call.

But wait, we're not done. This information is all online and searchable. If you search on "Error 39" on Dell's support forum, this answer comes up near the top. Apparently, a lot of people have done that because this answer was viewed 630 times. Let's just assume, conservatively, that of those 630 people looking, 100 found the answer to their question in this posting (and didn't have to call Dell). That's at least $1,000 that Jeff has saved Dell with this one post alone.

As it turns out, Jeff spends a lot of time on this forum. A *lot* of time. Since 1999, he's been logged into the forum for over 473,000 minutes, the equivalent of 123 working days a year.[5] (He told us that he leaves the Dell forum open on his desktop while he's working on other projects.) He has read nearly a quarter of a million of other people's messages, and he has posted over twenty thousand times. Those posts have been viewed over 2 million times by other people. Again, if one out of twenty of those people reading Jeff's posts has, as a result, had their question answered and not called Dell, then Jeff, by himself, has saved Dell over $1 million.

Why is Jeff so dedicated? "I actually enjoy helping people," he explained to us. "That's what got me hooked: when you help people and they say 'thank you.'"

Thank *you*, Jeff Stenski, for saving Dell a million bucks.

Amazingly, we see this impulse throughout the groundswell. Caterina Fake, cofounder of the photo-sharing site Flickr, called it "the culture of generosity."[6] We call it the search for psychic income.[7] As we described in chapter 3, psychic rewards come in several varieties, including good feelings from altruism, validation, and belonging to a community. People like Jeff participate for the gratitude. Others want recognition. Still others feel answering questions gives them influence. Psychic income is free—it's paid in love, not money.

The search for psychic income wouldn't be worth much if it were limited to Jeff Stenski. But in fact, there are thousands of customers on Dell's community forums, all helping each other and saving Dell money. They're happy—they're getting answers without hanging on the phone. Dell's happy—many of its customers love the forums, and they call support less. The desire for psychic income is widespread—there are Jeff Stenskis everywhere you look in the groundswell, helping people out.

Understanding how to tap the desire for psychic income is a central element of groundswell thinking. In the rest of this chapter, we'll show you how people like Jeff Stenski can help *you*.

the economics of community forums

Sean McDonald, director of Dell's global online community team, let us in on a few secrets about how the community works for Dell. According to Sean, about seven thousand of Dell's customers log in every week, generating nine thousand new posts. "It's the power of thousands and thousands," he says.

These people aren't visiting for fun—they're visiting to get answers. Of 4 million posts on the forum, somewhat less than 1 million could be characterized as answers (versus questions and commentary). But these answers work pretty well. When Dell surveys people leaving the site, between 20 percent and 50 percent say they got an answer to their question (and remember, that doesn't count people who ask a question and get a response when they come back later). Since those visitors solved their own problems, they're far less likely to be calling Dell's support lines.

The economics of support forums are hard to argue with (see table 8-1). As a result, this form of groundswell application has become well established, especially with technology companies.

TABLE 8-1

ROI of a community support forum

This analysis examines a community support forum for a company with a technologically sophisticated product (e.g., a gadget or piece of software). We assume a company with 5m customers. Costs include technology and moderation. All numbers rounded to nearest thousand.

Start-up costs	Costs
Planning and development	$25K

Ongoing costs (annual)	
Forum software platform (e.g., Lithium)	$60K
Moderation and management (5 full-time staff)	$500K
Advertising to drive traffic (10,000 clicks/month at $1 per click)	$120K
Total costs, year one	*$705K*

Benefits here include only avoided support costs.

Benefit analysis (annual)	Value of benefit
Customers participating in support forum annually (assume 1% of all customers)	50K
Additional customers viewing content, without contributing to forum (assume 5% of all customers)	250K
Total support calls these customers would have made (estimate average of 1 call per customer)	300K
Support calls avoided because of forum (assume 33% find answers on the forum)	100K
Cost savings from avoided calls (assume $10 per call—lowest possible estimate)	*$1M*

new support applications, new benefits

Forums work. Applications range from iRobot, which uses them to help owners of its robot vacuum cleaners solve each others' problems, to Fair Isaac, where people help each other understand the ins and outs of credit scores. Any company whose product raises a lot of questions should consider forums.

And it's not just saving money, as Tarik Mahmoud, who runs support forums for Linksys, told us. Linksys makes routers for home networks—a line of products that tend to generate a lot of technical questions, which is why the company set up a support forum a lot like Dell's. But that support forum ended up saving a lot more than money.

On Christmas 2006, tens of thousands of people found Linksys routers under their Christmas trees. Thousands called Linksys. Normally, this wouldn't have caused a problem. But an earthquake had struck in Asia the night before, severing the phone lines that connect 80 percent of Linksys' support representatives in places like the Philippines to people in North America.

Linksys dodged a bullet that day. Its on-hold system automatically reminds people to check the support forum. Christmas day saw registration, search, and posts in the support site all surging. People got the answers they needed. And amazingly, customer complaints didn't spike.

For Linksys, the groundswell saved Christmas.

You may be looking at these examples and saying, "Sure, that works for the kind of geeky people who need help from Linksys and Dell." But forums are helping media companies, too—look what they did for CBS.

forums for supporting passion

Some people don't want support so they can get their gadgets working. Instead, they want support—solidarity—with others who share their passion. That's what happened at CBS.

When forums meet media, you enter the astounding world of fan phenomena. Henry Jenkins, MIT's amazing media studies professor and keen observer of fan phenomena, has written a whole book about this: *Convergence Culture*. He uses the term *participatory culture* to describe the new media world in which consumers do far more than consume—they create as well. According to Henry Jenkins:[8] "Increasingly . . . the Web has become a site of consumer participation that includes many unauthorized and unanticipated ways of relating to media content . . . [T]he Web has pushed [a] hidden layer of cultural activity into the foreground, forcing the media industries to confront its implications for their commercial interests."

Often, media companies run screaming from the groundswell, threatening lawsuits over inappropriate use of copyrighted materials (and Jenkins' book is filled with examples of this). But there's another path. Why not let your fans buzz about you and build passion for your programs?

A great example is what happened with *Jericho*, a mysterious post-apocalyptic TV series in the *Lost* mode, launched in 2006 by CBS. Tapping into the fan base, CBS and the producers of *Jericho* created a fan forum at and a wiki on cbs.com. Thousands of fans posted tens of thousands of comments, indulging in speculation about who dropped the bombs that created the apocalypse and what motivated various characters on the show. The discussion board energized the fans, similar to what Lego did for its fans as described in chapter 7. But the producers went beyond just setting up a discussion board—they actually answered fan questions every week, further fueling interest in the show.

In May 2007, CBS announced that *Jericho* would be canceled. But it didn't count on the powerful force it had created by enabling its viewers to support each other. TV networks look at viewers as demographics and must be ruthless with shows that don't perform. But TV viewers—especially viewers in forums—see themselves as people with a common cause. In this case, that cause was bitter disappointment over the show's demise. Supporting took the form of a powerful, collective, impossible-to-ignore action—a groundswell in the classic sense. Fans banded together to send $50,000 worth of peanuts—twenty tons—to the producers of the show.[9] (Why nuts? A character in the show used the epithet "Nuts!" to protest the absurdity of life, clearly a sentiment the fans of the canceled show identified with.)

It worked. Here's what CBS posted on the fan forum soon after the tons of nuts began arriving:[10]

June 6, 2007

To the Fans of Jericho:

Wow!

Over the past few weeks you have put forth an impressive and proba-bly unprecedented display of passion in support of a prime time televi-sion series. You got our attention; your emails and collective voice have been heard.

As a result, CBS has ordered seven episodes of "Jericho" for mid-season next year. In success, there is the potential for more. But, for there to be more "Jericho," we will need more viewers.

A loyal and passionate community has clearly formed around the show . . . But that community needs to grow . . . We will count on you to rally around the show, to recruit new viewers with the same grass-roots energy, intensity and volume you have displayed in recent weeks.

On behalf of everyone at CBS, thank you for expressing your support of "Jericho" in such an extraordinary manner. Your protest was creative, sus-tained and very thoughtful and respectful in tone. You made a difference.

Sincerely,

Nina Tassler

President, CBS Entertainment

P.S. Please stop sending us nuts.

Take a good look at what happened here. By enabling their fans to support each other—and by participating themselves—the producers saved the show. But because they'd set up a supportive dialogue with these enthusiastic viewers, they could ask for something back. They asked the fans to recruit more viewers, turning supporting into energizing.

CASE STUDY

bearingpoint: using a wiki to reassure clients

Is it possible to do more than just corral your customers into a community? Can you get them to build something together?

Consider Wikipedia as an example. Thousands of people have created millions of entries. The search for psychic income, multiplied across all these contributors, has built a major Internet institution. And while the accuracy is certainly not 100 percent, chances are that whatever you're looking for, you'll find it described there.

Surely, anyone who has visited Wikipedia has asked, "Could I harness a technology like wikis for my own customers?" The answer is yes—if you can find a topic that engages them.

Take MIKE2.0. MIKE stands for "Method for an Integrated Knowledge Environment." The people who invented it supply this definition: "An Open-Source methodology for Enterprise Information Management that provides an organizing framework for Information Development."[11]

Still confused?

If you were a CIO, this might be central to one of your most important initiatives—gluing together all your information systems to deliver a dependable picture of how your business is doing. But let's be fair—scratch the surface, and you'll find this is hellishly complex stuff.

BearingPoint is a large consulting firm that makes millions selling companies on information management solutions and implementing the complex technologies involved. Naturally, it competes with other big system integration service providers like Accenture, IBM, and HP. Robert Hillard, global leader of BearingPoint's information management solutions, needed a way to lay out his solution to the problem of information management and prove it was better than the other guys'.

BearingPoint, the creator of MIKE2.0, had masses of intellectual property (IP)—methods, philosophies, principles, definitions—applicable to the problem. But it was all over the place. "People were sharing information in white papers and custom communications with clients," explains Robert. "A lot of IP was being given away in a haphazard way. There was a lot more value that was hidden, being referred to in PowerPoints, but clients couldn't confirm what it looked like." Robert's problem was this: how could he pull this mass of spaghetti together where clients and prospects could not only see it but even potentially collaborate on it?

This was the genesis of the MIKE2.0 wiki.

The MIKE2.0 wiki looks a lot like Wikipedia. (If you're a CIO in the market for information management solutions, give it a once-over—it's at www.openmethodology.org.) It works just like Wikipedia—it was built on the same software. And it's full of the information that makes BearingPoint stand out, if you peel it back, layer by layer, and observe how the company solves business problems.

The wiki started as an internal information repository. Using wikis is a common way for companies to harness the collaborative power of their employees, as we'll describe in chapter 11. But since May 2007, the wiki is open to everybody—BearingPoint clients, technology vendors, even competitors and their clients.

At first this seems counterintuitive. Why would a consulting company put its intellectual property out where anyone could see it—and even change it? But for a complex shared problem like information management, this approach turns out to make a lot of sense.

For one thing, it gets everybody singing from the same sheet music. It lays everything out where buyers can see it, which gives buyers a lot more confidence to make the multi-million-dollar commitment to Bearing-Point. "As in a lot of open-source initiatives, if you can create a try-before-you-buy scenario, it increases the market," says Robert.

But wikis are about collaboration, not just publishing. By opening up the wiki to outsiders, BearingPoint puts itself at the center of an accruing collection of new intellectual property. Outsiders are contributing to the wiki in areas that BearingPoint doesn't cover. "It's not in areas where we would have put investment dollars," Robert says, "but it has added value to our clients."

The bottom line is this: by opening itself up to collaboration with its own clients, BearingPoint has enabled them to feel that they are solving problems together. Clients feel supported, just like Dell's customers and the patients at Massachusetts General Hospital. Support makes people comfortable. And people need to be comfortable to spend money.

BearingPoint's information management bookings have increased significantly, and Robert Hillard says the availability of the wiki is the main reason. So far, two or three hundred people have registered for the wiki, most from outside BearingPoint. This gives them the ability to add to the content. But for many others, the wiki is more for tire kicking and for reference, Spectator activities that don't require registration. The wiki site has seen well over a million hits already.

Visitors to the wiki come for information. Some turn into leads for BearingPoint's services. BearingPoint makes money from these leads, which are more likely to convert than leads it gets elsewhere. It makes money from appearing larger than it is, with the contributions of others. And by wrapping pieces of the wiki into information management projects, BearingPoint is actually selling the content of the wiki along with the project.

As you might imagine, BearingPoint keeps a close eye on the wiki and doesn't allow people to change it arbitrarily (in contrast to what can happen on Wikipedia). This takes management time. But the company had already developed savings from centralizing its information internally. Robert calls the amount of extra effort "a drop in the bucket." And it certainly is, compared to the benefits the company gets from making its customers feel supported.

is a wiki right for you?

Wikis are great. If you have customers who you think are ready to share in a common collection of information, you should certainly consider starting one. If it gets going, customers will like it, and it will keep them active and make you into a recognized authority. But understand that the risks are great.

Wikis are not easy to get going. They're a lot harder than support forums, to be sure.

Here are the ingredients for a successful outward-facing corporate wiki.

First, as always, you'll need people—in this case, people with a common interest in contributing. BearingPoint had its clients and vendors. Intuit, which has started a very successful wiki at taxalmanac.com (it's the twentieth-most-trafficked wiki in the United States[12]) started with tax accountants. And eBay, which started a wiki about buying and selling stuff at ebaywiki.com, has hordes of homegrown eBay veterans contributing to its wiki.

All these groups are full of contributing experts. You'll need a core of those contributing experts if your wiki is to have any chance of succeeding. In fact, before you start, you really should connect with some of those active participants in your customer base and invite them to help you start it.

The second key ingredient is content. It takes a lot more content to get a wiki off the ground than a discussion forum. BearingPoint had masses of IP to kick things off. Intuit had the entire U.S. tax code, which forms the backbone of taxalmanac.com. And eBay had its rules for buying and selling. The wiki will, of course, grow and evolve from this starting point, but it needs a pretty substantial seed crystal to get started.

The final ingredients are patience and policy. Like all groundswell activities, you'll need to think this through. What rules will you make to ensure the integrity of information? (BearingPoint funds an editorial group that vets changes and reverses ones that aren't compatible with the goals of MIKE2.0 community; Intuit, of course, won't let you change the tax code.)

These rules for your wiki should be spelled out up front, and they should reflect a balance. Too lenient, and you'll run afoul of vandalism—as podtech.net and a top blogger, Robert Scoble, learned when they started a wiki around Scoble's content but had to shut it down because of rampant anti-Scoble edits.[13] Too strict, and people could be too intimidated to contribute.

To get these rules right, you need to think of the wiki not as your wiki, but *our* wiki—yours and your customers'. This lets you tap the creative, altruistic, and validation impulses—the search for psychic income— that made Wikipedia into the vibrant and massively useful content collection it is now. Thinking of the wiki as being for the good of your customers will help you understand where to draw the policy line.

profits from answers

When it comes to the groundswell supporting itself, perhaps the simplest paradigm of all is questions and answers. Why not let people just post questions and then let other people answer those questions? And why restrict those questions and answers to just one product? What would happen if anyone could ask a question about anything and anyone else could answer it?

Two companies set out to find out what would happen—Naver and Yahoo! Both are now driving significant profits from helping the ground-swell answer its own questions.

Naver, the largest search engine in South Korea, grew out of an international weak spot in the Internet—there's just too little content available in Korean. As a result, Koreans conducting a Web search wouldn't find what they were looking for.

Naver, a division of Korean gaming company NHN, decided to see whether people's goodwill could solve the problem. Naver created a Q&A system—anyone can pose a question, and anyone can answer.

The result: every day Koreans pose forty-four thousand questions to Naver—and receive a hundred ten thousand new answers.[14] This is big business: 77 percent of Korean Web searches go through Naver, and it generated half of NHN's profits for 2006. An article in the *New York Times* quotes one of the answer givers, Mr. Cho, on why he's so helpful: "When people I have never met thank me, I feel good . . . No one pays me for this. But helping other people on the Internet is addictive." Apparently, psychic income applies in Korea as strongly as in America.

In the United States and worldwide, the similar success story is Yahoo! Answers. As of July 2007, there were 350 million answers on the service in the countries where it operates.[15] What drives all this activity? While ordinary generosity plays a large part, Yahoo! also uses a point system, which costs Yahoo! nothing but allows participants to distinguish themselves. One of the top question answerers on Yahoo! Answers is the reclusive "Judas Rabbi," who has answered over a hundred thousand questions in a little over a year. When we tracked him down to ask him what motivates him (in the only way possible, by asking a question on Yahoo! Answers), all he would admit to was "Just trying to answer as many questions as possible."[16] But we did hear from many other Yahoo! Answers denizens who talked about him—he's a mysterious legend in the Yahoo! Answers community. Getting on top, staying on top, and being known to as many questioners as possible is generating psychic income for Judas Rabbi, whoever he is.

Could Q&A work for companies that sell stuff, not just portals? Sam Decker thinks so. Sam is CMO for Bazaarvoice, a company that makes ratings systems, as described in the previous chapter. Now Bazaarvoice is adding questions and answers to product pages on ecommerce sites. "Forums are great for support because of the threaded discussion," Sam explains. But in a commerce environment, versus a traditional support environment, you need to get answers fast, not to troll through forums. So Bazaarvoice puts Q&A on every product page of sites like shoes .com. "The big difference is, you never leave that product page," says Sam. So you get an answer just at the moment you need it, when you're buying a product.

It's not yet clear whether support of this kind could help sell, not just make customers happier. But based on our experience, it makes sense. That's because psychic income is ubiquitous—people in the groundswell want to help each other. And if you can tap into that desire, you can turn it into a powerful force, not just for satisfaction, but for new business as well.

helping the groundswell support itself: what it means for your company

Should *you* tap into the search for psychic income?

As always, it depends on your goals. Saving money is great, but if your dream is to move all your customers online and lay off those support reps, think again. Properly managed, helping your customers support each other will make them happier, save money, and generate insights. But it also requires a great deal of effort and will change your company. Before you start, you should examine three things: what problem you will solve, how you will participate, and whether you should create a support community or join an existing one.

what problem is your support activity trying to solve?

Imagine that you set out to create a support forum, a wiki, or some other form of community support. *Why* will people participate? Think about it from your customers' perspective. If your product is a significant part of their business (like TurboTax for accountants), or if it generates a lot of enthusiasm (like TiVo), or if you have so *many* customers that even a small percentage of fanatics represents tens of thousands (like Dell or eBay), then you can go forward and form a community or wiki around your product. But for most products, you'll need to think bigger, about the customer's whole problem. Intuit created a tax information wiki, not a TurboTax wiki, because Scott Wilder, who runs the company's online communities, realized that his customers wanted tax advice, not just software advice. What is your customers' biggest issue?

Psychic income is a lot more powerful when you tap into the problems people like to talk about most. So if you sell electric guitars, maybe you'd be better off with a support forum about the challenges of making it as a musician, not about whammy bars and wah-wah pedals.

groundswell support needs your participation

Support communities need activity—few will go to a forum that's not buzzing with activity. We've seen countless examples of people who created communities, forums, or wikis, only to watch them fizzle as activity tapered off. Take Special K's weight management community on Yahoo!, which declined from a promising start of 2,001 messages in January 2007 to only 185 in August.[17] For every community that takes off, there must be dozens that have languished.

Activity creates content, which creates traffic and links, which boosts search engine placement, which drives more traffic, and so on. To start this, you must prime the pump. Begin by figuring out whether your forum even has a chance of succeeding on a volume basis. Here's the math: 28 percent of all online consumers participate in forums, and two-thirds of those people say they actually contribute to the forums. Your customers will be different, of course—you'll need to do the research to determine whether your customers are more, or less, likely to be forum participants. But even if 40 percent of your customers participate in online forums, they won't necessarily participate in *yours*.

Even Intuit, the champion here, has only 5 percent of its Quick-Books customers in its forum. Companies should estimate that between 1 percent and 5 percent of their customers will participate in a support forum (depending on the customers' Social Technographics Profile and how committed they are to a companies' products), and that building that participation will take at least a year. And remember that many more visitors will watch than will provide answers—not everyone is looking for psychic validation. You need thousands of participants to get the forum going—can your customer base generate that volume?

During that first year, the support community will require your attention, with staff and resources dedicated to it. First, you will need to drive people to the forum with messages on your Web site, in your packaging, and on your telephone systems. But even more important, you need to *participate*—just like the producers of *Jericho*. At first, your own staff will have to provide some of the answers, monitor activity, and find ways to help people, modeling the activity that participants will provide themselves as the forum grows. Dell started with thirty staff who monitored forum activity and helped direct people to answers. Even though the forum is much bigger now, years later, it mostly moderates itself and Dell has reduced its moderator staff to five. The lesson: your participation is *crucial* at the start.

More exotic technologies like wikis and Q&A are even tougher to get going. Even in general purpose applications like Wikipedia and Yahoo! Answers, far more people are interested in *reading* the results than in contributing to them. If you're building on an existing customer community, your chances of success are greater. If not, you'll need to find other ways to involve your customers.

why build it if you can join it?

One last, obvious step: you should check whether there is an existing community for your customers. That's what TiVo did.

Out of 4.3 million owners of the TiVo digital video recorder, a hundred thirty thousand—about 3 percent—are registered at tivocommunity.com, a site with no official affiliation with the TiVo company. The member with the most posts, "jsmeeker," has posted forty-four thousand times since 2001.[18] Clearly, jsmeeker is getting psychic income from his TiVo knowledge.

TiVo owners are solving each others' problems on tivocommunity.com. TiVo didn't need to build a forum—it would be redundant. But Bob Poniatowski, a product marketing manager at TiVo, points out, "We loosely monitor what's going on over there." TiVo engineers will sometimes get bug reports linked to posts on tivocommunity.com, where TiVo owners have taken the time to clearly and neatly document stuff that doesn't work the way they expect. Bob also occasionally participates in the forum, where he's known as "TiVoPony." "If there is an issue, since we have a credible presence, I can share a bit more detail in the forum than in a press release," says Bob. "They will, in turn, evangelize our product and services to other people." So TiVo uses the forum in three ways—to *support* its subscribers, to *listen* to how people use its product, and to *talk* to community members who can spread the word about improvements. This connection is sufficiently valuable that TiVo has contributed to help tivocommunity.com with server and bandwidth costs when the community needed it.

We continue to be amazed at how many companies are afraid to dive in like this because they fear they'll pollute the community discussion. This is often an excuse used because companies are afraid of taking the first step, assuming that people don't want to hear from yet another marketer. In reality, the members of such a community are dying to hear from you—they are there explicitly to talk about your products and services. Posts by the company will garner a lot of attention. If there's a vibrant community around your product or service already, consider joining it, sponsoring it, or forming some other relationship so you can help your customers support themselves.

practical advice for getting started with a community

If you do decide to go forward with building a community for support, here are some suggestions:

- *Start small, but plan for a larger presence.* As in so many groundswell activities, starting small is the best way to succeed. If you have multiple product lines, you may want to start building around only one of them. Then learn what works for your type of customers before expanding your presence to support other products. But recognize that you'll be supporting people across multiple product lines before too long. Remember that changing support vendors—because yours didn't scale up—is highly disruptive to the community that you're starting.

- *Reach out to your most active customers.* How should your community work? Your customers know. Through your sales group, find your enthusiasts, and ask them how they'd prefer to participate. They will become important leaders in your online community, so keeping their support and enthusiasm is crucial. If you have celebrity customers (for example, Olympic stars for a snowboard manufacturer or home decorators for a furniture company), you can reach out and secure (and pay for) their participation in advance.

- *Plan to drive traffic to your community.* The moment you open the doors to your community, here's what will happen: nothing. Nobody knows you exist. Tarik Mahmoud at Linksys uses the company's on-hold system and Web site in a coordinated fashion to drive traffic—you should do the same. Advertise on sites where your customers shop; put the community's Web address on the cover of the owner's manual. And don't forget search engines. Once your support community or wiki is buzzing with activity, posts will show up high in search results; until then, you'll want to buy paid search listings at Google, Yahoo!, and MSN Live Search.

- *Build in a reputation system.* Allowing participants to build up a reputation is crucial. Ask Lyle Fong, the CEO and cofounder of Lithium Technologies, the company that built many of the forums you see on company Web sites, including the forum that saved Christmas for Linksys. According to Lyle, "Users will spend hours a day building their reputations in a community. A well-built reputation system encourages users to participate and behave in the right manner." The reputation system is what allows Jeff Stenski—with his twenty thousand posts on the Dell community forum—to be recognized as a contributor at the "Diamond level," which makes his advice more credible. And it's the accumulation of points that helps people like Judas Rabbi rise higher in the rankings at Yahoo! Answers. The community develops gamelike mechanics. This way, it isn't just the altruistic impulse but also the competitive impulse that drives participants.

- *Let your customers lead you.* Communities have opinions on everything. They'll not only tell you what product features to add; they'll also tell you how the community should run and what you are doing right—and wrong. Be sure to include a thread called "Improving this community," and pay close attention to what you hear, not just there, but throughout the forum.

So take the plunge. Let your customers support each other. But you'd better be prepared for how this will change the way you do business.

how groundswell support communities will change your company

A funny thing happens when you participate in community forums.

People expect you to listen and respond to them.

CBS and the producers of *Jericho* found this out in the most dramatic way possible—as they waded through nut deliveries in their offices. But regardless of the forums or wikis you create and participate in, be clear—you're creating your own little part of the groundswell.

Your forum or wiki will become a laboratory where customers talk about everything. Not just your products and how to use them, but also your pricing. Your competitors. Your salespeople's tactics. Your new product road map. Your company's stock. Everything from your logo to the labor practices in your factories.

Look at this as an opportunity. By owning or participating in a community, you get a front-row seat. Support departments don't typically gain a lot of influence in corporations—they're a cost center. But because support communities are so much richer in content, they can influence development and marketing. The owner of the community, with all this information in her pocket, gets a seat at the table.

Since you'll be communicating back to the people in these environments, you can ask them to clarify the meaning of their comments. This dialogue—especially with your most active customers—inevitably draws them into your development process. You end up collaborating with your customers to create better products. That's taking the power of psychic income and building it into your business.

Whether you start with listening to, talking with, energizing, or supporting the groundswell, you'll end up with customers in your business processes, especially those related to product development. That's what we mean by embracing the groundswell, the topic of chapter 9.

9. embracing the groundswell

In a tiny town in central Pennsylvania lives a guy named George. George loves his dog, Pooch. Pooch is a cockapoo, which is a fuzzy cross between a spaniel and a poodle. George and Pooch are very close. "We enjoy taking walks and running," says George. "We also go hiking and enjoy playing in the yard. I would be lost without my Pooch."

Gala Amoroso is very interested in people like George. Gala is senior consumer insights manager for Del Monte Foods. She's spent her whole career peeking into the psychology of people who buy products in grocery stores. She describes doing research on consumers as detective work. "That's what I love to do," she says. "Understand what the story is—how to connect the dots—and come up with an insight."

With help from the brand monitoring vendor Umbria, Del Monte had identified a segment of pet owners it calls "Dogs are people, too." We bet you know somebody like this. "Dogs are people, too" includes people who treat their pets like members of the family. They take them on trips. They play with them anytime they can. They make those dogs part of their lives, from sunup to bedtime. And they've got a soft spot for pet treats that fit their lifestyles.

That was a fair description of George. So when Del Monte and its community vendor, MarketTools, started up a private community called

"I love my dog/Dogs are people, too," George was easy to recruit. And an amazing conversation began.

On one side were Gala and the folks from Del Monte, trying to figure out what products to make, how to package them, and how to sell them.

On the other were George and his fellow pet lovers, who were happy to explain—in detail, with lots of back-and-forth—what they were looking for.

Gala (through a MarketTools moderator) asked:[1]

What if your dog was a person? Ok, I know your dog IS a person. Imagine that your dog could write out his or her fantasy of what to eat for one day. What would that look like? What would he or she write? Click the comments link below to write out what your dog would want to eat for [breakfast on] YOUR DOGGIE'S IDEAL PERFECT DAY.

George responded:

For breakfast she would definitely want bacon and eggs and she would want ketchup on her eggs. She loves ketchup!!!

A theme began to emerge from the responses of George and the other four hundred people in the community as they described the perfect breakfast for their dogs. Dog lovers want doggie treats that look like people food! One asked for "McDonald's breakfast pancakes, eggs, bacon, hash brown with a cappuccino." Another said "Breakfast . . . [w]ould have to be eggs with lots of cheese—Andy loves cheese!" The dogs had spoken (through their owners). They wanted bacon and eggs.

So Del Monte decided to give them bacon and eggs. Thus was born Snausages Breakfast Bites, a breakfast snack that looks just like little strips of bacon and fried eggs.

What should be in Snausages Breakfast Bites? How about vitamins? People take their vitamins in the morning, why not dogs?

Gala and Del Monte to the community:

Would you buy more treats if they had vitamins and minerals as ingredients?

George:

I would buy healthier treats over ones that didn't have vitamins and minerals . . . I try to look for amino acids and omega 3 and fish oils. I also take these and know they are essential. It is hard to find a variety of snacks that are healthy, so I look for the healthiest brands.

Fifty-four percent of the community responded that yes, they would definitely buy a snack with vitamins and minerals.

Next decision: what to put on the package. Gala posted a picture of the package on the community. In addition to a happy cartoon dog snacking on bacon- and egg-shaped treats, the package featured this text:

A healthy, great tasting start to your dog's day.
    * CALCIUM for healthy bones and teeth
    * ANTIOXIDANTS to promote a healthy immune system
    * OMEGA 3 AND 6 FATTY ACIDS for healthy skin

Again, George responded:

Dogs are like people 2. They need all the necessary vitamins and minerals to lead a long and healthy life, a lot of dog foods in the past were made of junk and fillers, now they are getting wise to the fact that owners [want] better nutritious foods 4 their animals and if they want to stay in business they better deliver. I love seeing what that package says because it shows they care.

George was not alone. The comments from the community poured in. Snausages Breakfast Bites were ready—they *would* sell. So Del Monte started making them. And it's early yet, but from all appearances, they *are* selling. Del Monte had found a way to make a few dog lovers happy.

Product development is hard. Why not let your customers help you with it?

embracing customers: a new kind of development

Innovating with help from your customers is such a great idea that there have already been at least three books written about it.

Eric von Hippel's groundbreaking *Democratizing Innovation*[2] goes into detail about the role of "lead users" in helping influence development of new products, from software to surfboards. Patricia B. Seybold's *Outside Innovation: How Your Customers Will Co-Design Your Company's Future*[3] provides dozens of examples of ways to harness "customer innovation" in development processes with tools like private communities, ratings, and reviews. And Don Tapscott and Anthony D. Williams's *Wikinomics: How Mass Collaboration Changes Everything*[4] looks at ways to use the collaborative Wikipedia model to tap the global community to create innovations.

These books are great, and the vision they demonstrate is spectacular. But when it comes to collaborating with your customers—really bringing them into your development and innovation processes—the one real truth is this: *it's challenging*. Your company almost certainly grew in ways designed to direct innovation into manageable places. You probably have a department that's in charge of product development, with a lot of smart engineers who have a lot of smart ideas. You probably have a market research department, with people like Gala Amoroso in it, that's charged with researching what your customers want. And it's not just products. When it comes to services or internal processes, there are probably people whose job it is to identify ways to improve those services and processes. If you want to open up new distribution channels, you need to work with a channel expert—and deal with pushback from the people in charge of the old channels.

But the fact is, as you've seen in all the chapters leading up to this one, your customers are chomping at the bit to tell you what to do. They're both complaining about and praising your products on forums. They're rating and reviewing your products on retail sites. They're blogging and making videos and analyzing your every move. Whether you're ready or not, they are now part of your process—they are leaning over your management's shoulders.

If you've already undertaken one of the goals in chapters 5 through 8—if you're listening to, talking with, energizing, or supporting the groundswell—then you've already opened up a channel of communication with those customers. And inevitably, the insights that come from that—the relationships you're developing with those customers—will lead them deeper into your company. We call this embracing the groundswell—making customers an integral part of the way you innovate, with both products and process improvements.

This chapter is about finding practical ways to tap into customers to help you innovate now—to increase the chances of developing something your customers want. And it's not just about better products and processes. It's about innovating *faster*.

why innovating faster is powerful

The cases in this chapter have one thing in common: they show how, by embracing the groundswell, you can move more quickly.

There are two reasons for this.

First of all, customers don't take long to tell you what they want. They use your product and interact with your company; they know what's wrong and how things can be fixed. They have ideas your development people and management haven't thought of yet. As soon as you're ready, you can tap into these sources of innovation. People who've connected with customers in this way are always amazed at how much more quickly they generate ideas. It's because they've just supercharged their dozens or hundreds of engineers with thousands or millions of other minds.

Second, with customers in the loop, innovation happens more quickly because you can iterate—make continuous improvements. Look at the conversation Gala Amoroso had with her customer community. First, she asked what the product should be. Then she asked whether the product should have vitamins. Then she asked about the packaging. That's three decisions, three iterations, in a few short weeks. When you're tapped into the customer community, you get feedback quickly, and once you've processed it, you can go back and ask the next question. It's as if we replaced an exchange of letters with a face-to-face conversation. Everybody knows you get more done face-to-face, and that's because conversations are more efficient than asking questions in a survey, conducting an engineering study, or having executives review every suggestion.

In this chapter we'll look at three cases: how salesforce.com uses an innovation community to involve customers in the design of new products, how a French credit union made customer suggestions a part of how it does business, and how a Canadian grocery store uses ratings and reviews to improve its products. In each case these companies are moving faster than they ever did before, which saves money and makes life difficult for competitors.

CASE STUDY

salesforce.com: embracing through an innovation community

Speed is important to Steve Fisher.

Steve is the VP in charge of the platform—basically, the foundation of the product and its development environment—at salesforce.com. Saleforce.com makes customer relationship management applications. If you're a salesperson, you open up salesforce.com on your PC and use it to manage the opportunities and leads you're working on. Salesforce .com also fills a similar role in service and marketing departments.

But salesforce.com itself isn't software. It's an on-demand service, delivered through the Internet. That means salesforce.com can deliver updated and improved capabilities far more quickly. And that's why speed is important to Steve.

Salesforce.com evolves rapidly. The company used to put out three new releases per year. But the process had developed some frustrating snarls. Developers—the tech wizards who build the application—and marketing people often disagreed about what made sense to add next. The obvious answer was to see what the customers wanted. The problem wasn't that salesforce.com wasn't listening—it was the blizzard of requests. Ten thousand customer requests had piled up. Some of those were great ideas; others weren't. The problem was telling which was which.

In 2006, one of the product managers at salesforce.com came across an application called Crispy News and saw what could be a solution to the problem. Crispy News works much like Digg, allowing visitors to vote entries up or down based on what they like.[5] But unlike Digg, Crispy News was an application that any company could license. "We were looking at doing this ourselves," said John Taschek, salesforce.com's VP of market strategy. "But Crispy had the technology to find out the kinds of things people wanted to know." And what people at salesforce.com wanted to know was which features would be most popular and relevant for customers.

In the fall of 2006, salesforce.com launched the salesforce.com Idea-Exchange (ideas.salesforce.com) and invited customers to itemize their development priorities. Before this, customers' ideas had fallen like snowflakes, enveloping the development process in an undifferentiated blanket of suggestions. Now the ideas were channeled and directed by the groundswell of Salesforce.com's own customers. In one year, over five thousand ideas arrived; now the best ones bubbled to the top. The customers were organizing their priorities for salesforce.com.

Not all of them were easy for Salesforce.com to swallow. One of the first and most popular suggestions addressed the "sawbanner," a text ad that popped up every time a customer logged in to salesforce.com. The sawbanner was beloved in Salesforce.com's marketing department, since it enabled the company to communicate directly with everyone using the software about new releases, conferences, and the like. But people attempting to get work done weren't so happy with it. Here's what a customer known as "fifedog" posted on the IdeaExchange:[6]

Be Gone Sawbanners Please [Be] Gone

[followed by a graphic of the sawbanner]

   I know I'm not [alone] on this however I want to bring this up and see if we can't get some relief from these annoying banners that show up on our screens every time we log into Salesforce.

   . . . [If] you would like to try and remedy the issue please vote YES on [this] idea to stop the insanity!

This was rapidly followed by over six thousand votes and hundreds of impassioned comments in favor of the idea of scrapping the sawbanners. And that caused a conflict at salesforce.com.

On the one side were Steve and many of the developers, who wanted to maximize the application's usability. On the other were salesforce.com's marketers, who had grown dependent on the sawbanner to connect with their customers.

Who won?

The customers did.

On this issue, both sides had compelling arguments. But in the end salesforce.com was trying to satisfy its customers, which added heft to Steve's side of the discussion. In the nine months it took to settle this argument, the company had learned that many of the customers' other suggestions were excellent and had begun to integrate those suggestions into its products. So when the time finally came to tackle the sawbanner issue, salesforce.com decided to trust its customers. And as fifedog had requested, it was "begone" to the sawbanner.

IdeaExchange has revolutionized the way salesforce.com develops products. Steve, who likes speed, got what he liked. In 2007, salesforce .com pumped out four new releases, in contrast to only two in 2006. New releases now include three hundred new features, three times as many as in previous years. Why did things change? Confidence.

Half the new features now come from suggestions in IdeaExchange. Instead of holding big meetings to wrangle over features, developers can move forward *knowing* what people want. This makes for less wasted effort and more progress. "We can help diminish the political pushing and make it [about] the quality of the ideas," says Steve Fisher. He describes the new process as "real debate about real ideas. You want to surface those and get rid of the crap." The crap, as he puts it—the features that were developed based on personal prejudices and guesswork—"won't survive true collaboration and social networking." He adds that IdeaExchange "gave us back our velocity." And for a man who likes speed in a company that moves briskly, that's worth a lot.

idea exchanges work if you can engage your customers

It's interesting to compare salesforce.com's experience embracing customers with Dell's.

Dell's IdeaStorm (www.dellideastorm.com) uses the same system that salesforce.com does—Crispy News. Just like salesforce.com, Dell has a high level of participation: seven thousand ideas and five hundred thousand votes cast as of this writing. And like salesforce.com, Dell has taken advantage of the ideas coming from the community.

As a company that sells to consumers, Dell naturally has a harder time connecting with customers in an idea exchange. Most of Dell's customers aren't interested enough in its products to contribute (in contrast to salesforce.com, which had convinced nearly 10 percent of its customers—in businesses—to join IdeaExchange). But even so, Dell has been able to get thousands of its customers into IdeaStorm, enough to make the site a productive source of ideas for the company.

One was a PC running Linux, the open-source operating system, instead of Windows.[7] With the confidence that came from IdeaStorm, Dell tapped the community to decide on features, support methods, even the type of Linux to install. As a result, the Linux PC went from idea to finished product in just two months, versus the nine to fifteen months it usually takes to ship a new machine at Dell.

Nobody at Dell believes that IdeaStorm is a representative collection of its customers. Dell knows that IdeaStorm is filled with the more technical members of its customer community and treats the suggestions accordingly. (Even so, the Linux machine is selling above expectations.)

Could you create an idea exchange at your company? If you have impassioned customers, they'll be happy to join a forum and influence your product development. While this could be a good source of ideas, recognize that it doesn't hit everybody in your audience. The concept works, but it reaches a skewed subset of the customer base. And for many companies, there simply aren't enough enthusiastic customers to support an idea exchange. These companies need another, simpler way to tap into their customers' desires. They should just ask customers how they can be better, as Crédit Mutuel did.

CASE STUDY

crédit mutuel: asking your customers for ideas

Crédit Mutuel is a French regional cooperative bank with 10 million customers. Its slogan is *la banque à qui parler* ("the bank you can talk to").

Recently, the company was testing an ad campaign on a focus group. Respondents thought the slogan was hollow. "What do you mean, the bank you can talk to?" they asked. "How can we talk to you? And if we do talk to you, what happens next?"

The amazing thing about this story—and the reason that Crédit Mutuel lives up to its slogan—is this: the bank decided it *would* listen. It would ask people what they wanted. And it would act on their suggestions.

Early in 2007, Crédit Mutuel began its ad campaign. Viewers were directed to a Web site with the unlikely name sijetaisbanquier.com (*Si j'étais banquier* means "If I were a banker.") The Web site invites people in with a voice that says (in French, of course), "If I were a banker, I would give my customers a say in things, and together we would build the bank of tomorrow." From there, there are two main choices—enter a suggestion, or see other people's suggestions. Once a week, the bank randomly selects one person who made a suggestion to receive an iPod.

Now, logic says this shouldn't work. Nobody wakes up and says "If I were a banker" in the morning (except maybe people really hoping to get a job as a banker). And the bank took a risk. What if all the suggestions were useless? What if people flooded the site with obscenities? Steeling itself, Crédit Mutuel began to run the ads and designated ten staff to sort through the suggestions and weed out the useless ones.

But as so often happens in the groundswell, people defied expectations. Crédit Mutuel received tens of thousands of suggestions. Fifteen percent of them were useless (like "If I were a banker, I would change jobs"), but the rest were interesting. Some were very interesting.

The bank picked the thirty best suggestions. One was this: "I would explain the fees better to my customers." Not drop the fees—just explain them. The bank realized that charges on its statements were mystifying its customers. This one's getting fixed already—all branches will be distributing a pamphlet with all the fees listed on it. That's easy.

How about this one: "Create a fictitious account that children could manage on the Internet, so that children get used to managing a bank account." Would Crédit Mutuel's staff have thought that one up? That's a parent talking, and it's a pretty interesting idea—completely out of left field.

The top ideas are all completely different and all reasonable. Like "I would commit to a deadline to reply to questions sent by email or left at the reception desk." Or "I would discount insurance for young drivers whose parents the bank has been insuring for years." In September 2007, the bank put all thirty of the top ideas online and let people vote on them. And it's already beginning to implement many of these suggestions.

If this sounds a lot like salesforce.com's IdeaExchange, it is. But unlike salesforce.com's customers, the bank's aren't likely to spend a lot of time coming back to a site whose only purpose is to evaluate banking ideas. The whole reason the campaign is called "If I were a banker" is that most people don't normally think like a banker. So a site that lets you submit a suggestion quickly and move on makes more sense than a banking idea exchange.

There's a lot right with this plan.

First of all, the bank has aligned itself on the same side as its customers. Instead of saying "Tell us what to do," it said, and the difference is subtle, "What would you do if you were us?" By encouraging the customers to develop empathy for the bank, even momentarily, Crédit Mutuel gets much more realistic suggestions.

Second, the bank has tapped into a major source of innovation here. Its customers know what has to be improved. All it had to do was to ask the right question and be ready to listen—and sort through suggestions, of course.

Third, the bank is listening. It says it's listening. People are noticing it's listening. "The bank you can talk to" are no longer just words. The next time a French citizen needs to pick a bank, that could make the difference.

Finally, the bank has not abdicated its responsibility to develop good services anymore than Del Monte has forgotten how to make pet products or Dell has forgotten how to design computers. It's still the bank's responsibility to figure out how to be a great bank. Bank employees can ignore some of those suggestions. But now that they have just a little help from their customers, it may be easier to prioritize ideas for improvement.

The cost of the ads is large—but Crédit Mutuel would have spent this money on some type of brand advertising regardless. For the incremental cost of ten staffers and twenty-six iPods over six months—probably less than $350,000—the bank improves itself and it improves its image.

What happens next? Let's assume that Crédit Mutuel decides to act on many of these suggestions.

Along one path, Crédit Mutuel becomes a different organization. After acting on the suggestions, it could publicize what's been done. Having seen that the bank is improving, Crédit Mutuel could make listening and acting—embracing its customers' suggestions—a regular part of how it does business. *Si j'étais banquier* would become a permanent part of the company's culture. And from that point on, Crédit Mutuel would improve itself continuously with its customers' help. In a world where banks are pretty much alike, it would be demonstrably more responsive.

Alternatively, Crédit Mutuel could stop embracing its customers when the ad campaign ends. "The bank you can talk to" would go back to being just a slogan, and one that people would stop believing. All the brand equity the bank had built up would ebb away, and worse, it would cease to tap into its customers' innovations and go back to business as usual.

a few words about crowdsourcing

The Crédit Mutuel story is an example of crowdsourcing—asking the groundswell to provide you with ideas.

Crowdsourcing is all the rage right now. It's especially popular with advertising agencies, which are increasingly asking people to create television ads as part of some sort of contest.[8] Frito-Lay's Doritos ad in the 2007 Super Bowl was crowdsourced.[9] It was pretty good, too.

Crowdsourcing by itself is not the same as embracing your customers. Crowdsource an ad campaign, and you might save a few bucks on ad production—but you won't have to do the hard work of changing the way you interact with customers.

Salesforce.com has permanently changed how it innovates. Del Monte thinks very differently about creating new products now. And Crédit Mutuel, if it keeps going in the same direction, will be a very responsive bank in the future.

On the other hand, Frito-Lay probably learned very little from crowd-sourcing its Super Bowl Doritos commercial. It's unlikely to turn over significant parts of its ad creation process to consumers on a regular basis. Its customers are not changing the company's product development pipeline, supporting each other, or energizing each other in any sustainable way. Crowdsourced ads are a flash in the pan—they tap the groundswell for a moment, rather than move the company in a positive direction.

CASE STUDY

loblaw: reviews that drive continuous improvement

Jim Osborne is helping turn a grocery store and its store brand into a hotbed of innovation.

Jim is VP of ecommerce and online marketing for Loblaw, a huge Canadian grocery chain and Canada's largest retailer, with over a thousand stores coast to coast. Loblaw is not just a retailer but also a manufacturer. Its President's Choice store brand accounts for more than 20 percent of all sales throughout the chain. Loblaw creates a thousand new President's Choice brand products a year.

A central part of the President's Choice brand is that Loblaw listens to—and responds to—its customers. In chapter 7 we showed how ratings and reviews can boost sales on a Web site. At Loblaw, the focus is also on ratings and reviews, but not for Web sales—the company uses ratings and reviews by Baazarvoice to close the loop in the store.

If you shop at Loblaw, reviews are everywhere. "PC rated by you" is a trademark of President's Choice, and the logo is visible throughout the stores. Loblaw drives and supports reviews, and the strategy works— over three hundred thousand customers are registered on its Web site. Loblaw even has the guts to ask in every review, "Do you love this product?" and post the answers—both positive and negative comments— right on its site.

On the store flyer, the PC Vegetable Lasagna gets four and a half stars out of five. "We ALL enjoyed it . . . even my 'vegetable-hating' 17-year-old son!" raves a customer, right on the flyer. (With all the reviews, Loblaw flyers can look a little more like movie ads than food ads.) Walk down the aisle in the store, and you'll often see big signs with similar messages, including a customer quote.

Just like eBags in chapter 7, Loblaw lets every site visitor see every review. And also like eBags, Loblaw gets about 80 percent positive reviews. But what sets Loblaw apart is that with its own store brand selling so well, it can continuously improve its own products.

The Greek moussaka was good, but not good enough. People wanted more eggplant. Loblaw doubled the eggplant. And bragged about it in the advertising flyer and on the package.

The chicken breast stuffed with mushrooms and provolone wasn't as popular. People complained it leaked when you cooked it. Loblaw fixed it.

Making improvements based on customer suggestions is now baked into the process at Loblaw. "We'll take the feedback, and pipe it right back to the product developers, and pat ourselves on the back" says Jim Osborne. "The ones that tank, they may discontinue, but often [they will] analyze, reformulate, and rerelease." Failed products at Loblaw are just an opportunity to try again and fix things.

Our favorite story is about PC Smokin' Stampede Barbecue Sauce. Loblaw took it to the Ozark Hawg Barbecue Championship in Batesville, Arkansas—not normally a hotbed of Canadian cuisine. A film crew recorded a local who tasted the sauce, loved it, and put it on his brisket—which went on to win the barbecue contest. Loblaw knew it had a great product and brought it back to Canada, where it proceeded to get an average rating of 9.4 out of 10, promoted with video from Arkansas. What's not to like?

The cap! Turns out that the bottle was too tall for some refrigerator shelves, and the spring-loaded cap was driving people crazy. Customer reviews revealed the flaw. Loblaw improved the packaging and fixed the problem. The customers still love the taste, and they're no longer complaining about the bottle.

For Loblaw, increasing market share for the President's Choice store brand increases profits. Improving products boosts that equation—there isn't a PC product that's immune to the benefits of suggested improvements coming in from customers.

But there's more to this story than that. Loblaw and President's Choice are listening, and customers know it. Everyone who shops knows products have problems, but it's the rare retailer or manufacturer that actually fixes them. Loblaw has that reputation now, which means a lot to its customers.

can you learn from loblaw?

Are you ready to change your company's reputation? Do you want people to think of you as a company that listens?

President's Choice and Loblaw have some special advantages over their competitors. A powerful brand and store under the same corporate ownership make this example work. Wal-Mart could do this—its store brands outsell many national brands. So could Sony, L. L. Bean, Sears, and countless other brands that have their own stores. But they'd have to prove they're ready to listen to their customers and act on those customers' suggestions, right at the point of sale, like Loblaw. Most stores and brands aren't humble enough to do that.

Even brands and manufacturers without their own stores can get feedback. For example, eBags provides reports to its suppliers about what its customers are saying. What about your brand? Are you scrutinizing weekly point-of-sales data to evaluate how well your promotions are doing? Maybe you'd be better off investing a little of that effort into reading customer ratings and reviews from your retail partners. Then you'd learn *why* things are selling—or aren't.

how humility and creativity can coexist, whatever business you're in

When it comes to embracing your customers, there are two things to remember.

The first is that it doesn't matter what kind of business you're in—if you have customers, they can help you. If you're in a consumer service business—like a restaurant chain—you can ask for suggestions, like Crédit Mutuel, or set up a private community, like Del Monte. If you sell to businesses, as salesforce.com does, your customers may have suggestions on how to improve your processes, your pricing, your billing, or your services. The key is, you need to do more than just ask for feedback. You need to *show* that feedback online, good and bad, where people can see that you are ready to act on it, that you are committed to improving things. While it's tough to put all that feedback out for everyone to see, it's worth the risk (and face it—as we saw in chapter 1, your customers are out there dissing you in the groundswell anyway—so you might as well keep the discussion where you can see it). You'll innovate faster and look responsive, and in the long term, that's going to bring more business your way.

The second thing to remember is that embracing your customers takes a balance between skill and humility. Take a company like Apple, which generates a lot of loyalty but doesn't have a highly visible feedback mechanism. Apple has brilliant engineers and marketers. But will it get every single product right every time? Sooner or later the hot streak is going to end.

We're not suggesting that a company like Apple turn its development over to its customers—that would be a tragic waste of talent. No, the companies that win by embracing their customers incorporate those suggestions into their own development and process strengths. The customers don't tell these companies what to do—they just make suggestions. The difference is, these companies are listening to and acting on many of those suggestions. That's what accelerates innovation—starting a conversation with your customers and using your skills to understand and exploit their knowledge.

So work on both fronts in your company—muster up the humility to listen and tap into the skill to take what you've heard and make improvements. That's embracing the groundswell, and it pays by shortening the distance between you and your next successful innovation.

You've reached the end of the strategy section of this book. But as you've seen in all these chapters, once you introduce the groundswell into your company, things change. It's irreversible. In the next three chapters, we'll reveal how those changes happen and what the future will bring.

part three.

the groundswell transforms

10. **how connecting with the groundswell transforms your company**

Rob Master knows how to market when it matters.

Rob is U.S. marketing director for skin care products for the brand colossus Unilever. When he proposed to his girlfriend, he started by creating an elaborate trail of rose petals that led her across Manhattan to the site of their first date. There, Rob popped the biggest question of his life. "She always teased me that I wasn't such a romantic guy," Rob said. "But I'm a marketing guy. I recognize the importance of how to position things."[1]

Rob's ability to position products and ideas turned out to be central to a transformation in how Unilever's Dove brand approached marketing.

Rob, working together with Unilever's U.S. media director Babs Rangaiah, helped Unilever not only to accept the Internet as a marketing vehicle, but to gradually give up some control of the brand, embracing the power of the groundswell and energizing consumers to make their own contributions.

The culmination of that cultural change came when Dove's "Evolution" video debuted on YouTube in the fall of 2006. While Rob and Babs didn't create the video—it came from Dove's agency in Canada, Ogilvy/Canada—they did help create an environment in which new approaches were welcomed and marketers could take risks. That culture paid off when "Evolution" became a viral success. The 75-second video, which shows a time-lapse view of how an average-looking woman is transformed into the epitome of airbrushed fashion "beauty," was distributed primarily on sites like YouTube; over 5 million people saw it in less than a year.[2] It also garnered advertising's highest awards at the advertising festival in Cannes. Best of all, it caused a surge of traffic to Dove's Campaign For Real Beauty Web site—more than double what Dove's 2006 Super Bowl ad drove.[3] The cost of airing a 30-second ad on the Super Bowl? Two and half million dollars. And the cost of distributing the "Evolution" video on YouTube? Zippo.

Let's put this idea into context. In 2006, Unilever spent $2.1 billion on marketing in the United States, with 40 percent of that spent on media like TV, print, and the Web.[4] Moreover, traditional media spending, even when it's online media, has been a highly centralized and controlled process. A YouTube video is really about letting go of control and trusting that your creativity will engage the groundswell. So how did one of the largest advertising spenders come to embrace low-cost, low-control social technologies, which, in many ways, are the antithesis of mass marketing?

It didn't happen overnight.

how the groundswell spreads with a customer-centric organization

This chapter will look at two case studies—Unilever and Dell—where big companies transformed a traditional marketing and customer support organization into one that is led by the groundswell.

It sounds so logical, so easy—keep the customer at the center of your organization. But the reality of departmental priorities and ingrained marketing and customer service practices keeps us far from this ideal. Think about it—how many companies have "customer managers" instead of "product managers"?

One of the benefits we've seen of engaging with the groundswell is that your organization goes through a mental shift—you become so engaged with your customers that you walk in step with their needs and wants. The key to this transformation is taking an idea that typically starts with a few employees who understand the groundswell and making it an organization-wide movement. In essence, you want to create your own mini-groundswell within the company to embrace the groundswell of customers outside it.

There are three essential elements to this transformation. First, it's important to take this step by step. A mental shift takes time and practice and requires building a repertoire of shared successes. Building these stepping-stones is also essential to giving people in your organization an opportunity to adjust their concepts of how things *should* work. Like a diet plan built on quick weight loss, quick hits and wins can rapidly evaporate if groundswell thinking doesn't become a regular part of a company's processes. And trying to do all the strategies we outlined in the previous chapters *at the same time* would be foolhardy.

Second, each of these stepping-stones leads in a natural progression to the next step. Supporting strategies can lead to talking, which can lead to embracing. You'll need a plan and vision about where you want to take your organization, building a firm foundation from which you can push it up to the next challenging level of groundswell thinking.

Third, you have to have executive support. Realistically, you may have to cobble together skunk-works projects to get something off the ground, but you better have in mind how you're going to sell someone in upper management on groundswell thinking if you want your efforts and ideas to catch fire within the organization.

In this chapter we'll look at how organizations can master these three key elements of groundswell thinking to transform how their companies work with customers. Then in chapter 11 we'll look at how companies can do this with their own employees, as members of the internal enterprise groundswell.

unilever: letting go of control to win over the groundswell

As the parent company of brands like Axe, Lipton, and Vaseline, Unilever is synonymous with brand marketing, where grand messages and media plans are meticulously planned, coordinated, and executed over several months. This requires a command-and-control structure where everything is planned and monitored centrally, especially when several internal and external teams need to be coordinated.

One of Unilever's key brands is Dove. When the company and its agency Ogilvy and Mather launched Dove's Campaign For Real Beauty in 2004, they took a big risk with the message, going against the industry norm of using young, slender, perfect models and instead featuring everyday, average women. But the radical message was well researched, and it was delivered through traditional channels like any other brand campaign, with a mix of TV, print, and outdoor ads. And it worked—people were definitely talking about the ad campaign and Dove.

Next step: learn to give up control of the brand message. Here's where Babs Rangaiah enters the story. Babs and Rob conceived the idea of working with the NBC reality television show *The Apprentice*, in an episode where teams created ads for a new Dove product. "It took an external opportunity like *The Apprentice* to create a need for real innovation," Babs recalled. "There is always some nervousness about how it will turn out." The Dove ads created by the teams on *The Apprentice* were pretty bad; it wasn't the best way to showcase and launch a product. But the Dove team took advantage of the *Apprentice* miscues and the buzz around them to launch their own version of the ad, introduced by *Apprentice* host Donald Trump himself, which generated a flood of visits to dove.com. In the end the *Apprentice* gamble and the subsequent ad paid off—Babs told us that Dove Cool Moisture Beauty Body Wash had strong sales results after the episode aired.

By 2005, Rob was eager to push the envelope again, and this time the Web was central to this plan. Rather than trying to capture a person's attention with thirty seconds of video between sitcom segments, Rob wanted to engage with consumers who *wanted* to hear from Dove. His proposal: create a set of Web-based videos to launch a new product line, Dove's Calming Night, designed to soothe women at the end of a hectic day. He lined up great talent, with Penny Marshall directing *Desperate Housewives* star Felicity Huffman. His plan also stacked the decks for dovenight.com[5] to succeed by supporting it with full-fledged television, print, and online portal campaigns to drive awareness and word of mouth about the brand and site. And he built in measurable results by offering free trials on the site. With 3 million visits to dovenight.com, the company was able to show it could put digital media at the center of an ad campaign. This was a turning point in Unilever's recognition of the power of online.

All these experiences had to precede the "Evolution" video, preparing Dove's management for more and more innovative messages delivered in new ways. Back in 2003, something like the "Evolution" video on YouTube would have been shot down. Instead, Rob, Babs, and innovators from other teams encouraged the cultural change—Babs mentions his boss Philippe Harousseau and Axe marketers Kevin George and David Rubin, for example. These leaders built Unilever's confidence in the groundswell bit by bit, each time loosening the control reins a little more. "It took a lot for us to do that program, a lot of pushing from me and Rob. Once we got it through management, it was the results of the business that allowed us to push that success into other things. Needless to say, it was big and got people at Unilever thinking that, wow, this is a different perspective and can have a major impact on how we can market our brands."

We told you that in addition to talking to the groundswell in steps, managers need to build executive support. As the director in charge of coordinating media across all Unilever brands, Babs Rangaiah provided the executive support to spread ideas about how to incorporate digital technologies into media plans. Today creating and positioning campaigns with the groundswell in mind is spreading across different product groups at Unilever, led by teams at Axe and Dove. "I would say that culturally, we are definitely a different company," says Babs. "It takes a few people to ignite that change. We were always a company that wanted to think of itself as creative. But we were a giant company. Companies like ours have a corporate way about them. We wanted to be more innovative, more nimble."

what you can learn from unilever

Think your marketing organization could never transform like Unilever to embrace the groundswell? Such a change typically requires a lot of pain and cajoling, and never happens quickly. Here's how you can use Unilever's example to incorporate the three elements of groundswell thinking into your organization:

- *Take small steps that have big impact.* The Dove team initiated a series of campaigns that were revolutionary in *one* area—innovating on the message with the Campaign For Real Beauty, letting go of message control with *The Apprentice,* and rethinking distribution with the "Evolution" video. The key was that they all had measurable success metrics that were tied to key marketing goals. These primed the pump for the more innovative, more challenging campaigns that came next. You should look for shortcomings in your current marketing and communications program and apply groundswell thinking to solving these particularly hard business problems. Don't try to take on the entire customer relationship all at the same time—you'll gain more support for groundswell thinking if you can show a series of successes that have impact.

- *Have a vision and a plan.* Transformational thinking can be maddeningly slow. Rob and Babs demonstrated tremendous patience in getting executives to take small steps forward—in all, two years passed between the launch of the Campaign For Real Beauty and the "Evolution" video. But both Rob and Babs personally had a vision of Unilever's potential with groundswell thinking, a vision that kept them going through the rough patches. You should have in your mind a three-year outlook of where you want to take the organization—and the simplest way to do that is to describe what the relationship with your customer will *feel like* in the future. You won't necessarily know what technologies you'll use, or what kind of message you'll have, but you should have a vision of the kind of conversation you want with your customers.

- *Build leaders into the plan.* It took leaders like Rob and Babs to have the guts to take Unilever all the way to the top. The Dove team was relentless in hammering on one point—the need to let go and embrace emerging media and give the consumer a voice in the brand. Rob and Babs shared this vision and backed it up with persuasive and planning skills to drive innovative marketing to another level.

how *not* to succeed in the groundswell

Sometimes business books make it look easy by showing only success stories. Let's take a quick look at what one company's failure to engage the groundswell looked like.

One of our clients decided to start a corporate blog. Several of the company's marketers looked at blogs like GM's FastLane, where several top executives regularly blog, and decided that they needed something similar—a jointly authored executive blog. Led by someone who had both corporate communications and investor relations experience, the small team then went into planning mode. For *eight months.*

Yes, that's eight months of planning without a single blog post seeing the light of day. Team members were intent on having several executives blog several times a week and knew that they had to make a watertight case for why the executives should invest the time to do this. But the executive team rejected the grand blogging strategy, despite a plan with plenty of backup data slides and blog mock-ups. Why? Partly because the executives couldn't internalize the value of blogging—they didn't buy into the numbers they were presented because they had never seen anything like the groundswell before. Moreover, the executives were concerned about the loss of control over their marketing message and the prospect of negative comments from customers.

Although beautifully conceived and planned, the grand blogging strategy never had a chance—these executives were being asked to live in the middle of the groundswell when they had not the faintest idea what the groundswell was. The plan was a total abject failure, and it looked as if the team had shattered any hopes of ever getting a blog launched.

Sounds like yet another casualty of old-world thinking, right? Wrong. The team within the marketing department just wouldn't give up. Team members learned from their failure and realized that they had taken the wrong approach, trying to force groundswell thinking from the top. Instead, they started from scratch and looked for someone who was already embracing groundswell thinking in everyday activities. They decided to approach the company's original founder, who was already regularly having discussions with customers and employees about new products under development. He was removed from day-to-day operations and had the time and bandwidth to devote to a blog. But most important, as the founder, he had a unique perspective—what the company stood for and where it was headed—that he wanted to share with customers and that customers wanted to hear about.

By changing the person responsible for content, the blog project was revived. You can't force executives to blog—hence the eight months of waffling. You *can* take someone who wants to blog and build a strategy around him.

Having won the support of an executive champion, the marketing team then crafted a communications plan that addressed executive concerns around the loss of control. A public relations/investor relations person would review posts to ensure they didn't disclose inappropriate information. The same person would review blog comments and delete any that were considered inappropriate—but would publish negative comments as long as they were respectfully written. Satisfied, the executive team gave its blessing. Within two months after the rejection of the grand blogging strategy, the company had a blog up and running with the full backing of the executive team.

We use this case study to illustrate a key point—that even though you may have a clear vision of what the company needs to do, getting the company to embrace the groundswell is going to take a lot of small steps and a lot of time. One of the best practices we ever saw was a small company that had all its interactive media team go through change management training—the manager realized that if these employees were going to have to spread social technologies throughout the organization, they needed to be prepared to change thinking, as well as to educate people about the new technologies. You would do well to prepare yourself and your team to follow suit.

dell: going through hell on the way to transformation

We've taken a look at how the groundswell transformed a marketing organization. Let's now look at Dell, where groundswell thinking started in marketing and support and moved into development. We've showcased Dell in several chapters already. Based on what you've read, you may think Dell is pretty advanced in using the groundswell to its advantage.

In fact, Dell's entry into the groundswell began as a real trial-by-fire crisis.

Built on a direct sales model, Dell relied on low costs, flexible products, and easy ordering to drive its growth and profitability. But without a traditional bricks-and-mortar presence, it had to rely on excellent phone and online customer support to connect with its customers. It also had a program where customers could subscribe to a service to have engineers come to their homes to provide support. In 2001, the company started offshoring its customer support. According to the American Customer Satisfaction Index, customer satisfaction began to decline in 2005.[6]

In the summer of 2005, journalism professor and noted blogger Jeff Jarvis wrote in his blog, BuzzMachine, about the abysmal customer service he was receiving from the company:[7]

June 21, 2005

Dell lies. Dell sucks.

I just got a new Dell laptop and paid a fortune for the four-year, in-home service.

The machine is a lemon and the service is a lie.

I'm having all kinds of trouble with the hardware: overheats, network doesn't work, maxes out on CPU usage. It's a lemon.

> But what really irks me is that they say if they sent someone to my home—which I paid for—he wouldn't have the parts, so I might as well just send the machine in and lose it for 7–10 days—plus the time going through this crap. So I have this new machine and paid for them to F***ING FIX IT IN MY HOUSE and they don't and I lose it for two weeks.
>
> DELL SUCKS. DELL LIES. Put that in your Google and smoke it, Dell.

Jeff then proceeded to descend into Dell hell. Despite having purchased an expensive warranty and on-site service contract, Jeff had to send his laptop back to Dell. Three days later, he had his new machine—and it didn't work. On June 26, Jeff wrote:[8]

> Is anybody at Dell listening? I know you are. What do you have to say, Dell?
>
> While you're at it, Dell, go <u>here</u> and <u>here</u> and <u>here</u> and read the comments and see how y our customers hate you. (And that extra space in "your" is because of your broken keyboard, by the way.)
>
> A snarker in the comments says, "Buyer beware."
>
> No, we are in the new era of "Seller beware." Now when you screw your customers, your customers can fight back and publish and organize. I just sent this link to Dell's media relations department and told them to read the comments and see what their real public relations look like.

Finally, and only after emailing Dell's chief marketing officer, did Jeff get someone to resolve the issue and give him a full refund. Throughout the process, Jeff and many other bloggers and journalists fully documented the actions and inactions of a company that was clueless about the groundswell.

listen first, then act

Dell's hell wasn't just a PR nightmare. The company was very publicly floundering. In November 2005, Dell announced that quarterly profits had dropped 28 percent. In May 2006, the company warned that it would not meet its earnings guidance. And then, on June 21, 2006, a

Dell notebook caught on fire at a conference in Osaka, Japan.[9] As you can certainly see, the formation of a social strategy was *not* the company's top priority.

But with Jeff Jarvis mouthing off about Dell hell, Dell's VP of corporate group communications, Bob Pearson, and his team began tracking blog posts. As is the case in most large companies, they didn't have the ties back to customer service to act on complaints. There was also no one whose job was specifically to reach out actively to bloggers with problems. There was no efficient mechanism in place to deal with these pesky but highly visible service problems in the groundswell.

In March 2006, Michael Dell charged Bob's team with figuring out a way to proactively find customers having hardware problems and connect them with Dell technicians. That job fell to Lionel Menchaca, who was ideally suited for the job. Lionel had started at Dell in 1993 as a product technician and fell into product PR in 1997, when Dell needed someone who was highly technical to run their server review program with journalists. As a product PR person, Lionel had spent nine years working with engineers in all lines of Dell's business. He had not only the knowledge but also the connections within Dell to make the new team work.

With Michael Dell's support, Lionel figured out a way to monitor blog posts and hired a cross-departmental "blog resolution" team trained to offer both customer service and technical support. When team members found a blogger writing about problems with Dell products, they reached out and were able to follow through with the entire issue—no painful "please hold while I connect you with another department" experiences here.

onward to blogging

For Dell, listening and then acting was the crucial first step for its new social strategy. The company had already long been using community forums to support customers, as we described in chapter 8, but that had largely been a separate initiative that didn't touch day-to-day operations. Listening was the crucial first stepping-stone needed to get key players in marketing, customer service, and technical support focused and coordinated on identifying and solving customer problems.

After listening, the most natural next step was for the company to talk. Bob Pearson recalled, "Dell had over 3 million customer contacts per day. Our customers were already coming to us looking for a solution. But with a blog, we would be talking with people who are *not* coming to us with a problem but are still interested in hearing from us."

This is where Lionel Menchaca comes back into the picture. In the course of his blog resolution work, he picked up an important skill. "We had to figure out what kind of support we needed to have to make the blog outreach work. That included being able to identify and address issues that repeatedly affected hundreds of customers. Whether the discussion is with one person or a thousand, the conversation is very similar. Figuring out all of those nuances helped me to evolve into the role of a blog manager."

This time, buoyed by the successes of the blog resolution team and with the right people in place, Dell moved much faster. The corporate communications team put together a digital media plan with a blog, written by Lionel, in a central role and showed it to Michael Dell. Michael not only approved it but told them to have the blog up and running *in two weeks.*

The team missed the deadline by a whole week.

It was a rough start. Bloggers like Jeff Jarvis and Steve Rubel blasted Dell for their first blog posts. On the day of the first blog post, as Lionel sat at his desk, trying to keep up with the flood of blog comments pouring in, many of them negative, he saw an email from Michael Dell pop up in his inbox at 1:00 a.m. According to Lionel, Michael wrote, "You're doing a great job, and it's great to see this coming to life."

That email from Michael was a huge lift for Lionel and enabled him to find his footing. It also gave him the confidence a few days later to write a pivotal post that showed that Dell was serious about engaging in an open conversation. What follows is the entire entry (and note the audacious title):[10]

Flaming Notebook

Beyond what you've seen in the blogosphere, there is no update on the now infamous "flaming notebook" from Osaka. We replaced the customer's computer and are still investigating the cause. We think it was a fault in a lithium ion battery cell. Dell's engineering teams are working with the Consumer Product Safety Commission and a third-party failure analysis lab to determine the root cause of this failure and to ensure we take all appropriate measures to help prevent a recurrence. By the way, lithium ion batteries are used in billions of notebooks, mp3 players, PDAs and cell phones these days.

Not everyone within Dell was thrilled to see this post go live. Lionel told us, "When I published that post and linked to the Engadget article that showed the flaming notebook, people came to me and asked what in the heck was going on." But Dell's followers were overwhelmingly positive. Here are the two initial comments responding to that post:

> We posted on this . . . a while back and wondered when you folks were going to join the conversation. And now here you are, blogging about it. I almost never thought I'd see the day.

> Big kudos for starting the blog. Glad to see you join the conversation(s) that have so frequently revolved around you but have not been able to include you.

transforming dell, one person at a time

After this, there was no stopping Lionel. He was on a mission to demonstrate that Dell was listening, taking action, and what's more important, admitting that he and Dell were making mistakes along the way. This very human, transparent approach was hard for Dell. Bob Pearson explains, "That level of transparency at the company—well, we weren't used to sharing at that level."

Lionel and Bob realized that they had to do this one person at a time. Lionel was allowed to go anywhere in the company to get managers to post on the blog. After these managers wrote their posts, they realized that they then had to keep track of what was being said on the blog by their customers and critics—and respond. Bob explained, "We're integrating blogging and talking with customers into people's normal jobs—if you're speaking to the customer, it's part of your job now to be more transparent."

The result: Dell's organization started to change, one employee at a time, from the inside out. Dell's history of supporting community forums gave it the foundation to listen to blogs, which then allowed employees to blog openly and honestly. It's a sequence of stepping-stones, and the natural next step was IdeaStorm.

taking it to the top

Amid all this turmoil, CEO Kevin Rollins stepped down on January 31, 2007, and company founder Michael Dell returned once again to the role of CEO. Michael wasted no time getting his executives lined up with the groundswell. He took an idea from his friend Mark Benioff, CEO of salesforce.com, to create IdeaStorm, the idea community described in chapter 9. He felt that the time was ripe to do this at Dell because of the foundation Lionel and Bob had laid with their successful blogging initiatives. Manish Mehta, Dell's global director of ecommerce and Bob Pearson in corporate communications worked together with the corporate IT team to get IdeaStorm launched on February 16, 2007, just days after the idea was first presented.

But it wasn't just the technology that was important. Michael made sure that his executive team was paying attention to the ideas that would impact the business and assigned a cross-departmental team to review results from IdeaStorm every week. Corporate strategy was deeply involved and helped figure out which ideas got the green light—and who would be responsible for them.

In the end did Dell have a coherent social strategy, or did it fall into one? By its own admission, Dell didn't have IdeaStorm or even a blog in its strategy plans in 2005, during the days of Dell hell. But the company clearly had top leadership support and individuals like Lionel, Bob, and Manish who were willing to push departmental boundaries aside to get things done. The key is that these critical people took smart, small moves that built a foundation for groundswell thinking. Dell's future plans in social media include integrating community directly into dell.com, as well as taking Dell into communities of interest and social networks.

what you can learn from dell

To recap, how did Dell shake off its stupor and jump into action at the executive ranks?

- *It took a crisis or two to get Dell started.* It wasn't a pretty process. It took a series of disasters, culminating in the flaming notebook, to get the company to jump into the cold water. Once there, it started swimming, and swimming hard. This is one way to get started. But don't imagine that groundswell thinking is only for losers with customer perception problems. Otherwise, you'll be losing out as your competitors engage and you don't.

- *Dell mastered one thing at a time, starting with listening.* Dell had deep experience with community forums, but the company's role was passive. Before its employees could decisively act, they felt they needed to understand the dialogue that was taking place. It just took a long time for them to get engaged because they were unsure how to act. But from listening to blogs, to solving bloggers' problems, to blogging themselves, to IdeaStorm, they pulled themselves up into the groundswell.

- *Executive push and cover made the difference.* Michael Dell provided support from the top, giving Bob and Lionel the ability to break down departmental silos and change processes to get things done. Michael also realized that transformation was crucial for Dell's future success, so he supported and pushed groundswell efforts no matter what the perceived cost. He realized that this was no one-off campaign. It could and should be part of the corporate strategy, and if corporate transformation was crucial, then the groundswell could be a powerful catalyst.

- *Authenticity was crucial.* Dell couldn't get anywhere in the groundswell until it honestly admitted its flaws. The blog became successful when it began to deal with real problems like the flaming notebook. That sense of authenticity extended to all of Dell's groundswell activities, including IdeaStorm, where the company frankly recognizes which ideas it will adopt and which it won't.

how organizations can prepare for a transformation

If you're reading this, you could be the person to start your company on the path to benefiting from the groundswell. Or you could be the person who loses your job for screwing it up.

It's a minefield. But you can succeed—if you take the right steps in the right order. Look at what worked at Dell and Unilever—and what didn't work with the grand blogging plan at the unnamed company. Here's what you should do to make sure you and your company have the best chance of succeeding.

- *First, start small.* We've said this throughout the book, but it's even more crucial in company transformation. The change will take time, and you typically only have so much political power to use at any one time. So pick your battles strategically.

- *Second, educate your executives.* Some of them think this is for their kids, not their customers. Show them otherwise with research (use one of the Social Technographics Profiles in this book, or generate one with the tool at groundswell.forrester.com). To the extent that you can, get them to *use* the technologies themselves. A great place to start is to launch internal blogs, social networks, and collaboration within a department (as described in the next chapter) to demonstrate the specific benefits for the company.

- *Third, get the right people to run your strategy.* Don't pick the person with the most time on his or her hands (you've got to wonder why!) or a senior executive. Pick the person who has the most passion about starting a relationship with your customers. (You'll be able to spot him because he uses the word *customer* in most of his conversations.)

- *Fourth, get your agency and technology partners in sync.* If they don't understand the groundswell, get them to invest the time and resources—or change agencies.

- *Fifth, plan for the next step and for the long term.* You want to know where this is going to take the company.

We've taken a look at how a social strategy and groundswell thinking can change how an organization works with customers. In chapter 11 we'll take a look at how groundswell strategies are changing the way companies manage and support their employees.

11. the groundswell inside your company

How would you feel if one of your employees wrote something like this?[1]

> I work retail. I inspire creativity and fun with my employees. I grand open stores, as many as possible, really. And I have never before loved a job and a company the way I love this one.
>
> My name is Ashley Hemsath, and I am Best Buy.

Ashley works at the Charlotte, South Carolina, Best Buy, one of twelve hundred Best Buy electronics stores. She's a Blue Shirt—that's what everybody at Best Buy calls the sales associates (if you've been to a Best Buy store, you've seen them working in their blue polo shirts). She's also a member of Blue Shirt Nation (blueshirtnation.com), an internal community site for Best Buy's employees—this quote comes from her profile on the community. The idea of Blue Shirt Nation attracted her, and she's one of the site's most-read contributors. "I can share my thoughts on how we should fix the company, and I can also post about my day," she says. "I then get support from other people, and not just at the local level. I can relate to people outside of my own store."

In any company, on any given day, employees may or may not feel committed to their company's goals. But with some forethought, internal groundswell applications like Blue Shirt Nation can make them feel empowered, connected, and more committed on a day-to-day basis. As Ashley says, "It feels like I'm making a difference. It makes me feel better at work, and I have a greater sense of responsibility to not just point out what's wrong but to come up with ways to fix things that are wrong. That's because what I'm saying could impact what someone thinks who just started a few days ago." Ashley credits her activities on Blue Shirt Nation for giving her a bigger picture of the company's goals. And that, in turn, led to her promotion to supervisor.

tapping the groundswell inside your company

In the first ten chapters of this book, we talked about how you can connect with your customers in the groundswell. But what about your employees? They're a natural constituency for social connections. They obviously have something in common: they work for you. And they ought to have a common goal: your company's success.

The bigger a company is, the more of a problem internal communication becomes. Information flows down the management ladder, but getting insights back up to management and encouraging collaboration among people throughout the enterprise is harder. Email boxes fill with a combination of urgent requests, irrelevant "cc's" and offers of free kittens. If Dell can get its customers to support each other and salesforce .com can get its customers to prioritize feature suggestions, why can't your employees work together in the same way?

They can.

Throughout corporations around the world, employees are connecting on internal social networks, collaborating on wikis, and contributing to idea exchanges. Some of these applications came from management and others began as skunk-works projects, but what they have in common is this: they tap the power of the groundswell of ideas among the people who know best how your business runs, your employees. It's a little scary to put this power in the hands of your workers. It doesn't fit into a nice, neat org chart. But if you want to run faster and smarter, you ought to take a look at it.

In this chapter we look at three kinds of internal groundswell applications: the community at Best Buy; wikis at Avenue A/Razorfish, Organic, and Intel; and an idea exchange at Bell Canada.

best buy: connecting far-flung sales associates

Blue Shirt Nation was started by two corporate marketing guys, Steve Bendt and Gary Koelling, who wanted to gather customer insight on what kinds of advertising worked. Best Buy's Blue Shirts are on the front lines and have, collectively, a lot of insight into what's really working at the stores. Steve and Gary, who aren't known for doing things in traditional ways, decided to give the Blue Shirts a voice. As Steve told us, "We wanted to get insight into what's really happening at the store, not just when the store is spic and span for corporate visits."

Gary started in August 2006 by finding a spare server, stashing it under his desk, and loading it with Drupal, an open-source suite of community-building software. He and Steve opened the site up to a few colleagues for testing and got feedback. "We had a lot of posts that said it sucked," Gary remembers. The project took off when they showed it to the senior VP of marketing, Barry Judge, who told them that they weren't thinking big enough—and promptly offered them a generous budget to build out the community.

But it turned out, money wasn't what they needed to make Blue Shirt Nation a success—participation was. "We thought this could be really awesome," Steve says, "but then we realized we didn't needs hundreds of thousands of dollars. We knew that something coming down from corporate wasn't going to fly and that this needed to grow organically." So they turned down most of the money.

Instead, Steve and Gary went on the road, participating in "chalk talks" in the stores and giving away Blue Shirt Nation T-shirts to employees. They took store teams bowling, getting feedback on what worked on the community and encouraging employees to participate. By the time the site went live to all employees in February 2006, there was already enough activity to see it as an early success, and the employees greeted it with enthusiasm. By October 2007, Blue Shirt Nation had grown immensely, with fourteen thousand employees logging in each month, 85 percent of them sales associates in stores.

Despite this success, Steve and Gary are still the irreverent guys who started the site on a server under Gary's desk. When we pointed out to them that their little community now had 10 percent of Best Buy's employees as members, they high-fived each other. "Dude," Gary exclaimed, "we're at 10 percent!"

the impact of blue shirt nation

Blue Shirt Nation was created to listen to what employees had to say. What Best Buy didn't anticipate is that it would not only educate management but also enable employees to help *each other*. For example, Blue Shirts had clamored for email addresses so that they could communicate with each other more effectively than leaving a note at the cash register and to follow up with customers. Someone posted that this wasn't possible because it would cost Best Buy close to $1 million to implement. Somebody else checked with IT and found the price was closer to $58,000 for all full-time associates. Soon after, the Blue Shirts got email. Chalk one up for the groundswell in Blue Shirt Nation.

Some managers worry that connecting their employees will create a revolt. And sometimes it does. When Best Buy pushed through a change in the employee discount, one poster wrote, "Don't like the changes? Let your opinion be heard! . . . We may not be able to stop the change from happening, but we can definitely let our company know exactly how displeased we are about it." Three days later, responding to a surge of impassioned comments in Blue Shirt Nation, a management staffer posted this: "We heard you. You made it very clear how valuable the employee discount is, and based on that feedback we have decided NOT to change it." The company realized that the discount was crucial to attracting and retaining employees and decided that it had better keep the discount as it was.

Blue Shirt Nation also solves mundane but impactful problems. An employee named Chris posted that a new SLR camera display case was too tall, included a picture with his post, and asked whether anyone had a similar problem. Within two hours, the case's original designer responded, writing, "There are two variations of the case . . . [Y]ou apparently got one that has an extra toekick in it . . . I will immediately follow up with this to make sure the right cases got ordered for the right stores." What normally would have taken weeks to wind its way through company bureaucracy was resolved in just a few days—and the case designer was proactively preventing others from suffering the same problem. That's the power and speed of the groundswell within companies—the ability for people to find what they need from each other.

internal groundswell benefits touch on many objectives

In chapter 4 we told you to build applications with a single objective in mind: listening, talking, energizing, supporting, or embracing. This approach also applies within the enterprise, but as Blue Shirt Nation shows, these objectives tend to blend together in internal applications. Management's relationships with employees—and employees' relationships with each other—are multidimensional. For example, here's how Best Buy's Blue Shirt Nation accomplishes all five objectives:

- *Listening.* Steve and Gary set up Blue Shirt Nation to listen, but its utility goes beyond the merchandising feedback they were seeking. With employees, listening can turn rapidly into problem solving. Management listened and then restored the employee discount. And it's not just management—the SLR camera case designer got to hear how his display was being used in stores and to fix problems with it.

- *Talking.* Now corporate can post policy changes where everyone can read them and see how they're playing in Peoria.

- *Energizing.* How much is an enthusiastic employee like Ashley Hemsath worth to Best Buy? Not only does Blue Shirt Nation give Ashley a platform, but it also amplifies her voice across the entire Best Buy employee base. She spreads her positive thinking and advice, which has an impact on stores everywhere.

- *Supporting.* A key part of Best Buy's success is its commitment to support and promote employees from within. According to Ashley, "My biggest goal is to get my team members promoted. I remember the names of everyone I hired and I know what store they are at now. It's really cool seeing them interacting with me and each other directly on BSN [Blue Shirt Nation]." The online forum on Blue Shirt Nation is a natural extension of that mentoring culture, where employees can find the support they need from around the company, not just from within their store or district.

- *Embracing.* In the summer of 2007, Ashley was invited to attend a Best Buy women's leadership forum in Chicago. She ended up sitting down with someone named Kal and talked with him for four hours straight about improvements. As she recalls, "I found out later that he was Kal Patel, Best Buy's EVP of strategy. He saw my posts on BSN and said to his assistant, 'I need to meet that girl!'" The community turned out to be a way to surface both ideas and great talent.

Blue Shirt Nation brought Blue Shirts together for listening and problem solving. But some companies need more than that—they need a full-fledged collaboration environment. That's what wikis are good for.

CASE STUDY

avenue a/razorfish: collaborating on a wiki

Just before Christmas in 2006, Clark Kokich sat down at his computer and wrote this blog post:[2]

> [A colleague] just sent me an email asking me to post my favorite guitar solo of all time. He thought there would be lots of people with opinions on this subject. Given that it's the day before the holidays and I haven't received [another] email all morning . . . , it seems like a good time to have some fun.

The quick and easy answer: I still get chills when I hear Cream play *Crossroads* live. But after thinking about it for a few minutes, I'd have to say that the ONE guitar solo that still surprises and amazes me every time I hear it is *Man in The Box* by Alice In Chains.

Sounds like a thousand other blog posts on the Net. But this one was written by the CEO of Avenue A/Razorfish, one of the largest interactive agencies in the world, and it appeared on his company intranet. Why is the CEO of a busy agency wasting time writing about guitar solos? Clark explains, "This post didn't serve any specific business purpose, but it was an opportunity [for our employees] to be connected to the leadership. You can do this with a few people over a beer, but how do you accomplish that with a whole company? If you look back on our history five to ten years from now, this connection is going to be one of the things that will get us to where we'll be."

Avenue A/Razorfish's internal intranet site, which is a wiki with blogs and collaboration spaces, is for lots more than sharing opinions on guitar solos. Since the company is organized around projects, the whole place increasingly runs on the wiki. Over nineteen hundred staff in nineteen offices needed to get out from under clogged email boxes and files scattered on various servers. Now those staff have pages where they share their ideas and skills and blog about their work or, as Clark did, about anything else. More important, projects have pages featuring project summaries, team members' roles, meeting notes, documents on which those team members collaborate, and schedules.

It works. Technologies have cut the time spent looking for sample tech architectures and third-party tools from hours or days to minutes. One of the company's consultants in Fort Lauderdale posted a request for insight into the company's expertise with a tool called RedDot. Within hours, the consultant aggregated case studies from London, Frankfurt, and Paris and used that information on the client's project. Similarly, new employees can get up to speed quickly as they learn about their colleagues' skills—and vice versa.

Rather than create a top-down imperative, Avenue A/Razorfish created features so that teams found using the wiki a whole lot easier than doing things the old way. When the wiki started in January 2006, pages in it were viewed fifty-seven hundred times. Nearly two years later, pages on the wiki had been viewed 1.8 million times. Over 90 percent of the employees have logged in, uploading three thousand files and contributing to seven thousand pages.[3]

It works not just for the employees but for Clark. Every morning he spends fifteen minutes reviewing employees' blogs, wikis, and book-marked articles. "The biggest benefit is being able to listen in on what people are working on, what they are concerned about, and where they are focused. It's the virtual equivalent to management by walking around."

Clark's ability to monitor the pulse of the organization became crucial on May 20, 2007, when Microsoft announced that it was acquiring aQuantive, Avenue A/Razorfish's parent company.[4] Clark knew that employees would be concerned about what the acquisition would mean for them, their clients, and more important, their ability to make independent technology choices.

He wrote a blog post addressing these concerns and then addressed comments and questions as they came into the blog and wiki. "I could have made the announcement by email," Clark explained, "but this was more conversational. That kind of dialogue is comforting to people because change is stressful. There is openness, and things aren't happening in secret. They are reassured that there's no diabolical plan that they didn't know about." As he toured around company offices following the announcement, he regularly checked the wiki and blogs to keep tabs on the latest concerns and complaints and then addressed them at live meetings. The result: by the time the acquisition closed in August 2007, employees felt more assured that the acquisition would be good for them.

The key here is that in creating a collaboration tool, the company had also created a communication channel. Not all the communication among employees is hearts and flowers, of course. But Clark's ability to carry his company through an acquisition, using the blogs and wiki for communication, demonstrates leadership through groundswell thinking. Rather than flinch at the negative sentiments about the acquisition, he chose to address them in a shared space. This skill—talking *and* listening—enables him to remain close to his employees while guiding the company through a crucial transition period.

wikis are spreading through the corporate world

Because they're so effective at enhancing collaboration, wikis are catching on with lots of companies. Take the case of Intelpedia.

In the fall of 2006, Intel product support engineer John G. Miner wrote a blog post on his internal Intel blog, asking, "Wouldn't it be cool to have something like Wikipedia inside of Intel?" Readers responded with skepticism, including comments like "It will never happen" or "It will take 2-3 years."[5] Except for Josh Bancroft, an engineer specializing in social media at Intel, who wrote back saying, "Give me a server and I'll get it running in a day." Josh found a server, loaded it with Media-Wiki (the open-source wiki software that's used to run Wikipedia), and enlisted his friends to start adding content. By the time John got back to Josh two weeks later, offering to try to find a server, it was too late; Josh had already launched Intelpedia. "It was one of the most enjoyable moments at Intel to tell John that Intelpedia was already up," said Josh. "He was blown away."

Two years after Intelpedia was created, it contained twenty thousand articles and generated seven hundred page views every month. The articles range from helpful references (such as how to configure Macs on Intel's corporate network) to the whimsical (such as the schedule for pickup soccer games near Intel campuses). The key to Intelpedia's success is that the articles are more than a static encyclopedia—instead, the wiki is an integral part of daily life at Intel. Oliver Young, a Forrester analyst looking at the application of social technologies within the enterprise, explains, "Out-of-date information is a serious problem with wikis. When you start living and breathing in these social tools, that's when they become a way to tackle business problems. They become part of the context in which you do daily work, instead of a separate island of information."

At Organic, an international interactive agency, staff faced exactly this problem—the internal wiki that they launched wasn't effective because few people were using it. "It wasn't that the wiki was difficult to use; it was just asking us to work differently," said Chad Stoller, executive director of emerging platforms at Organic.

To re-energize employee collaboration, top management took an hour to sketch out the guiding principles for a new intranet at a 2006 off-site meeting. They planned (1) to provide employees, or "talent" as Organic liked to call them, with their own profile on an internal social network called Organism; (2) to support people trying to locate expertise across six offices in the United States and Canada; and (3) to encourage people to upload and share their work on their profiles. They also wanted employees to connect in the same way as the people using their applications did—on a social network.

Organism combines elements of social networks, collaboration software, and corporate intranets. According to David Feldt, a senior vice president in the Toronto office who drove the creation of Organism, "It helps the teams really get to know each other and ultimately work more effectively together."

Organic realized that people's business process revolved around knowing each other and, more important, around the work that each person did. "Organism became an entry point for the wiki," Chad explained. "Anything that gets updated on your profile is documented in the wiki."

Now whenever new employees join Organic, they get a page on Organism and are expected to keep it up to date with their client deliverables. Because Organism is tied directly into the company directory, anyone looking for a programmer with, say, experience creating widgets, will make Organism his first step. This, in turn, encourages employees to update their profile and upload client work—because it very likely will lead to their next project. Finally, Organism also has lightweight social networking features—employees can list their "friends," allowing project leaders to get informal referrals and recommendations for new team members.

Intel and Organic learned that wikis and social networks don't solve problems by themselves. Just as in external groundswell applications, you have to start by thinking about the *relationships*, not the *technologies*. There—as at Avenue A/Razorfish and at Best Buy—technologies succeeded in the enterprise only because the company nurtured them into useful business tools.

The examples we've describe so far show how companies can improve communication and collaboration. What about innovation? That was the goal Bell Canada pursued.

CASE STUDY

bell canada: driving cultural change from the bottom up

In early 2005, Rex Lee, director of collaboration services at Bell Canada, was holding a series of informal coffee sessions with small groups of employees. As is typical in many companies, these degenerated into gripe sessions, filled with complaints and criticisms about the company. Rex found it frustrating that these employees, asked how they would solve the problems they had surfaced, often responded, "It's not my problem." When employees finally did come up with some good ideas, they asked Rex what he was going to do about it. Rex had reached his limit. "Bell Canada has forty thousand people, and honestly, I didn't know how to move forward or who to go to with these ideas," he told us.

Rex needed a better way to corral the ideas and put them where appropriate managers could see them. So he turned for inspiration to ... *American Idol*. That's right, the hit TV show. On *American Idol*, the audience votes for the winners. Could that work at Bell Canada? To find out, Rex and a small team of volunteers created ID-ah!, which allows anyone in the company to submit an idea and then have the employees vote on it. (It's similar to salesforce.com's IdeaExchange, which we described in chapter 9.)

In the year and a half that ID-ah! has been in place, employees have submitted more than a thousand ideas and shared more than three thousand comments. Fifteen thousand employees (out of forty thousand Bell Canada employees) have visited the site and six thousand have voted. Obviously, not all thousand ideas are worth pursuing—but that's what the voting is for. As a result of ID-ah!, over a six-month period in 2007, twenty-seven of the top ideas have been "harvested" for review and twelve have been implemented.[6]

But this is just the beginning of the cultural change that ID-ah! ushered in at Bell Canada.

Top management, led by Eugene Roman, group president, systems and technology, and Mary Anne Elliott, SVP of human resources, championed ID-ah! not just to generate ideas but to change employee attitudes. As Rex recalled, "We wanted each person to be personally invested in Bell, to feel a sense of accountability. And we saw ID-ah! as one of the key ways we could do this."

It was rough initially. According to Rex, "ID-ah! got the attention of executives pretty quickly because they were concerned—after all, people could post anything that they wanted to. What if someone posted something false or slanderous?" To get comfortable with letting go of that control, executives became intimately involved early on, carefully reviewing ideas that were submitted in the beta release. It was only after several months of testing with more and more employees that executives felt comfortable rolling it out to all employees.

The success of ID-ah! as a driver of cultural change at Bell Canada stems from the commitment to make it available to all employees and, even more important, from the commitment from senior management to review the top ideas. That's why it's working. With ID-ah! in place, employees no longer felt that they couldn't make a difference. Instead, they felt empowered by the groundswell. This was Rex's dream and vision—that the sense of company ownership and responsibility would permeate throughout the organization.

Rob Koplowitz, Forrester's workplace collaboration analyst, draws an important lesson from this story: that companies should deploy social technologies internally only when organizational change is both desirable and possible. "Don't bring collaboration tools inside if your company's not ready for it," Rob says. But clearly, Bell Canada was very ready—and the management team accomplished its objective with its internal idea exchange.

strategies for nurturing the internal groundswell

As the Bell Canada case study shows, the internal groundswell is all about creating new ways for people to connect and work together, and to that end, it's about relationships, not technology. Here's what you need to nurture the groundswell power of your employees: promote a listening culture from the top down, ease and encourage participation with incentives, and find and empower the rebels in your organization.

internal groundswells work only when management is listening

Internal social applications demand a high level of trust because employees have more at stake when they participate—after all, their jobs and livelihoods are on the line. Unlike external social networks, the participants can't be anonymous. They need to know that management will listen to their openly contributed opinions, rather than punishing dissenters.

This works only when the culture permits it. Clark Kokich from Avenue A/Razorfish and the managers at Bell Canada understood their role and got involved early in the process. They led not with just the allocation of money and resources but with their own personal involvement. When Avenue A/Razorfish employees saw Clark regularly incorporating material from internal blogs and wikis into his own communications, they knew that they had the ear of their CEO.

This is crucial—without management's active participation, your efforts will fail. For example, we recall one puzzled professional services company that approached us with a conundrum. It had deployed blogs, wikis, and social networking tools internally, specifically targeting newly hired college grads who all said they were very familiar with these tools. Yet several months into the rollout, there was hardly any participation. Why not? Because the company had deployed the technologies with little management sponsorship or involvement. While managers were not using the tools themselves, they expected the people at the bottom of the corporate ladder—those who were still trying to figure out what it means to communicate professionally in an organization—to stick their necks out into the unformed corporate groundswell. As you can expect, no newly minted college grad picked up the flag to lead the internal charge.

There is no substitute for management involvement. The fact that a VP references an employee blog post in the course of everyday business discussions speaks louder and truer than any mandates or exhortations to use the technologies. Within a company groundswell thinking does not come naturally. Count on contributing significant executive time and sponsorship to nurture it, support it, and market it.

plan to ramp up in stages and ease people's participation

Having the right culture in place and an engaged management team is a good start, but it's not enough, especially if a key goal is to foster better communication and collaboration. Externally, as long as applications can attract thousands of participants, the mass of nonparticipating Inactives rarely gets in the way. Inside a company, however, Inactives are like the control rods in a nuclear reactor—they dampen the participation and keep the idea generation from heating up.

The critical level of participation varies based on your application. If only half of Organic's employees were actively managing their profiles and portfolios, for example, then Organism would be useless. Contrast this with Blue Shirt Nation, where 10 percent participation was enough to create a vibrant self-supporting community. Best Buy could survive with lots of employees missing because its application was mostly about listening. But Organic was targeting a groundswell of collaboration, which only works when nearly all the collaborators are present.

What strategies can you use to goose participation? Here's one that won't work: coercion.

One company we worked with was hoping to get close to 100 percent participation in its social collaboration technologies. As with the company's previous deployments of knowledge management and customer relationship management tools, executives mandated participation. An executive or manager would refuse to read files delivered via email and instead insist that they be loaded into the corporate wiki for him to retrieve and review. But the wiki was difficult to use, required a separate authentication sign-on, and had little structure. Forcing people to use nearly unusable tools doesn't work so well, and as a result, the company had a very difficult time getting employees to buy into the social strategy.

Contrast this with Avenue A/Razorfish's approach. It launched its wiki and encouraged, but did not require, participation. Each office had a "wikivangelist" whose job was to explain and encourage participation. One by one, teams decided to connect with the wiki for projects, found it useful, and became believers. Word began to spread, especially since the teams on the wiki were more productive. The early teams, with help from IT, helped improve the design so that as later teams got on board, they found the wiki easier to use.

This staged approach is far more likely to succeed than strong-arming people. As Avenue A/Razorfish's David Deal explains, "People need to *want* to use the wiki." If your early participants aren't finding your social application valuable or usable, you'd better fix it first, rather than force it on the rest of the organization.

One way to encourage participation is to create easy "on-ramps." One law firm knew that its lawyers would resist using RSS, so it set up RSS folders within Outlook rather than make them use a separate RSS aggregation application. If it's important for everyone to participate, then you'll have to make some accommodations for people who would otherwise be Inactives.

Note that the technologies that are most effective at generating participation within the enterprise differ from the external customer-oriented efforts. For example, a blog is an effective tool for talking, but it doesn't help teams much. Instead, teams need support and collaboration tools like wikis, which allow them to stay up to date on a project, to share competitive market intelligence, and to collect and vote on promising ideas.

Once teams are more productive, you'll gain the participation of even those legendary corporate curmudgeons—you know, the guy who until last year insisted that all his emails be printed out by his assistant for him to review.

find and encourage the rebels

Because groundswell thinking is hard, it's important to find people like Intel's Josh Bancroft and Best Buy's Steve Bendt and Gary Goelling. You probably already know who these people are within your organization— they have been pestering you for the past year to do something, anything. Rather than think about the things that can go wrong, think about the opportunity cost—namely, the lost opportunity of creating a groundswell of enthusiastic employees like Ashley Hemsath.

To do this, companies need to be ready to fail often, fail quickly, and most important, fail cheaply. When Procter & Gamble launched its internal blogging program, the system was built over a weekend and housed on a server underneath someone's desk, just like Best Buy's Blue Shirt Nation. Bell Canada's ID-ah! was built entirely with volunteers. Almost every example of internal groundswell initiatives began as skunk works.

As a senior manager, your job is to direct this energy productively. Help your rebels with political and technical resources. Help them figure out where in the organization change can happen most quickly—and where it will be resisted. Help them try things, pick them up when they fall down, dust them off, and help them learn from mistakes. And most important, use your management experience to see, when success begins, *what it is* that is succeeding, and duplicate *that*.

On the other hand, managers should stem the inherent corporate impulse to put in place processes, controls, and guidelines for everything. Instead, set some ground rules in advance. Just as companies have phone, email, and more recently, blogging policies, some basic rules of engagement are a good place to start. We've seen guidelines range from "slanderous name-calling will not be tolerated" to technical specs detailing which areas of corporate information or servers are off limits. You may have to adjust the ground rules over time as your experience with the groundswell increases, but once your rebels know how big of a box they have to play in, they won't have to go looking for approval each time they want to try something new.

culture and relationships trump technologies

In this chapter you've seen how social networks can help spark employee communication, how wikis can stoke collaboration, and how idea exchanges can harness innovation.

No matter what you're after, in the internal groundswell, the secret to thriving is culture. This is not about technology implementation but about managing and changing the way organizations work, a change that needs the blessing—or, even better, the active participation—of top echelons of management. It's nearly impossible to force social technologies on organizations from the top down, because by their definition, these technologies require the participation of your employees. You can't force them to adopt groundswell thinking, anymore than you can convince reluctant managers to deploy social technologies with your customers. But it sure helps if the social technologies have an executive or two behind them.

We'd all like to work in companies filled with Ashley Hemsaths. To get there, start on your internal groundswell applications now.

You've come to the end of our strategy advice. What's left? A look into the future and some advice on how you, personally, should prepare yourself to live in the groundswell. All that's in chapter 12.

12. the future of the groundswell

Jason Korman makes wine. He's made wine his whole life. That's how he knows it's a terrible business.

Success in running a small winery is pretty close to impossible. There are thousands of new wineries all around the world. Distribution is challenging. Awareness tends to come from magazines like the *Wine Spectator*, where it can take months to get a review—*if* you're lucky.

So when Jason Korman started his winery, Stormhoek, in South Africa in 2003, he knew he needed a different approach to reach people. He decided his wine would be the first to succeed through the groundswell.

Jason realized the key was to concentrate on the experiences wine is a part of, not the wine in the bottle. "Wine is a social lubricant," he says. "While we care passionately about wine quality, we really believe that wine is about what happens after you open the bottle." The groundswell thinking in Stormhoek's approach was to encourage people having a good time with his wine to talk about it. That's why one of his first strategies, in June 2005, was to send bottles of Stormhoek vintages to 185 bloggers in the United Kingdom and Ireland. "Try our wine," he told them in a little booklet that came along with the wine, suggesting that they write about it if they liked it, or even if they didn't.

The result of all this activity was that by the end of 2005, 305 blog posts mentioned the wine. Stormhoek had created a new meaning for "wine buzz."

One key to this success was the connection Jason made with Hugh McLeod, an American blogger who draws devastatingly sarcastic little cartoons on the back of business cards and posts them regularly on his blog at www.gapingvoid.com. Hugh partnered with Stormhoek. The assets Hugh brought were his international following, his catchy graphics (which now grace many of Stormhoek's bottles), and his intuitive feel for what works in the groundswell. Hugh's little pamphlet that accompanied the gift wines gave the whole exercise credibility and authenticity, which probably led to the wine being featured in so many blog posts.

Two years later, Stormhoek's $1 million wine business had grown to a $10 million business. Jason has continued to build on the success among bloggers with a Facebook group, YouTube videos, and Flickr photos (he suggests you post mementos of your "geek dinner" with Stormhoek wines, or a photo of yourself outside the local Tesco food store with a bottle you bought). And all these activities have generated their own cloud of publicity, with mentions on CNN and in *Advertising Age*. Stormhoek even managed to get Microsoft employees interested in a private-label vintage featuring a Hugh McLeod illustration with the words "Change the world or go home," a sentiment many Microsofties embrace.

Stormhoek lives in the groundswell. The Internet is Jason Korman's marketing department. Jason and Hugh have created a company firmly embedded in the social fabric across multiple countries, and it's not some ethereal start-up—it sells a real physical product that takes sweat to produce and comes in bottles. Jason Korman is not a stubble-faced Internet entrepreneur, either—he's forty-seven. The difference between Stormhoek and nearly every other company in this book is this: Jason and Hugh live in the groundswell and know they will grow as it grows. They're natives.

You should learn to think as they do.

the ubiquitous groundswell

Groundswell technologies are exploding, as we described in chapter 1. They're cheap and easy to create and improve, they tap easily into the Internet advertising economy, and they connect people who naturally want to connect.

The net result of all this accelerating activity is that the groundswell is about to get embedded within *every* activity, not just on computers, but on mobile devices and in the real world. This is the ubiquitous groundswell. What does that mean?

It means social networks will connect people with the groups they care about. Transactions will be constantly rated and reviewed. Tags, supplied by ordinary people, will reorganize the way we find things. Feeds will alert us to any changed content, and feed readers will be as much a part of the online experience as e-mail or browsers are now.

It's hard to imagine what this world will be like. So rather than explain it, we'll take you on a tour. Let's spend a day in that future.

a day in the life of the ubiquitous groundswell

The net effect of all these changes will be much broader than the individual parts. When the groundswell surrounds you like a cocoon, when you breathe it like air and depend on it always, the world will feel very different.

Imagine for a moment that you're in marketing at a shoe company. You wake up on December 1, 2012. What will your day be like?

As soon as you wake up, your phone (now a much more sophisticated mobile device) tells you things it's learned from the groundswell, things you want to know. To start, your favorite social network tells your phone that a college friend is coming to town next week on business. You text that you're interested in getting together—word will get back to her, along with others from your circle of college friends. Next thing you know, a spontaneous mini-reunion is being organized by the group.

Your phone is also telling you that the Federal Trade Commission is thinking of blocking your two top competitors from merging with each other, and that the two hot colors for next spring look like mauve and canary yellow—because you've set the device up to bring you information from the *Wall Street Journal*, *Footwear News*, and *Women's Wear Daily*. The feeds are smart—they watch what you've been reading and bring you more of the stuff they know you, and others similar to you, would like to know.

Alongside those feeds are the top posts from shoeblog.com and shoeaholicsanonymous.com. You key in a comment on shoeaholics, right from your phone—can't let them get away with calling those cute pumps your company just had shipped in from Mexico "cheap." Downing the last of your morning coffee, you receive an alert that warns the interstate is backed up again—better take the alternate route. You make sure your phone's GPS tracking system is on so that you can add your own commute progress to the traffic database.

Arriving at the office, you plug the laptop in and check your monitoring dashboard. Mauve is on fire—according to your groundswell monitoring service, shoe buzz is up 25 percent today, and 11 percent of the posts mention mauve, mostly next to positive indicator phrases like "gotta-have" and ";-b." Canary yellow, on the other hand, is getting dissed with words like "lame" and "ten minutes ago." The spring color choices need to get finalized this week—this is a big decision. Is it a fad, or is it real? You decide to test the theory.

On your own blog, nextgenshoetrends.com, you float a trial balloon. It takes just a moment to take some designs from last season and color a few of them mauve. "We're thinking of something like this for next spring— but with a different strap, something you've never seen before," you post. Let's see what happens when your little cadre of shoe followers sees that. For fun, you do a search on ShoeTube and find the source of the buzz—it's a video of the twenty-two-year-old singer-celebrity of the moment, leader of the superficial friends, Helena Trampp. She was hitting the club circuit last night in mauve stilettos and a skimpy midriff-baring outfit. You drop a link in your blog and, to supercharge things, ask your pal Manny down in community relations to put a link to your post out on SuperShoe, the private community of shoe fanatics your company runs. Before lunchtime you go to your internal wiki to add a quick note that ties together the files and activities from the morning that have already been uploaded and logged, so that manufacturing and retail relations know what you're up to.

Lunchtime. Time to drop off the grid. You turn your phone on private so that it stops tracking you and buy a gift for your honey's birthday in the shop around the corner. The groundswell can wait a moment. You grab a sandwich, and it's back to work.

By afternoon the word is back. Of the 191 comments on your blog, 75 percent are positive, and they're going nuts over Helena's stilettos—ShoeTube already shows nine other videos of Helena wannabes strutting their stuff. The competitors can see this, too, but you've got an edge—your designers have already got the heel designs ready, and your manufacturer, in addition to being fast on new designs, is a whiz at color. To top it off, the buzz in SuperShoe is sizzling—sure, that community is filled with out-there shoe fanatics, but they definitely seem to want mauve.

With a great deal of confidence, you place the order; you know the feed of your orders will go straight to your boss and operations, so there's no need to contact them. Your suppliers and retailers have also subscribed to your order feed, so their start pages and mobile devices will soon be showing you're on top of the mauve trend, too.

You'll post the news with a little more spin on your blog a week or two from now; *Footwear News* will probably pick it up, but that's too late for your competitors to catch up, especially when they're distracted by their pending merger. You decide to drop a few advance pairs to a couple of up-and-coming actresses you know in Hollywood—you call them your shoe ambassadors—who make a sideline of blogging fashion and commenting on fashion forums. You call one to make sure she'll be at the movie premiere next February and shoot off the new designs, appropriately colored, to her phone to whet her appetite.

Just before heading home you see a note that your daughter's chatter on FaceSpace.soc is way up. But clicking through, you find out she and her friends are talking about . . . algebra. Hey, if that's how they solve problems in high school now, it's pretty good college prep.

Time to head home with a smile on your face. Sure, it's hard to keep up with all that information flowing your way, but the flow of insight to and from the groundswell is crucially valuable to the decisions you make—and it's manageable thanks to the intelligence built into your browsers, both mobile and computer based. Just another day immersed in the groundswell.

how the ubiquitous groundswell will change companies

The scenario we've just described is completely plausible. Every single part of it—the mobile Internet, the feeds, the communities, the blogs, the wiki—is already working right now. All that's missing is participation—by more people, and by more companies—and that's coming. Rapidly.

Within a few years, a company that doesn't engage in this sort of activity will look dated. What would you think of a company that had one static graphic and no links on its home page? In 1995, that was typical—now it's laughable. And in the same way, companies that aren't wired into the groundswell in 2012 will look very twentieth century—which is to say, out of touch.

You might think this connection to the market would result in an unhealthy focus on the short term. But based on what we've seen—like Dell developing its Linux product in two months—we think this future will instead foster a culture of responsiveness that's needed to create effective long-term strategies. Companies will make moves incrementally, see what works, and evolve their products in positive directions with confidence from the constant feedback that says they're making the right moves. When they make the wrong moves, they'll learn quickly and correct those mistakes just as quickly. They will be so secure in their relationship with customers that they know they can make a mistake—and not only survive, but thrive.

It's not just about the short term. Strategically, you will *need* that connection to the groundswell. Companies need connections to their markets to create long-term loyalty. They need those customers for intelligence about what's coming up. They need experience dealing with the groundswell to know the difference between a momentary hiccup and the start of a major trend. Companies that have figured out how to make the groundswell a resource will have all this. The rest won't—and they won't be able to build it in a week or a month once they realize they need it.

Product cycles will speed up. For example, the consumer electronics industry typically works on products for a year or more, debuts them in January at the huge International Consumer Electronics Show in Las Vegas, and then delivers them in October and November of the same year, in time for holiday buyers. With constant feedback, the cycle will be more continuous. If we were a consumer electronics manufacturer, we'd watch what was at the show in January, put that information together with knowledge gained from observing the groundswell, and begin building and selling products that match that online feedback, months before the other guys are ready to go. Instead of the big ad campaign, we'd start with influential electronics bloggers. Sales might not be as big as the huge product introductions, but our products would be way better suited to what people really wanted and reap a better profit margin.

In this world of constant feedback, one element of some corporate cultures is definitely going away. Strategies based on deception are doomed to failure. If your high-speed Internet offering is slower in real life than your competitors', skeptics will point a finger at the stream of online reviews and discussion groups, and people will know. If your new mop looks great and costs less but the refills are expensive, people will know. If your mortgage company underestimates how long the paperwork takes, *people will know.*

It's an exciting but scary future. None of us is truly prepared to live in this future because everything about it is so new. But some people, like Jason Korman and Hugh McLeod at Stormhoek, are thriving in it.

Before we leave you, we want to do our best to prepare you to live in this future.

attaining groundswell thinking

Something struck us in our interviews with the successful groundswell thinkers in this book—Memorial Sloan-Kettering's Ellen Sonet with her research community, Procter & Gamble's Bob Arnold with beinggirl .com, salesforce.com's Steve Fisher with his IdeaExchange, and all the rest.

These people took a different approach. They have all learned something, and they have all gained a higher profile in their companies, but they don't swagger. Instead, they seem to reflect a down-to-earth quality because they know they are in touch with something bigger than they are.

We used Sony's Rick Clancy to introduce this book. Rick, who's just beginning to get his feet under him on a corporate blog and is looking to extend that success within the company, has a great chance to succeed, but like everyone entering this world, he needs the right approach. The groundswell swallows up people who don't have the right approach.

So we'll finish with some advice, not on what to *do*, but on how to *be*. This is the essence of the groundswell thinking we've been describing throughout the past eleven chapters—developing the right attitude. Here are some lessons we learned from groundswell thinkers, lessons that will help you make this amazing transition.

First, never forget that the groundswell is about person-to-person activity. This means you as a person must be ready to connect to people you haven't met, customers of yours. You need to be willing to talk to people like cancer patient Lynn Perry or luggage buyer Jim Noble. Blogging, connecting in communities, "friending"—these are all personal activities. Develop empathy for the people, and you unlock their secrets.

Second, be a good listener. Marketers sometimes have trouble with this—they think their job is about talking to customers (or shouting at them). But success in the groundswell means listening not just to customers but to others in your company, and to people who've built applications at other companies. We're all learning here; the best listeners will end up the smartest.

Third, be patient. The technology moves so fast it's easy to think you're about to fall behind. But these applications touch so many parts of your company that it takes time to get everybody to buy in. It took four years for Maureen Royal to launch her community at Constant Contact. All Rick Clancy wanted to do at Sony was to launch a blog, and it took six months. But in the end they got to where they wanted to be because they took that first step to begin the journey.

Fourth, be opportunistic. We've told you throughout this book to start small. This means seeking places to build applications that make progress on connecting with customers, even in a small way. Then seek opportunities to expand that success. When you get a green light or have a great idea, get moving. You may not have another chance.

Fifth, be flexible. If there's one thing we've learned about the groundswell, it's that it always surprises people. Events happen that you don't expect, like Wal-Mart bashers invading the retailer's Facebook page or Dell laptops catching on fire. Groundswell thinking means constantly adjusting to and learning from these events.

Sixth, be collaborative. In your company there are others who think like you. You'll need their support to get past entrenched resistance, and their ideas to help you accomplish your goals. Rob Master and Babs

Rangaiah couldn't have transformed Unilever's advertising except by working together and backing each other up.

Seventh, and last, be humble. People connecting together are a hugely powerful force. You work for a company, which is not quite as powerful. Sure, you can take advantage of the groundswell, but it's the people's groundswell—you're just trying to be a part of it. The true irony, the ultimate jujitsu, is that in this world power comes only to those who are humble.

These are the principles of groundswell thinking. Aspire to these qualities, and you can use the strategies we've laid out to your advantage—or invent your own. You'll be able to build on your successes, both with customers and within your company. And then, as the groundswell rises and becomes ubiquitous, you will be ready.

acknowledgments

A book—this book—is a strange and incredible thing. It begins as an ethereal idea in the minds of a couple of people and ends up as a very real physical object, destined, we hope, to touch the minds of many more.

Along the way we needed to listen to, talk with, energize, gain support from, and embrace—and inspire, persuade, challenge, beg, charm, and collaborate with—an awful lot of people. We had to build our own groundswell around this book, and as we say in these pages, it changed us just as much as we influenced it. We truly do feel we are a part of that groundswell, and we're grateful to everyone in it.

We need to start with George F. Colony, founder and CEO of Forrester Research. When, as analysts, we came to him with the idea to write this book, the rational decision would have been to say no, that we should stick to what we were doing. Instead, George embraced the idea and, in the eighteen months it took to make it happen, never wavered in his enthusiastic support. George is in his heart an idea person, and he wanted to see what ideas we could create, given the chance to concentrate on them. We hope we have lived up to that promise.

Ike Williams, our agent (or as the *Boston Globe* puts it, *über* agent), deals equally adeptly with publishers and authors—without his counsel there would be no *Groundswell*.

Jacque Murphy, our editor, and the amazing collection of people at Harvard Business School Publishing not only made the book better but managed to finish it without compromising quality on a schedule that would make most publishers blanch. Thanks also to our anonymous peer reviewers, who made great suggestions.

The biggest portion of gratitude goes to our colleagues at Forrester Research. Forrester has always been a very collaborative environment, and we shamelessly exploited that culture to get the book done. The data you see in these pages sprang from the relentless dedication and attention to detail of Cynthia Pflaum. The graphics are beautiful because of the sparkling Sarah Glass. The core group of analysts concentrating on social technologies—Jaap Favier, Brian Haven, Rebecca Jennings, Mary Beth Kemp, Peter Kim, Jeremiah Owyang, and Chloe Stromberg—collaborated selflessly. We expanded this team by tapping into analysts with other areas of specialization, including Victoria Bracewell-Lewis, Lisa Bradner, Jonathan Browne, Charlie Golvin, Henry Harteveldt, Elizabeth Herrell, Carrie Johnson, Rob Koplowitz, Harley Manning, Chris Mines, Sucharita Mulpuru, Laura Ramos, Shar VanBoskirk, Oliver Young, and probably a few more we can't recall. It's a very heady experience to have such a broad collection of experts on call, and busy as they all are, none of them ever said no to us. We'd also like to thank the people who provided additional indispensable support in research, data, graphics, and marketing: Dia Ganguly, Dawn Habgood, Jennifer Joseph, Jens Kueter, Karyl Levinson, Gail Mann, Francie Mathey, Reineke Reitsma, Jackie Rousseau-Anderson, Roxana Strohmenger, Tracy Sullivan, and Kevin Turbitt.

Forrester's senior managers were handed this project by George and, to their credit, embraced it excitedly. We'd especially like to thank our bosses—Christine Overby, Elana Anderson, and Cliff Condon—as well as senior managers in the company who made the project possible, despite obstacles: Brian Kardon, Dennis Van Lingen, and Charles Rutstein. Ted Schadler, who runs Forrester's Technographics data service, deserves special mention because he shared our vision for the Social Technographics Profile and steadfastly shepherded it through his global organization.

Four people, no longer at Forrester, shaped us into the analysts and writers we are today through mentoring, leadership, and relentless editing. If you like our writing and the quality of our ideas, these people had a lot to do with it. We raise a glass to Chris Charron, Emily Green, Mary Modahl, and the late Bill Bluestein and hope we have met their high standards.

We gratefully accept the indulgence of our endlessly supportive families—Côme, Ben, and Katie; Kimberley, Rachel, and Isaac—and are looking forward to "friending" them once again.

Unconventionally, we'd like to thank each other. Coauthoring a book would test any relationship. We're very glad to have come to the end of this project as close friends, rather than, say, having strangled each other.

And finally, anyone reading this should recognize that the broader groundswell is what makes a book like this possible. All the entrepreneurs, technology vendors, executives, and regular people in this book indulged us by sharing their stories and connections. And the broader groundswell of our clients and others who connected with us on our blog and in person contributed endlessly, as the groundswell always does.

See you in the groundswell.

—Josh Bernoff and Charlene Li
Cambridge, Massachusetts and
Foster City, California

notes

Much of the information in this book comes from direct in-person, telephone, and email interviews by the authors with the people and representatives of the companies described in the book. Facts and quotes that do not have a note come from these personal interviews.

In these notes, when citing a long Web address, we typically use an equivalent address of the form groundswell.forrester.com/site$x$-y. We created these site references for the convenience of the reader. Enter the Web address into your browser and you will be redirected to the appropriate site online.

Please note that as in all cases with Web addresses, people sometimes change or remove content that we have cited. Web content cited was visible at the time the book was written.

Except where otherwise noted, the consumer statistics cited in this book come from these consumer surveys:

- U.S. data comes from Forrester's North American Social Technographics Online Survey, Q2 2007, an online survey with a sample of 10,010 adults in the United States.

- U.S. youth data comes from Forrester's North American Technographics Retail And Marketing Online Youth Survey, Q4 2007, an online survey of people ages twelve to eighteen with a sample of 5,359 people in the United States.

- European data comes from Forrester's European Technographics Benchmark Survey, Q2 2007, a mail survey with a sample of 24,808 adults.

- Asian data comes from Forrester's Asia Pacific Technographics Benchmark Survey, Q1 2007, a mail, online, and in-person survey with a sample of 6,530 adults.

Because of the differences in survey methodology and survey timing, comparisons across surveys must be made with caution.

If you are a Forrester client, you can see Forrester research reports at the indicated Web addresses. Full Forrester reports are not available for free to nonclients. However, if you go to the indicated Web address, you can see an abstract of the report, and you can also buy the report.

chapter one

1. BusinessWeek *put his picture on its cover:* See "Valley Boys: Digg.com's Kevin Rose leads a new brat pack of young entrepreneurs" by Sarah Lacy and Jessi Hempel, *BusinessWeek*, August 14, 2006. The *BusinessWeek* cover is visible at groundswell.forrester.com/site1-1.

2. *It started when a blogger named Rudd-O put this on his blog on April 30:* See Rudd-O's April 30, 2007, blog post "Spread this number" on the blog Rudd-O .com at groundswell.forrester.com/site1-2.

3. *The encryption for the new high-definition DVD format had been broken:* In fact, this encryption key had been used in many of the DVDs in both high-definition DVD formats: HD DVD and Blu-ray Disc. Once the key was broken, studios began to use a new key, but it's inevitable that the new key will be broken as well, eventually.

4. *Digg removed the link (and posted an explanation on the Digg blog):* See Digg CEO Jay Adelson's May 1, 2007, blog post "What's Happening with HD-DVD Stories" on the blog Digg the Blog at groundswell.forrester.com/site1-4.

5. *By the end of the same day, there were 3,172:* This analysis comes from Google Blog Search (blogsearch.google.com). Because some blog posts have been taken down since we did this research, it's no longer possible to duplicate this analysis.

6. *A YouTube video posted by "keithburgun":* See the YouTube video "Oh Nine, Eff Nine" at groundswell.forrester.com/site1-6.

7. *That's like trying to take pee out of a swimming pool:* See Grant Robertson's May 1, 2007, blog post "HD-DVD key fiasco is an example of 21st century digital revolt" on the blog downloadsquad at groundswell.forrester.com/site1-7.

8. *Kevin wrote this on the company's blog that same evening:* See Kevin Rose's May 1, 2007, blog post "Digg This: 09-f9 . . ." on the blog Digg the Blog at groundswell.forrester.com/site1-8.

9. *By the next day, there were 605 news stories:* The count of news stories comes from a date-bounded search in Nexis.

10. *Ben McConnell and Jackie Huba's book* Citizen Marketers: McConnell and Huba's book includes a fine account of how these Internet situations can blow up—the authors call such situations "firecrackers." See *Citizen Marketers: When People Are The Message* by Ben McConnell and Jackie Huba (Chicago: Kaplan

Publishing, 2007). The authors' blog, Church of the Customer, is well worth following at www.churchofthecustomer.com.

11. *Attempts to remove content from the Internet cause it to spread broadly instead:* See Mike Masnick's January 5, 2005, blog post "Since When Is It Illegal To Just Mention A Trademark Online?" on the blog Techdirt at groundswell.forrester .com/site1-11.

12. *More than a million viewers have watched a YouTube video posted by law student Brian Finkelstein:* See the YouTube video "A Comcast Technician Sleeping on My Couch" at groundswell.forrester.com/site1-12.

13. *An unauthorized blog, Snakes on a Blog:* See www.snakesonablog.com.

14. *She documented the event on her blog:* See Jennifer Laycock's February 1, 2007, blog post "Overzealous Big Pork Stomps on Breastfeeding Blogger" on the blog The Lactivist at groundswell.forrester.com/site1-14.

15. *Soon more than two hundred other blogs were linking to it:* One way to count blog references is by using Google—type any URL into the box at blog search .google.com. The list of blogs linking to Jennifer Laycock's post at www.the lactivist.com is at groundswell.forrester.com/site1-15.

16. *Couldn't stop the spread of the conversation in reactions from other bloggers:* See Hyejin Kim's May 4, 2007, blog post "Korea: Bloggers and Donuts" on the blog Global Voices at groundswell.forrester.com/site1-16.

17. *The entire episode was covered by the* Korea Times: See "Dunkin's Production Faces Sanitation Criticism" by Kim Rahn, *Korea Times,* May 4, 2007, visible at groundswell.forrester.com/site1-17.

18. *In 2006, Forrester Research released a report called "Social Computing":* Forrester's report was called "Social Computing: How Networks Erode Institutional Power, And What to Do About It." In this report we argued that technology-driven social phenomena—including blogs, wikis, social networks, file sharing, customer ratings, citizen journalism, and the like—are part of a single trend toward people connecting and depending on each other, rather than on institutions. (We now call that trend the groundswell.) According to the report, "To thrive in an era of Social Computing, companies must abandon top-down management and communication tactics, weave communities into their products and services, use employees and partners as marketers, and become part of a living fabric of brand loyalists." The surge of client interest in the topics flowing from this report convinced us that there was a broad audience for these ideas—hence this book. See the February 13, 2006, Forrester Report "Social Computing: How Networks Erode Institutional Power, and What to Do About It" by Chris Charron, Charlene Li, and Jaap Favier, available at groundswell.forrester.com/site1-18.

19. *73 percent of Americans:* Online penetration figures for the United States come from Forrester's North American Technographics Benchmark Survey, Q1 2007. See the September 7, 2007, Forrester Report "The State of Consumers and

Technology: Benchmark 2007" by Charles S. Golvin, available at groundswell .forrester.com/site1-19.

20. *64 percent of Europeans:* Online penetration for Europe is a five-country weighted average from the United Kingdom, France, Germany, Spain, and Italy based on Forrester's European Technographics Benchmark Survey, Q2 2007. See the August 22, 2007, Forrester Data Chart "Profiling European Internet Avoiders" by Reineke Reitsma, available at groundswell.forrester.com/site1-20.

21. *It's the technology in the hands of almost-always-connected* people *that makes it so powerful:* The difference this makes is dramatic. In 1996, Forrester Vice President Mary Modahl described the Internet this way in *Wired* magazine: "Right now it's like a neutron bomb went off on the Web. All the buildings are there, but you don't have a sense of people . . . The way-out vision for the Web is that when you go to a site, there will be people." Well, it's not such a way-out vision anymore. Go to MySpace or Digg, and people are visible all over, connecting merrily and drawing pleasure and support from those connections. See "Touchstone: If you want to know what's really new in new media, you ask Mary Modahl" by Harvey Blume, *Wired*, May 1996, visible at groundswell.forrester.com/site1-21.

22. *Online advertising had reached $14.6 billion in the United States alone:* Forrester publishes an annual projection of online marketing spending based on surveying advertisers about their spending and intentions. The $14.6 billion number is a 2007 projection and includes search engine marketing, online display advertising, and online video advertising, but it omits email marketing spending. See the October 10, 2007, Forrester Report "US Interactive Marketing Forecast, 2007 To 2012" by Shar VanBoskirk, available at groundswell.forrester.com/site1-22.

23. *And approached €7.5 billion in Europe:* Forrester creates its European online advertising projection using the same methods as it does for the United States. The €7.5 billion number is a 2007 projection and includes search engine marketing and online display advertising. See the July 12, 2007, Forrester Report "European Online Marketing Tops €16 Billion In 2012" by Rebecca Jennings, available at groundswell.forrester.com/site1-23.

24. *An amazing short story called "Microcosmic God":* Theodore Sturgeon's "Microcosmic God" was first published in 1941. The story appears in *The Science Fiction Hall of Fame, Vol. 1,* edited by Robert Silverberg (New York: Orb, 2005).

25. *Seven weeks, for a total investment of $12,107.09:* See Guy Kawasaki's June 3, 2007, blog post "By the Numbers: How I built a Web 2.0, User-Generated Content, Citizen Journalism, Long-Tail, Social Media Site for $12,107.09" on the blog How to Change the World at groundswell.forrester.com/site1-25.

26. *As Chris Anderson, author of* The Long Tail: See *The Long Tail: Why the Future of Business Is Selling Less of More* by Chris Anderson (New York: Hyperion, 2006). The author's blog is at www.thelongtail.com.

27. *Here's what one FastLane reader, for example, said about the new Pontiac GTO:* See Bob Lutz's January 25, 2005, blog post "Sharpening the Arrowhead" on the blog GM FastLane at groundswell.forrester.com/site1-27.

28. *Here's how he put it, just four months after starting the blog:* See Bob Lutz's April 29, 2005, blog post "Building the World's Biggest Car Market" on the blog GM FastLane at groundswell.forrester.com/site1-28.

chapter two

1. *Think of it as jujitsu:* Some reviewers of this chapter reminded us that among martial arts experts, the martial art of aikido is better known for turning the attacker's force against him than jujitsu. Fair enough—but in common parlance, people attribute this quality to jujitsu. Rather than confusing the reader, we'll use *jujitsu* and offer up this note for purists.

2. *User-generated content:* In July 2007, one of us (Josh) posted an entry on our blog entitled "I'm sick of users." This post reflects our perspective that we are all users of technology now, and the word *user*, by putting a focus on technology rather than people, obscures the real trend here—the trend of people connecting with other people. "Try, just for a day, to stop using this word," the post says. "You'll be amazed at how differently you think about the world." In avoiding the word *user* whenever possible in this book, we've attempted to focus on the power of relationships. (The single exception is in the term *user-generated content*, which, for better or worse, is now an established part of the discussion—rather than fight the groundswell, so to speak, we'll go along for now with this terminology.) In a great demonstration of how ideas spread in the blogosphere, our blog post was cited by the very popular blogger Steve Rubel in his Micro Persuasion blog, after which it was picked up on dozens of other blogs and then cited on prominent pages on the BBC and *Wall Street Journal* Web sites. "I'm sick of users" was viewed by over ten thousand visitors and is among our most popular posts ever. Here's what we learned: technical developers cling tightly to the word *user* and objected strenuously to its removal, but many marketers and others closer to the relationship with customers agreed with us. See Josh Bernoff's July 25, 2007, blog post "I'm sick of users" on the blog Groundswell at groundswell.forrester.com/site2-2.

3. *Some bloggers have also created video blogs, like Martin Lindstrom on the* Advertising Age *site:* Martin Lindstrom's video blog BRANDflash is visible at groundswell.forrester.com/site2-3.

4. *One in four online Americans reading blogs:* Except where otherwise noted, all the statistics cited in this chapter come from Forrester's North American Social Technographics Online Survey, Q2 2007 (U.S. data); Forrester's European Technographics Benchmark Survey, Q2 2007 (European data); and Forrester's Asia Pacific Technographics Benchmark Survey, Q1 2007 (Asian data). Because of the differ-

ences in survey methodology and survey timing, comparisons across surveys must be made with caution.

5. *Wayfarer sunglasses are thrown and caught on a man's face in increasingly unlikely settings:* See the YouTube video "Guy catches glasses with face" at groundswell .forrester.com/site2-5. This video is part of Ray-Ban's Never Hide campaign, which has other similar videos that are visible on YouTube at groundswell.forrester.com /site2-5a. A number of other videos on YouTube claim to debunk the video, showing it was done with string and film run in reverse, but this does not appear to have affected the number of people viewing it.

6. *Second Life is a popular 3-D simulated environment with more than 10 million members:* See Second Life's membership statistics at the company's "Economic Statistics" page, visible atgroundswell.forrester.com/site2-6.

7. *22 percent of teenagers check in* daily, *for example:* This data comes from Forrester's North American Technographics Retail And Marketing Online Youth Survey, Q4 2007.

8. *Apache is the dominant Web server software on the Internet:* Netcraft tracks Web server market share. You can see its October 2007 survey at groundswell.forrester.com/site2-8.

9. *Firefox has gone from zero to over 25 percent of market share in less than two years:* W3Counter is one of a number of sites that track browser market share. Browser market share figures vary greatly based on methodology—for example, self-report surveys of consumers give entirely different statistics from statistics collected from Web sites. The October 1, 2007, browser share report from W3Counter is visible at groundswell.forrester.com/site2-9.

10. *It's the eighth-most-popular site on the Web, according to Alexa:* The Alexa rankings of sites by popularity are visible at Alexa's home page: www.alexa.com.

11. *Companies should carefully monitor pages that describe them or their products:* We got so many questions about how to protect a company's reputation on Wikipedia that we wrote a report about it. Even though you can change anything you want on Wikipedia, those changes won't stick unless you work with the community of ordinary people who edit articles there. As a result, we recommend that companies treat Wikipedia as they would, say, the *New York Times*—as an important information source that you can influence but not control. Companies should designate a single person, probably someone in public relations, to monitor articles about the company and its products. That person should track when changes are made in those articles, participate openly in the "talk pages" for those articles, and create content on the company's own site that Wikipedia articles can reference. More active participation—like attempting to promote the company within Wikipedia's pages and hiding your identity in an attempt to seem more objective—is likely to backfire. The changes won't stick, and you may be banned from further participation on Wikipedia. See the October 23, 2007, Forrester Report "When And How To Get Involved With Wikipedia" by Charlene Li, available at groundswell.forrester.com/site2-11.

12. *Owners of products upload their own video reviews of items from cosmetics to remote car-starters:* ExpoTV recruits people to review products for a minimal amount of compensation and then syndicates those reviews back to the manufacturers. See www.expotv.com.

13. *884 people to vote that her review was helpful:* The review of *Harry Potter and the Half-Blood Prince* by Argentinean Belen Alcat is visible at groundswell .forrester.com/site2-13.

14. *David Weinberger explains in his book* Everything Is Miscellaneous*:* See *Everything Is Miscellaneous: The Power of the New Digital Disorder* by David Weinberger (New York: Times Books, 2007). The author's Web site is at www.evident.com.

15. Folksonomy, *a term coined by Thomas Vander Wal:* For a history of the term *folksonomy,* see Thomas Vander Wal's February 2, 2007, blog post "Folksonomy" on the blog vanderwal.net at groundswell.forrester.com/site2-15.

16. *A construction funded by Wal-Mart's PR agency, Edelman:* The blog was formerly at www.walmartingacrossamerica.com. Going to that address now yields an error. But if you tag it on del.icio.us, you can still see how others have tagged it—and "fake" is one of the most popular tags. The del.icio.us tags for the site are visible at groundswell.forrester.com/site2-16.

17. *On the latest versions of browsers like Firefox or Internet Explorer:* One place to get an excellent explanation of how to use RSS is from Common Craft in its video "RSS in Plain English." You can see the video at groundswell.forrester.com /site2-17. Common Craft has other simple tutorials worth checking out—see them at www.commoncraft.com.

18. *21 percent of online consumers have interacted with a Web-based widget:* The press release from comScore reporting widget usage numbers is visible at groundswell .forrester.com/site2-18.

19. *Delivers a subtle UPS branding message:* You can download the UPS widget from www.ups.com/widget. Unless you live in the United Kingdom, France, or Germany, you won't be able to track packages with it, but it has several other amusing features, including an RSS reader.

20. *The Discovery Channel created a Shark Week widget:* To download the Shark Week widget, go to groundswell.forrester.com/site2-20.

21. *Closed platforms like Digg don't evolve as fast because they don't tap into the well of innovation that is the Web 2.0 development community:* To be fair, digg.com is set up as a destination site, not a platform. But since it's not a platform, others are copying it for their own purposes. (The salesforce.com IdeaExchange and Dell IdeaStorm innovation communities we describe in chapter 9 use a mechanism much like digg.com, for example). A list of over three hundred Digg-like sites and applications is visible at groundswell.forrester.com/site2-21.

22. *So students don't have to waste a trip to see if a washer is free:* Assuming it's still running, Olin College's laundry room application is at www.twitter.com /laundryroom.

chapter three

1. *Let's collect them all here in one place, in figure 3-1:* Except where otherwise noted, all the statistics cited in this chapter come from Forrester's North American Social Technographics Online Survey, Q2 2007 (U.S. data); Forrester's European Technographics Benchmark Survey, Q2 2007 (European data); and Forrester's Asia Pacific Technographics Benchmark Survey, Q1 2007 (Asian data). Because of the differences in survey methodology and survey timing, comparisons across surveys must be made with caution.

2. *Placing them into one or more of six groups:* The Social Technographics Profile is an extension of Technographics, a survey program and segmentation that Forrester has been running since 1997. The first definition of Social Technographics appeared in the April 19, 2007, Forrester Report "Social Technographics" by Charlene Li and Josh Bernoff, available at groundswell.forrester.com/site3-2. We've changed the definitions of the Social Technographics groups slightly since the report was published, to account for a more refined set of questions in our surveys about consumers' participation in social activities.

Except where otherwise noted, the cases in this chapter (for example, L. L. Bean) are based on actual consumer data, but don't reflect actual work with clients. At the time this was written, we were not developing strategy for them based on the data. We include them to demonstrate how companies can use the Social Technographics Profile to develop strategies.

3. *An article in* USA Today *describes them this way:* See "Alpha Moms leap to top of trendsetters" by Bruce Horovitz and Alex Newman, *USA Today*, March 27, 2007, visible at groundswell.forrester.com/site3-3.

4. *An optimistic attitude toward technology and are family motivated:* Technology optimism and primary motivation are basic elements of Forrester's Technographics segmentation and are based on proprietary questions and scoring that are included in all our surveys.

5. *Its advertising features pop star Takuya Kimura:* For a Fujitsu commercial, see the YouTube video "Kimura Takuya—Fujitsu FMV" at groundswell.forrester.com/site3-5.

6. *One in five online singles has viewed or participated in online dating in the past year:* See the June 6, 2007, Forrester report "Why Marketers Should Court Online Daters" by Charlene Li, available at groundswell.forrester.com/site3-6.

chapter four

1. people, objectives, strategy, *and* technology: We debuted the POST method at Forrester's Consumer Forum in October 2007 and have used it with many clients. See the October 9, 2007, Forrester report "Objectives: The Key To Social Strategy" by Josh Bernoff and Charlene Li, available at groundswell.forrester.com/site4-1.

chapter five

1. *He'll be dead in less than six months:* We're pleased to report that in our latest communication in September 2007, Lynn Perry said he has no further evidence of disease and is happily riding his Harley throughout the United States.

2. U.S. News & World Report *ranks it tops in the nation:* The *U.S. News & World Report* 2007 rankings of cancer centers are visible at groundswell.forrester .com/site5-2.

3. *It just spent $125 million on a proton therapy cancer treatment center, the most advanced technology there is:* See "Proton Therapy Center Opens To Patients," *Medical News Today,* July 9, 2006, visible at groundswell.forrester.com/site5-3.

4. *He says brands belong to customers, not companies. In his words:* The quote from Ricardo Guimarães comes from a personal interview conducted on July 5, 2007.

5. *Companies pay over $15 billion annually for market research:* Source: "Honomichl Global Top 25: The World's Leading Market Research Firms (2006)," available at groundswell.forrester.com/site5-5. The report was published with the August 15, 2007, issue of *Marketing News.* The Nielsen and IMS Health research revenue numbers are also from this report.

6. *Here's a comment from "Tracy D" in the Communispace forum:* This quote comes from NCCN's private community of cancer patients managed by Communispace. Since this community is proprietary to NCCN, it's not available for viewing without a password. We gratefully acknowledge Communispace and NCCN for allowing us to review and quote from this community. The remainder of the quotes from cancer patients in this chapter comes from this community.

7. *"For Axe star, it sure helps to think like guy":* See "For Axe star, it sure helps to think like guy" by Jack Neff, *Advertising Age,* November 6, 2006. This article is available to subscribers only.

8. *Payoff: 32 percent more Generation X investors over the previous year:* The information about Charles Schwab's private community of Generation X investors, which was powered by Communispace, comes from its submission for the 2007 Forrester Groundswell Awards. Charles Schwab and Communispace won the award in the listening category.

9. *Mini owners scored well above average on community activities, like sharing pictures and joining local clubs. Here's a typical comment:* This quote and subsequent quotes from Mini owners come from the presentation "MINI WOMMA Case Study: Managing & Galvanizing Brand Community," presented by Ed Cotton of Butler, Shine, Stern & Partners and Mark Witthoefft of MotiveQuest in May 2007.

10. *Mini outranked every other brand in owners' likelihood to recommend the car to others:* The J.D. Power and Associates rankings are available at www.jdpower.com.

11. *Analyst Peter Kim, Forrester's expert on brand monitoring:* See the September 13, 2006, Forrester Report "The Forrester Wave: Brand Monitoring, Q3 2006" by Peter Kim, available at groundswell.forrester.com/site5-11.

chapter six

1. *Some nut had put an Apple iPhone—the hottest technology product out there, just released—into a blender:* See Joshua Topolsky's July 10, 2007, blog post "Will it Blend: the iPhone smoothie" on the blog Engadget, available at groundswell.forrester.com/site6-1.

2. *[If] you need to get some fiber in your diet, this is perfect:* This Jay Leno quote is taken from the package for Blendtec's *Will It Blend?* DVD.

3. *Worldwide, marketers spent more than $400 billion on advertising in 2006, according to PricewaterhouseCoopers:* See "Global Media Outlook: $2 Tril. by 2011" by George Szalai, *Adweek,* June 21, 2007.

4. *Marketers no longer dictate the path people take, nor do they lead the dialogue:* "The marketing funnel is a broken metaphor that overlooks the complexity social media introduces into the buying process. As consumers' trust in traditional media diminishes, marketers need a new approach. We propose a new metric, engagement, that includes four components: involvement, interaction, intimacy, and influence." This is from the executive summary of the August 8, 2007, Forrester report "Marketing's New Key Metric: Engagement" by Brian Haven, available at groundswell.forrester.com/site6-4.

5. *Trust in ads continued to plummet:* See the November 26, 2006, Forrester report "Consumers Love To Hate Advertising" by Peter Kim, available at groundswell .forrester.com/site6-5.

6. *Consider "Greg the Architect," an extremely cheesy video series from Tibco about service-oriented architecture (SOA) solutions:* See the YouTube video "Greg the Architect—SOA This. SOA That." at groundswell.forrester.com/site6-6. The whole series is also at www.gregthearchitect.com. Tibco's Dan Ziman insists the videos are not cheesy but "entertaining."

7. *And since 74 percent of college students are Joiners:* All adult consumer statistics in this chapter come from Forrester's North American Social Technographics Online Survey, Q2 2007.

8. *E&Y's careers group on Facebook had 8,469 members, of which 68 had joined that day:* The Ernst & Young careers page on Facebook is visible (to Facebook members) at groundswell.forrester.com/site6-8.

9. *According to Market Evolution—a consultancy that analyzed the campaign for MySpace and Carat in a 2007 report called "Never Ending Friending":* "Never Ending Friending" has its own MySpace page at www.myspace.com/neverendingfriending. The PDF of the report is available at groundswell.forrester.com/site6-9.

10. *It insisted on shutting down Joe Anthony's Barack Obama profile on MySpace:* See "Obama Campaign Asks: Is It MySpace or Yours?" by Jose Antonio Vargas, *Washington Post,* May 3, 2007, visible at groundswell.forrester.com/site6-10.

11. *Vince Ferraro, an HP vice president who heads worldwide marketing for HP's LaserJet printers, explained how to solve the Vista problems on his blog:* See Vince Fer-

raro's February 26, 2007, blog post "New HP Universal Print Driver Solves Vista Printing Problems for LaserJets" on the blog The HP LaserJet Blog at groundswell .forrester.com/site6-11.

12. *Sun Microsystems CEO Jonathan Schwartz put this on his blog:* See Jonathan Schwartz's August 17, 2006, blog post "Acquiring Hewlett Packard's Legacy" on the blog Jonathan's Blog at groundswell.forrester.com/site6-12.

13. *So Eric Kintz responded with this blog post:* See Eric Kintz's August 18, 2006, blog post "Something new under the Sun" on the blog The Digital Mindset Blog at groundswell.forrester.com/site6-13.

14. *After studying blogs for years, we came up with the model in table 6-1:* The model in this book is based on Forrester's reports on the ROI of blogging. The January 24, 2007, Forrester report "The ROI Of Blogging" by Charlene Li and Chloe Stromberg, available at groundswell.forrester.com/site6-14a, examines the costs, risks, and benefits of blogging and lays out a methodology for evaluating blog ROI. The January 24, 2007, Forrester report "Calculating The ROI of Blogging: A Case Study" by Charlene Li and Chloe Stromberg, available at groundswell.forrester .com/site6-14b, estimates the ROI of GM's FastLane Blog. For a humorous look at the same topic, see Hugh McLeod's December 13, 2005, blog post "What's Blogging's ROI" on the blog gapingvoid at groundswell.forrester.com/site6-14c.

15. *Carol owned up to the company's inability to compete with all the other marketing blogs in the blogosphere:* See Carol Meyers' September 24, 2007, blog post "Requiem for a Blog" on the blog The Marketers' Consortium at groundswell .forrester.com/site6-15.

16. *We . . . are still investigating the cause:* See Lionel Menchaca's July 13, 2006, blog post "Flaming Notebook" on the blog Direct2Dell at groundswell.forrester .com/site6-16. For more on how Dell embraced the groundswell, see chapter 10.

17. *It means girls can share their most embarrassing experiences, like this one:* This story is available at groundswell.forrester.com/site6-17.

18. *Here's a typical example from "Ask Iris":* This advice from Iris is available at groundswell.forrester.com/site6-18.

19. *Spends $7.9 billion per year to advertise its products worldwide:* Source: page 73 of Procter & Gamble's 2007 annual report.

chapter seven

1. *The most honest form of marketing, building upon people's natural desire to share their experiences with family, friends, and colleagues:* The Word of Mouth Marketing Association's Web site is at www.womma.org. This quote is from its "Word of Mouth 101" and is available at groundswell.forrester.com/site7-1.

2. *Fred Reichheld in his book* The Ultimate Question: Driving Good Profits and True Growth: Reichheld persuasively makes the point that the Net Promoter

Score is correlated with growth across many industries. See *The Ultimate Question: Driving Good Profits and True Growth by Fred Reichheld* (Boston: Harvard Business School Press, 2006). The author's blog, Net Promoter, is at groundswell.forrester.com/site7-2.

3. Fred Reichheld estimates the value of each promoter's positive word of mouth at $42: See *The Ultimate Question: Driving Good Profits and True Growth* by Fred Reichheld (Boston: Harvard Business School Press, 2006), pp. 50–54.

4. *A Massachusetts company, BzzAgent, will be happy to sell you a word-of-mouth program:* Some people have denigrated BzzAgent as false word of mouth. We're not so sure. BzzAgent distributes products to people who agree to talk about them, but if those people don't like the products, they won't spread buzz. In any case, genuine spontaneous word of mouth is far more powerful. You can see BzzAgent at www.bzzagent.com.

5. *1151 of 1185 customers said they would buy this product again:* You can see the eBags Weekender Convertible and all its customer reviews at groundswell.forrester.com/site7-5.

6. *76 percent of customers use online reviews to help them make purchases:* This statistic comes from the May 11, 2007, Forrester Report "Five Immediate Opportunities For eCommerce Improvement" by Sucharita Mulpuru, available at groundswell.forrester.com/site7-6.

7. *96 percent of the sites that have them rate them as an effective merchandising tactic:* This statistic comes from Forrester's shop.org report "State of Retailing Online 2007," available at groundswell.forrester.com/site7-7. This report is available free to members of shop.org; others must pay a fee.

8. *Visitors to Petco's pet supplies site who browsed specifically by highest-rated products were 49 percent more likely to buy:* This statistic comes from Bazaarvoice's case study of Petco, available at groundswell.forrester.com/site7-8.

9. *About 80 percent of reviews tend to be positive:* Forrester examined reviews on amazon.com in the electronics category and the home and garden category, and found 80 percent were positive. See the January 10, 2007, Forrester Report "How Damaging Are Negative Customer Reviews?" by Sucharita Mulpuru, available at groundswell.forrester.com/site7-9.

10. *It's highly active, with over six thousand posts in thirty-nine forums:* Constant Contact's ConnectUp! user community is visible at community.constantcontact.com.

11. *Constant Contact's revenues grew 88 percent between 2005 and 2006, beating the previous year's 82 percent growth:* These figures are calculated from the revenue figures in the prospectus for Constant Contact's IPO filing. The company went public in October 2007. The prospectus is available at groundswell.forrester.com/site7-11.

12. *Kelly Rusk (known in the Constant Contact community as "cardcommunications"), a twenty-three-year-old Canadian woman working for an email services firm,*

feels good when she gets to answer posts like this: You can see this exchange on Constant Contact's ConnectUp! user community at groundswell.forrester.com/site7-12.

13. *Lego has even included these active customers in product design discussions:* See "Geeks in Toyland" by Brendan I. Koerner, *Wired,* February 2006, visible at groundswell.forrester.com/site7-13.

chapter eight

1. *We're going to let them pick up the story from here (what you're reading is an on-line posting):* This text and other excerpts regarding the Howleys are taken directly from TJ and Michelle Howley's CarePages, with their permission. These entries are accessible only to friends of the Howleys who are invited to share their page. As of October 2007, the Howley twins were both breathing on their own and doing great.

2. *In a recent study of cancer patients by the Kaiser Family Foundation and the Harvard School of Public Health:* See "The USA Today/Kaiser Family Foundation/Harvard School of Public Health National Survey of Households Affected by Cancer," November 2006, available at groundswell.forrester.com/site8-2.

3. *3.4 million American jobs and 1.2 million European jobs will go offshore by 2015, many of them jobs in call centers:* This estimate of American jobs going over-seas comes from the May 14, 2004, Forrester report "Near-Term Growth Of Off-shoring Accelerating" by John McCarthy, available at groundswell.forrester .com/site8-3a. The European estimate comes from the August 18, 2004, Forrester report "Two-Speed Europe: Why 1 Million Jobs Will Move Offshore" by An-drew Parker, available at groundswell.forrester.com/site8-3b.

4. *You might post this query on Dell's community forum (www.dellcommunity .com):* This thread on the Dell community forum is visible at groundswell.forrester .com/site8-4.

5. *He's been logged into the forum for over 473,000 minutes, the equivalent of 123 working days a year:* Dell representatives provided us with these statistics on Predator's time spent and postings on the Dell community forum.

6. *Caterina Fake, cofounder of the photo-sharing site Flickr, called it "the culture of generosity":* See, for example, "Web Content by and for the Masses" by John Markoff, *New York Times,* June 29, 2005, visible at groundswell.forrester.com/site8-6.

7. *We call it the search for psychic income:* The term *psychic income*—meaning nonmonetary compensation—entered the lexicon through the work of the econo-mists F. A. Fetter and Irving Fisher in the 1920s. In the groundswell it becomes a crucial form of currency. See, for example, this page for a definition: groundswell .forrester.com/site8-7.

8. *Consumers do far more than consume—they create as well. According to Henry Jenkins:* From *Convergence Culture: Where Old And New Media Collide* by Henry

Jenkins (New York: New York University Press, 2006), p. 133. The author's blog, Confessions of an Aca-Fan, is at groundswell.forrester.com/site8-8.

9. *Fans banded together to send $50,000 worth of peanuts—twenty tons—to the producers of the show:* The owner of Nuts Online, which took most of the nut orders, brags about it at www.nutsonline.com/jericho.

10. *Here's what CBS posted on the fan forum soon after the tons of nuts began arriving:* See this post on the *Jericho* wiki at groundswell.forrester.com/site8-10.

11. *An Open-Source methodology for Enterprise Information Management that provides an organizing framework for Information Development:* See http://www .rodenas.org/blog/2007/10/23/mike20-methodology/.

12. *It's the twentieth-most-trafficked wiki in the United States:* Source: Scott Wilder, group manager of Intuit's QuickBooks online community.

13. *Started a wiki around Scoble's content but had to shut it down because of rampant anti-Scoble edits:* Source: Forrester analyst Jeremiah Owyang, who worked on the Scoble wiki when he was at PodTech.

14. *The result: every day Koreans pose forty-four thousand questions to Naver— and receive a hundred ten thousand new answers:* The facts about Naver cited here come from the article "South Koreans Connect Through Search Engine" by Choe Sang-Hun, *New York Times,* July 5, 2007, visible at groundswell.forrester.com /site8-14.

15. *As of July 2007, there were 350 million answers on the service in the countries where it operates:* These facts about Yahoo! Answers come from a personal communication with Yahoo! PR.

16. *Just trying to answer as many questions as possible":* You can't see our question to Judas Rabbi—asking a question directly to a member violates Yahoo!'s terms of service, so Yahoo! deleted it. But no one knows who Judas Rabbi is, and there is no way to find out his e-mail address. We posted the question "What drives you, Judas Rabbi?" and he answered it before Yahoo! removed it. (Many other Yahoo! Answers participants, having seen others try to smoke him out, told us we'd never find him, and we never really did.)

17. *Take Special K's weight management community on Yahoo!, which declined from a promising start of 2,001 messages in January 2007 to only 185 in August:* The Special K Challenge Group on Yahoo! is visible at groundswell.forrester.com /site8-17. Scroll down to see a history of the number of messages in each month. Messages picked up again in September, probably because of marketing activity by Special K and additional moderation effort in the forum. But this community still has a key weakness—the design doesn't encourage people to network with each other, so they have less incentive to come back.

18. *The member with the most posts, "jsmeeker," has posted forty-four thousand times since 2001:* Statistics on posts and frequently posting members on tivocommunity.com are visible at groundswell.forrester.com/site8-18. You have to become a member of the community and log in to see this information.

chapter nine

1. *Gala (through a MarketTools moderator) asked:* This quote comes from Del Monte's private community of pet owners managed by MarketTools. Since this community is proprietary to Del Monte, it's not available for viewing without a password. We gratefully acknowledge MarketTools and Del Monte for allowing us to quote from this community. The quotes from pet owners in this chapter come from this community.

2. *Eric von Hippel's groundbreaking* Democratizing Innovation: See *Democratizing Innovation* by Eric von Hippel (Cambridge, MA: MIT Press, 2005). The author's Web site is available at groundswell.forrester.com/site9-2.

3. *Patricia B. Seybold's* Outside Innovation: How Your Customers Will Co-Design Your Company's Future: *Outside Innovation: How Your Customers Will Co-Design Your Company's Future* by Patricia B. Seybold (New York: Collins, 2006). The author's blog is available at groundswell.forrester.com/site9-3.

4. *Don Tapscott and Anthony D. Williams's* Wikinomics: How Mass Collaboration Changes Everything: *Wikinomics: How Mass Collaboration Changes Everything* by Don Tapscott and Anthony D. Williams (New York: Portfolio, 2006). The authors' Web site is available at www.wikinomics.com.

5. *Crispy News works much like Digg, allowing visitors to vote entries up or down based on what they like:* Salesforce.com subsequently acquired Crispy News and will be selling the IdeaExchange application to other companies that want to deploy it.

6. *Here's what a customer known as "fifedog" posted on the IdeaExchange:* You can see this post on salesforce.com's IdeaExchange at groundswell.forrester.com/site9-6. You'll notice we've corrected the customer's spelling, which is awful.

7. *One was a PC running Linux, the open-source operating system, instead of Windows:* The post by "dhart" on IdeaStorm that led Dell to offer a Linux computer is visible at groundswell.forrester.com/site9-7. It received 148,000 "points," which puts it at the top of the list of suggestions.

8. *It's especially popular with advertising agencies, which are increasingly asking people to create television ads as part of some sort of contest:* The *New York Times* examined this phenomenon and noted that not only is crowdsourcing commercials sometimes an expensive proposition, but it also leads to expressions of the brand that the company might find less than ideal. See "The High Price of Creating Free Ads" by Louise Story, *New York Times*, May 26, 2007, visible at groundswell.forrester.com/site9-8.

9. *Frito-Lay's Doritos ad in the 2007 Super Bowl was crowdsourced*: The Frito-Lay's 2007 Super Bowl ad site, powered by Yahoo! Video, is visible at groundswell.forrester.com/site9-9.

chapter ten

1. *"But I'm a marketing guy. I recognize the importance of how to position things":* This story and these quotes come from "Weddings/Celebrations; Lori Blackman,

Robert Master," *New York Times*, December 14, 2003, visible at groundswell. forrester.com/site10-1.

2. *The original video on YouTube was seen by over 5 million people in less than a year:* See the "Evolution" video on YouTube at groundswell.forrester.com/site10-2.

3. *Triple what Dove's 2006 Super Bowl ad drove:* According to Alexa, the reach of campaignforrealbeauty.com in January 2006 was 0.03 percent of the global Internet users versus 0.07 percent in October 2006, when the "Evolution" video appeared online. See statistics at groundswell.forrester.com/site10-3.

4. *In 2006, Unilever spent $2.1 billion on marketing in the United States, with 40 percent of that spent on media like TV, print, and the Web:* Source: "Special Report: 100 Leading National Advertisers," *Advertising Age*, June 25, 2007.

5. *His plan also stacked the decks for dovenight.com:* The site dovenight.com is no longer available. However, you can see the trailer for the videos, "Felicity Huffman and Brady Bunch MashUp," on YouTube at groundswell.forrester.com /site10-5.

6. *According to the American Customer Satisfaction Index, customer satisfaction began to decline in 2005:* These customer satisfaction scores are visible at groundswell .forrester.com/site10-6.

7. *The abysmal customer service he was receiving from the company:* Jeff Jarvis's June 21, 2005, blog post "Dell lies. Dell sucks." on the blog BuzzMachine is visible at groundswell.forrester.com/site10-7.

8. *Three days later, he had his new machine—and it didn't work. On June 26, Jeff wrote:* Jeff Jarvis's June 26, 2005, blog post "Dell still sucks. Dell still lies." on the blog BuzzMachine is visible at groundswell.forrester.com/site10-8.

9. *And then, on June 21, 2006, a Dell notebook caught on fire at a conference in Osaka, Japan:* See "Dell laptop explodes at Japanese conference" by Paul Hales, *Inquirer,* June 21, 2006, visible at groundswell.forrester.com/site10-9.

10. *What follows is the entire entry (and note the audacious title):* Lionel Menchaca's July 13, 2006, blog post "Flaming Notebook" on the blog Direct2Dell and the comments that follow are visible at groundswell.forrester.com/site10-10.

chapter eleven

1. *How would you feel if one of your employees wrote something like this?:* This quote is from Ashley Hemsath's profile on blueshirtnation.com. Blue Shirt Nation is available only to Best Buy employees. We gratefully acknowledge the permission of Best Buy to allow us to see and quote from this site.

2. *Clark Kokich sat down at his computer and wrote this blog post:* This quote is from Clark Kokich on Avenue A/Razorfish's intranet. The intranet is available only to company employees. We gratefully acknowledge the permission of Avenue A/Razorfish to quote from this site.

3. *Over 90 percent of the employees have logged in, uploading twenty-nine hundred files and contributing to sixty-five hundred pages:* These statistics come from Avenue A/Razorfish's submission to the 2007 Forrester Groundswell Awards. The company and its wiki won the award in the managing category.

4. *Microsoft announced that it was acquiring aQuantive, Avenue A/Razorfish's parent company:* See the May 23, 2007, Forrester Report "Microsoft Buys aQuantive: The Future Of Avenue A/Razorfish Is Unclear" by Harley Manning, available at groundswell.forrester.com/site11-4.

5. *Readers responded with skepticism, including comments like "It will never happen" or "It will take 2–3 years":* For more on the details of the creation of Intelpedia, see "'Wikimaniacs' debate corporate acceptance of wikis" by Phil Hochmuth, *InfoWorld,* August 9, 2006, visible at groundswell.forrester.com/site11-5.

6. *twenty-seven of the top ideas have been "harvested" for review and twelve have been implemented:* These statistics come from an interview with Rex Lee. For detailed background on ID-ah!, see "Collaboration only blooms with employee cultural shift" by Paul Weinberg, *ConnectIT,* October 10, 2007, available at groundswell.forrester.com/site11-6.

case index

subject index

about the authors

CHARLENE LI is one of the leading voices in the area of social comput-ing and Web 2.0 through her work over the past nine years with the re-spected technology and market research company Forrester Research. She is one of Forrester's most quoted analysts. An accomplished and fre-quently requested public speaker, she often appears at industry events and delivered the keynote speech at Forrester's Consumer Forum in 2007.

Charlene analyzes how companies can use technologies—like blogs, social networks, RSS, tagging, and widgets—to meet business objec-tives. She started her own analyst blog in 2004 and is regularly cited as America's most influential analyst blogger. She currently shares a blog with Josh Bernoff at www.forrester.com/groundswell.

Previously, Charlene led the marketing and media research team at Forrester and ran its San Francisco office. She has also been publisher of interactive media for Community Newspaper Company, a group of news-papers in Massachusetts, and served on the board of directors for the Newspaper Association of America's New Media Federation. Charlene has managed new-product development for the *San Jose Mercury News* and has also been a strategy consultant for Monitor Company. She holds an MBA from Harvard Business School.

Charlene lives in San Mateo, California, with her husband and two children, all of whom are happy, engaged members of the groundswell.

JOSH BERNOFF is one of America's most prominent and widely quoted technology analysts.

Josh has been a Forrester Research analyst for thirteen years and is currently a vice president at the technology and market research company. He created the Technographics segmentation, the foundation for Forrester's worldwide consumer survey business since 1997. Josh's analysis aims at a deeper understanding of people, how they use technology, and how that affects business. He shares a blog with Charlene Li at www.forrester.com/groundswell.

Currently focusing on social technologies, Josh has also created groundbreaking analysis of changes in the media industry with widely cited reports, including "Will Ad-Skipping Kill Television?" and "From Discs To Downloads." In an appearance on *60 Minutes*, Mike Wallace introduced him as "the top TV industry analyst at Forrester Research, the authority on where TV is going."

Josh has consulted on strategy with senior executives from global companies including ABC, Best Buy, Cisco, Comcast, L'Oréal, Microsoft, Sony, TiVo, and Viacom. He is a sought-after speaker, having key-noted conferences around North America and in Barcelona, Cannes, London, Rome, and São Paulo. Before Forrester he worked as an executive and a writer at several Boston high-tech start-ups.

Josh lives in Arlington, Massachusetts, with his wife and two children.

join the conversation

A book is a one way communication. We write, you read. But it doesn't have to be that way.

As we worked on this project it became clear that the people most interested in social technologies were a groundswell of their own. They wanted to connect with us, but even more, they wanted to connect with each other. So we took our own advice. We created a place for you to connect at groundswell.forrester.com.

How did we decide what to put there? We took our own advice and used the POST method (see Chapter 4).

The people—the readers of this book—are obviously highly inclined to participate online, but have a professional bent and may not be social technology experts. The site reflects that.

Our objective is to create a place where you can support each other, so we created a supporting community, like the ones we describe in Chapter 8.

Our strategy is consistent with Forrester's mission—to create business advantage for the members of our community. This book is just the first stepping stone, and we wanted to continue the conversation with an online community, coupled with professional research from Forrester. It's our way of making sure this book continues to deliver value for you, long after you've finished it.

As for the technology, it will constantly evolve based on what will serve the community best. Rather than read a detailed description that will be quickly outdated, why not go to groundswell.forrester.com and give it a try?

We look forward to meeting you in the groundswell.